A JUNGIAN LIFE

The family of the author, Tom Kirsch, Palo Alto, California, August, 2014

Left, from top: David Kirsch, son; Andrea Nagin Kirsch, daughter-in-law;
Susannah Kirsch-Kutz, daughter; not pictured, John Kutz, son-in-law

Seated, center, from top: grandchildren Isabel and Jacob Kirsch, children of David and
Andrea Kirsch; and Jasper and Hildegard Kutz, children of Susannah and John Kutz

Standing, right: Jean and Tom Kirsch, married for forty-six years

A Jungian Life

Thomas B. Kirsch

fisher king press

A Jungian Life

Copyright © 2014 by Thomas B. Kirsch
First Edition
ISBN 978-1-77169-024-9 Paperback
ISBN 978-1-77169-025-6 eBook

Published simultaneously in Canada, the United Kingdom, and the United States of America by Fisher King Press. For information on obtaining permission for use of material from this work, submit a written request to:

permissions@fisherkingpress.com

Fisher King Press
PO Box 222321
Carmel, CA 93922
www.fisherkingpress.com
fisherking@fisherkingpress.com
+1-831-238-7799

Many thanks to all who have directly or indirectly provided permission to quote their works. Every effort has been made to trace all copyright holders; however, if any have been overlooked, the author will be pleased to make the necessary arrangements at the first opportunity.

Front cover image, *Fog Near Black Mountain* © is from an original painting by Kit Colman.
www.kitcolman.com

DEDICATION

To my wife, Jean, who has not always agreed with me,
but has always supported my Jungian life.

ACKNOWLEDGMENTS

I have shown parts of this memoir to the following people, who have given me valuable insights: Andrew Samuels, Baruch Gould, Tom Singer, John Adams, Nancy Cater, and Murray Stein. Furthermore, I have presented parts of this publication to the Psychobiography Group in Berkeley, who have added penetrating insights into this memoir. Christa Robinson helped me when I was in a logjam. I want to thank Karen Farley, who has done a masterful job of editing the manuscript, which was in a primitive form when I first asked her to edit it. She has shaped it beautifully. I want to thank Mel Mathews at Fisher King Press for his enthusiastic support and direction. All the material in this memoir is from my own personal experience and reflections, and I take full responsibility.

CONTENTS

INTRODUCTION

As I write this, I am seventy-eight years old, and my entire life has been intimately involved with C.G. Jung and analytical psychology. My parents were in analysis with Jung when I was born, and I was imaged to be the product of a successful analysis. The title of my memoir, *A Jungian Life*, reflects the fact that from conception until the present, Jung, his ideas, and analytical psychology itself have been a central thread of my existence.

With the advent of World War II, my family crossed the "great water," the Atlantic Ocean, and ended up in Los Angeles. At that time the Los Angeles area was dominated by Hollywood and orange groves, a very different place from the Los Angeles of today. Over the next forty years, my parents became the founders of all the Jungian groups that formed in and around Los Angeles. My father became the intellectual leader, while my mother provided the relational glue to work out the many difficulties the new groups faced.

It was wartime, and for five years they were cut off from any contact with Jung. Looking back from my present perspective, that must have been extremely difficult, because they were dealing with the difficulties of a new land, a new and foreign culture, a difficult marriage, and the lack of friends and colleagues. Los Angeles, with its burgeoning freeways and the absence of natural landscape, made life itself seem alien, especially for my mother.

My parents had little sense of what American collective values were. My mother relied on my older half-brother, Jerry, to give her some sense of what was considered "normal." We lived in a predominantly Jewish neighborhood where many families had an older relative from Eastern Europe who primarily spoke Yiddish. My parents were from Germany, and there was a cultural differentiation between the German Jews and those from Eastern Europe. I did not realize it at the time, but all my Jewish friends came from an Eastern European background and had an inferiority complex in relationship to German Jews.

Being Jewish, and what that Jewishness has meant, has been a primary leitmotif throughout my life. I was given a Hebrew middle name, Mordechai, because it was thought that we might return to Palestine. I began Hebrew school at the age of six and continued with

Hebrew lessons until the age of fourteen, well after my bar mitzvah. However, we were never formally connected to any synagogue, and I have never been an observant Jew. On the other hand, I have always culturally identified myself as a Jew, and that has had a profound influence on me. Israel was important to my parents, and they were on friendly terms with some of its founders, many of whom came from a similar background to their own.

My parents, being on the one hand Jungian and on the other Jewish, were often attacked for supporting Jung, especially after the conclusion of World War II, when the full scope of the Holocaust became known. The rumors had gone so far as to indirectly implicate Jung in the actual Holocaust. My role professionally has in many ways been similar to that of my father, and I have written about it on a number of occasions. It has not been an easy position to be in.

Though my own relationship to my Jewishness has undergone considerable change throughout my life, it has been a constant thread and a strong part of my identity that is interwoven with my story.

It was a given that my parents wanted me to become a Jungian analyst. My mother teasingly said, "Tommy could become any kind of Jungian analyst he wanted to be." Growing up none of my other four half-siblings had much interest in Jungian psychology, while I seemed to have a natural affinity for it.

Jung was a large part of family life growing up. My father held a weekly seminar on various topics ranging from the Bible to untranslated works of Jung's, at times studying some of the more difficult alchemical texts line by line. In addition, there were extremely loose boundaries between their professional and personal lives. Often patients became best personal friends, and as a child I often could not make a distinction. I knew when I opened my practice that I wanted to have an office separate from my home. I did not want my patients to become the cornerstone of my social life.

My parents were interested in my dreams, and my mother was especially attuned to dream life. From time to time I would tell her a dream I'd had. Her understanding of my dreams, and therefore of me, was uncanny. She always seemed to know what was going to come up next for me in my life. Her interest did not seem intrusive, and, although I could not name it at the time, I was fascinated by the information she could garner from my dreams. It was only later in my analysis that I realized that, for all my fascination, my mother's insight into me hindered me from finding my own masculine way. This ambivalence between being both understood and encroached upon shaped our entire relationship, but I have always been aware that it was through my mother that I found my interest in the unconscious and analytical psychology, and for this I am indebted to her. On the other hand, it was only as I became an adult that I began to appreciate my father's approach to the unconscious, which truly was an acquired taste. I still do not find it easy to read most of Jung's work on alchemy, while for my father, Jung's alchemical works were the essence of his psychology.

When World War II ended and travel by air became commonplace, my parents invited many of the first generation of Jungians from London and Zürich to come to Los Angeles. They were often houseguests, and so they became part of my extended family. In 1953 my parents took me to Europe for the first time since we had departed in 1940 under extremely dangerous conditions. London and Paris were still feeling the effects of World War II, but when we arrived in Zürich, everything was in order. There were no destroyed buildings, all the church bells rang, streetcars functioned normally, and I fell utterly in love with the city. Palo Alto and the California coast are home to me, but I still consider Zürich a second home, and it has played a major part in my story.

Between graduating from college and beginning medical school in New York, I felt the need to go into therapy for the first time. I was in a relationship with a woman who wanted more from me than I was able to give. On the other hand, I was not ready to let go of the relationship. I sought out a Jungian analyst, and my parents recommended that I begin in Zürich with the psychiatrist and Jungian analyst, C.A. Meier. This began a sixteen-year history of being in analysis, first in Zürich, then in New York, and finally, from 1962 until 1973, in San Francisco with Joe Henderson. During this time I finished medical school, became a psychiatrist, finished my Jungian analytic training in San Francisco, opened a private practice in Palo Alto, got married, divorced, remarried, and had two children. Jungian analysis was the thread that guided me through this labyrinth.

In 1976 I became president of the Jung institute in San Francisco, and in 1977 I was elected second vice president of the International Association for Analytical Psychology, or IAAP, the professional organization of Jungian analysts around the world. As vice president and then president of the IAAP for eighteen years, I traveled the world and was able to meet Jungian analysts from many different countries. The position allowed me to serve a missionary function of sorts in new areas like China, South Africa, Mexico, Russia, and other former Soviet Eastern Bloc countries. The administrative center was in Zürich, so I traveled there frequently and had the chance to deepen established friendships and develop new ones. I became familiar with both the ins and outs of Zürich and the character of its people.

After I finished my eighteen years with the IAAP, I returned to a full-time private practice in Palo Alto. Some colleagues were worried that I would miss the IAAP terribly and that I would not know what to do without it. I decided to address this by writing a history of the Jungian movement from its inception in 1913 until the year 2000. Writing *The Jungians*, which was published in 2000 by Routledge, turned out to be a daunting task that required an intimate knowledge of the details of the individual Jungian societies. Of course, I lacked an inside perspective on the individual societies, and some of the members weren't completely happy with the way I described their groups in my book.

In the past decade I have become increasingly interested in the history of analytical psychology, Jung's life and work, psychoanalytic history, and the entire history of depth psychology. My parents introduced me at an early age to many of the first-generation analysts who surrounded Jung, and over time I became acquainted with them. Later, in my roles with the IAAP, I gained a broad knowledge of the developments in analytical psychology, and through both my early family history and in my later professional life, I came to learn much about the private affairs of many analysts which must remain forever secret. On the other hand, I have much to say about my experiences, what places felt like to me and the people I have met, both my impressions of them at the time and how they seem to me now, as I look back on them.

1

EARLY BEGINNINGS

I made my appearance at Middlesex Hospital in London on June 14, 1936, butt first. In those days a breach presentation meant that the obstetrician did an internal rotation of the fetus so that the head emerged first, rather than the behind or the legs. All the technology we have today to assess the status of the fetus did not exist then, and in the process of delivery, my left arm was broken. Luckily there was no nerve damage, a common complication of that procedure. My arm was in a cast for several weeks. According to those who saw me, I looked like an English policeman.

Not only was my birth physically traumatic, but it had been difficult for my parents psychologically as well. Although I was a wanted child, my parents knew that the clouds of another war were gathering in Europe, and that Hitler was a megalomaniac who could not be trusted. Was it right to bring forth a child in those turbulent times? Thoughts of abortion had crossed both their minds, but in the end their desire for a child won out, despite an uncertain future. But the future was murky at best, so, to see me through a range of possibilities, I was given three names, Thomas Basil Mordechai. Thomas was an international name that would work in many countries; Basil, although it meant "king" in Greek, was nonetheless very English and appropriate for a young English family; and Mordechai, my Hebrew name from the story of Esther in the Old Testament, was given to me in case we returned to Palestine.

At the time of my birth, Marianne Jacoby, a patient of my father's at the time, prepared an astrological chart for me. She and her husband were also refugees from Europe, and the two couples had become good friends in London. I have no memory of Marianne from the London days, but we reconnected more than thirty years later. By then she had become an individual member of the International Association for Analytical Psychology, or IAAP, and had been a founding member of the British Association of Psychotherapists. In 1974 we were both at the IAAP congress in London, and I asked her for a reading on my chart. What she said about my past made sense in terms of the difficulties with female relationships, and she said that in the future I would have more difficulty with men. I don't know if that has turned out to be the case, but in the second half of life I have taken some controversial stances which have embroiled me in conflict.

My parents had met in Germany and had made their way to London only a few months before my birth. My mother, Hildegard Klara Kirschstein, came from an assimilated German Jewish professional family whose roots could be traced into the fourteenth century. Her ancestors had fled religious oppression in Spain even before its formal expulsion of the Jews, moving to northern Germany to begin life again in exile. By the time my mother was born in 1902, her family was part of a large group of assimilated German Jewish professionals who no longer practiced traditional Jewish rituals. Her father was a dentist, and her uncle Leopold, whom I would know growing up, was a doctor. She had two older brothers, and one of them, Uncle Walter, or Welty as we all knew him, remained in close contact with my parents throughout their lives. He and his wife Lona ultimately achieved minor prominence as dentists in London, both because of their superior German training and because they had purchased expensive American equipment at a time when American machinery surpassed all the rest in excellence. My mother's other brother died in 1943 in London, and I have no memory of him. My mother had grown up in Berlin, thinking of herself as German with few conscious thoughts of her Jewish roots. She finished high school and soon after was engaged to Hermann Silber, a successful manufacturer of hats. At a young age she bore two sons, James Rudolph in 1923 and Gerhard Walter in 1927. Germany was in complete political and economic chaos, struggling to recover from World War I. Her husband Hermann was diagnosed with multiple sclerosis, and the disease progressed quite rapidly. By 1933 he was completely disabled and, despondent about his condition, he committed suicide. My mother, a typical German housewife with no advanced education, skill, or profession, was in a state of despair and, with two young sons, was left a widow who had little money due to the hyper-inflation of the German economy. She moved her family to a rooming house, where she met a young law student, Max Zeller, who was to become a lifelong friend and fellow Jungian analyst in Los Angeles. She was desperate, depressed, and at a loss about her future, when either Max or Kate Nottman, the twin sister of Hermann Silber, suggested psychotherapy and recommended James Kirsch, a local psychiatrist, as a therapist. This well-meaning referral had far-reaching consequences for everyone involved. My mother made an appointment with the man who was to become my father and rapidly formed a dependent erotic transference so powerful that it shaped her future.

My father, on the other hand, had come from an Orthodox Jewish background, and his family had only moved from Poland to Germany, and then to the Americas, in the late nineteenth century. The entire Kirsch family was oriented toward business, and some of the family members had gone to San Francisco to pursue business interests, while others, including my father's father, had gone to Guatemala. I never knew my paternal grandfather, who had settled in Guatemala City to establish a button business, but his choice of Guatemala, where my father was born on July 21, 1901, proved to be a boon to us all. When we moved to the United States in 1940, we were admitted under the quota for Guatemala rather than that of Germany or England, which paved the way for our entry into the United States.

My father was the fourth of five children, having three older sisters and a younger brother. Noting that my father was extremely intelligent, my grandfather decided to send his wife and family back to Germany, where young James could obtain a solid education of the sort not available in Guatemala. The family returned to Berlin via San Francisco in 1907, and my father received a classical European education. His father remained in Guatemala, with the understanding that he would visit Germany every two years. However, World War I intervened, and my father did not see his own father between 1912 and 1921. My father assumed that his father must have acquired a second family in Guatemala, but if so, he never met them, and his father died in 1931.

During his teenage years, my father became an ardent Zionist, and he continued that association while at the University of Heidelberg, where he joined a Zionist student organization called the Blau-Weiss. There he became lifelong friends with Erich Fromm and Ernst Simon, a close associate of Martin Buber. Ernst Simon later became a professor at the University of Judaism and was an important influence in my life as well as my father's. My father chose to study medicine at the University of Heidelberg, much to the chagrin of his family, who wanted him to join the family business. Instead he became a psychiatrist, opening an office at 3 Olivaer Platz in Berlin. He had two years of a Freudian psychoanalysis and then began a Jungian analysis with Toni Sussman. In 1928 he contacted Jung, and he arranged to begin analysis with him in Zürich in 1929. By 1931 he had become a founding member of the Berlin C.G. Jung Gesellschaft and had developed a thriving practice of psychiatry and Jungian analysis. His reputation in Berlin was excellent, which is why my mother was advised to seek him out for psychotherapy.

By the time my parents met, Hitler had come into power, and the situation for Jews in Germany was changing rapidly for the worse. My father, who was still a member of the Zionist Blau-Weiss, believed he saw the handwriting on the walls of history and recommended to all his family members and his Jewish patients that they leave Germany and settle elsewhere, preferably Palestine. He took his own family, a wife and two children, to Palestine in 1933, and my mother and her two boys quickly followed. The two families settled in close proximity in Tel Aviv, where friendly relations were established.

My father and his first wife Eva divorced in 1935, a process that required both of them to return to Germany for a short time. Eva had attended seminars in Zürich with my father from the late 1920s and had become a Jungian-oriented psychotherapist, so she decided to remain in Germany. By 1938, however, she realized that she, too, had to leave and did so with much difficulty. She began a new life in Wales, remarried, and had a practice of psychotherapy for many years, dying at the age of ninety-eight. She had attended some of Jung's seminars while she was married to my father, and one can see her name as one of the participants in the dream seminar from the late 1920s.

Meanwhile, my father was establishing a close romantic relationship with his patient Hilde Silber, although neither of them liked the lifestyle of Tel Aviv and Palestine in the mid-1930s. The Zionist movement was extremely strong and malaria and other diseases were rampant, so my parents were both uncomfortable with the politics and concerned for the health of their families. They began to consider leaving Palestine.

In 1935 my parents officially married and moved their blended family to London. This was not an easy task, as it was a time of mass movements of refugees from Europe, and the United Kingdom had established stringent limitations on entry. When my father made his application at the United Kingdom immigration office, the immigration officer was familiar with Jung, because Jung had just delivered his Tavistock lectures. My father brought with him a letter from Jung stating that he was in good standing and that he had learned Jung's psychotherapeutic methods, and the customs official, believing that England needed more Jungians, admitted my father and the family. I grew up hearing this story of the customs official, but it was validated for me more than fifty years later when I was lecturing in Wellington, New Zealand. The first New Zealand Jungian analyst, Dorothea Norman Jones, told me she had been living and training in London in 1935 and had been close friends with the customs agent who admitted my family.

From the time of my birth the following year until late September, 1940, our family lived in Golders Green, a predominantly Jewish enclave in north London. We lived close to Hampstead Heath, and I remember many walks on the Heath and in the Big Wood. When I was less than one year old, my mother received a call that changed her life, and the family's life along with it.

After my mother's therapy with my father, she had managed to work her way in to see Jung in 1935, and she did analysis with him off and on during her wanderings between Palestine and Europe and England. She quickly became a member of the Analytical Psychology Club in London, an adjunct society where those who had undergone Jungian analysis could become members. There she had met a young psychiatrist, Michael Fordham, who aspired to become a Jungian analyst. In May, 1937, my mother was still nursing me when she received a telephone call from Michael Fordham. He said that Professor Jung had recommended that he see her for analysis. She was quite taken aback with this request, having had no desire to become an analyst herself, but, nonetheless, she began to see Michael in analysis. Fordham had previously been in analysis with H.G. Baynes, and he had traveled all the way to Zürich, planning to see Jung. However, Jung did not have time and instead recommended my mother to him. This story, related to me by my mother and confirmed by reading Michael Fordham's autobiography, is how my mother's analytical practice began. In the next years she developed a number of other clients. When I first bumped into Michael Fordham again in the men's restroom at the third IAAP congress in London in 1971, I introduced myself. His immediate response to me was, "My rival!" harkening back to 1937, when I was an infant and his analysis was also in its infancy. In this way my mother's career as a Jungian analyst was launched, and she continued to have a large practice until her death in December, 1978.

By 1940 the situation in England had become rather perilous. The Germans had conquered France and the Low Countries, Belgium, Holland, and Luxembourg, and they were contemplating crossing the English Channel. During the late summer and fall of 1940, German airplanes were bombing London continuously. We were forced to sleep in air raid shelters, and somewhere along the line I got the idea that I would be safe if I slept in a chair. In fact, I was so traumatized by the bombing that I insisted on sleeping in a chair for many months after we had arrived in the United States, over a year later.

The Battle of Britain waged on, and each morning when our family emerged from the bomb shelters, we had to check to see whether our house was still standing. As the bombing raids continued, houses close to ours were destroyed, but somehow our house survived. At times the Germans bombed London by daylight, and we would rush into the cellar of our house until the raid was over. On a couple of occasions we were at the market when a bombing raid began, and my mother hurriedly pushed me up against the wall in order to protect me from bombs falling around us.

My father feared that England ultimately would fall to the Nazis as well. He began to investigate whether moving to the United States was feasible and discovered that, since he was Guatemalan by birth, our family would be counted under the US immigration quota for Guatemalans seeking entry rather than among the large numbers of Europeans hoping to obtain refuge. Since some of his family had settled in San Francisco years earlier, my father decided that we should immigrate to the United States. This was a tremendous undertaking, and initially the plan was for the entire blended family, the three of us, his two children from his marriage to Eva, who were named Ruth and Michael, and my mother's two children, to all go by ship to America. At the very last moment, Eva could not let seven-year-old Michael go, and he stayed in England with her. I was not to see him for another twelve years. Twelve-year-old Ruth made the crossing to America with us.

I remember leaving London and driving past Hampstead Heath, where I saw a downed Messerschmidt. We spent that night in Liverpool, and the city was bombed in the night. One bomb landed very close to our hotel, our first close call of the journey.

Late in September, 1940, we boarded a crowded ship full of refugees headed for New York. Our ship, the *Samaria*, was part of a large convoy, and we had air support accompanying us across the North Atlantic. German U-boats were sinking many of these ships, and we had daily drills on how to board the life boats. On several occasions we were attacked by U-boats, and our ship zigzagged back and forth to dodge the torpedoes. Luckily, none hit the *Samaria*, and we arrived safely in New York ten days later.

Upon arrival we disembarked at Ellis Island, which served as our introduction to the United States. Many previous refugee ships had been sunk by the U-boats, so our arrival was greeted with interest. Several passengers were interviewed by the press, including four-year-old Tom Kirsch, who offered one reporter a child's viewpoint. When asked how I liked Ellis Island, I replied that I liked this hotel very much. This made it to a daily New York paper, which was in turn picked up from the subway floor by Werner Engel, a close friend of my father's from Berlin who had arrived in New York a few months earlier. In this way he learned that we had made it safely to the United States, and he greeted us upon our release from Ellis Island.

When we arrived in New York, the question was whether we would stay there or go on to San Francisco, where my father had many relatives. My father had received a rather lukewarm reception from the Jungians in New York, and he felt he needed to see his relatives in San Francisco, because they had sponsored us so that we could come to the United States. So he ventured on to San Francisco to visit his family, and on the way back to New York stopped in Los Angeles. In those days Los Angeles was wide open and reminded him of Tel Aviv and Guatemala, and my father liked it immediately. Many refugees from Europe were settling there, and it was reasonably close to his relatives in San Francisco. And so we all took the train, the *Challenger*, to Los Angeles. We stopped in Chicago en route to visit my mother's cousin, Gerhard Danelius, with whom she had grown up in Berlin. At the time he was a radiologist in Chicago, but after the war he moved to Los Angeles to practice with a prestigious medical group in Beverly Hills. In 1960 he made another change and went to Zürich to train as a Jungian analyst. After his training he came back to Santa Barbara, where he practiced for the final twenty years of his life. He had expressed his total dissatisfaction with the practice of radiology to my mother, and she was a significant influence on his decision to go to Zürich.

2

GROWING UP IN LOS ANGELES

Our first weeks in Los Angeles were spent gaining a foothold, but by the beginning of 1941, our family found a home to rent which was the right size for the four children and where one or two of the rooms could be used for psychotherapy offices. The location was close to Beverly Hills in central Los Angeles, and the neighborhood was predominantly Jewish. Los Angeles at that time was already a sprawling city, and many refugees had found a home among the orange groves and glitz of Hollywood. My mother wasn't one of them. She found the culture of Los Angeles difficult to adjust to. In fact, when interviewed near the end of her life, she said she still felt like a stranger in the United States and especially in Los Angeles. Having been used to walkable European cities with their parks and greenery, Los Angeles still felt foreign to her, and she felt little connection to the land. Vacationing for both my parents meant going back to Europe, especially to Switzerland, where they had friends and could hike in the Swiss Alps.

Initially there were no Jungians in Los Angeles, and the only person from Los Angeles who had even gone to see Jung was Mary Wilshire, after whose husband the long and famous east-west boulevard is named, and she had seen Jung very early in his career, when he was still under the influence of Freud. My parents knew no one in Los Angeles at the time, yet they both began to build up private practices in Jungian psychotherapy and analysis. How they were able to build up their practices so quickly is a mystery to me, but the fact that they did was a credit to their resourcefulness.

The whole family settled in quite well to new lives in Los Angeles. Ruth and Jerry entered junior high school, and Jim went to the University of California, Berkeley, where he received an undergraduate degree in 1943. I began kindergarten at Carthay Center grammar school in September, 1941, and graduated from there in June of 1947. It was a traditional American grammar school of that era. All the teachers were women, and we addressed them by their last names only.

When I entered kindergarten, the first thing to go was my British accent, since the other kids teased me about it constantly. Reading, writing, and arithmetic came easily to me, though, and at the end of my first-grade year, I was promoted to third grade. As a result I was always the youngest person in the class. I was left-handed, although my fifth-grade teacher tried her best to make me right-handed. The effort to change me was a miserable failure, and I have continued to be left-handed in almost everything.

At age six I was signed up to the Jewish community center and began to learn Hebrew every day after school. I had an excellent teacher, Mrs. Shamir, with whom I learned the basics of writing and reading Hebrew. During those early lessons I had a child's fluency, but at the end of World War II Mrs. Shamir returned to Israel, and without her my enthusiasm for Hebrew declined. However, I continued to have Hebrew lessons of one sort or another until I was fourteen, and then I stopped abruptly. I just was not interested anymore. I did have a bar mitzvah with Rabbi Sonderling, a German Jew who looked like a prophet from the Old Testament. Because of my many years of Hebrew study, the preparation for my bar mitzvah was not difficult. It was followed by a small party at home for about thirty relatives and friends, nothing like the lavish affairs that I have gone to at different times in my life.

My family never belonged to any synagogue. My father had grown up in an Orthodox Jewish family, but he had rebelled against their narrow, materialistic outlook. He was supposed to go into the family business, and, when he went into medicine instead, his family considered it a betrayal. Later he joined the Zionist Blau-Weiss society at the University at Heidelberg, and that affiliation became a means of retaining a sense of Jewish identity in spite of rejecting his Orthodox background. Later, when he left Germany, those same feelings led him to choose Palestine, but in mid-1930s Palestine, the fanaticism of the Zionists reminded him too much of what he had just left behind in Nazi Germany, so he severed his connections to Zionism and left Palestine. Although his sense of Jewish identity remained important to him throughout his life and he did not rule out returning to Palestine at some point, he never returned to Zionism. Instead, he satisfied his deep religious impulses through his study of the collective unconscious, and in his old age he returned to the study of Hebrew and Jewish subjects.

My mother, on the other hand, had grown up in a completely assimilated German household, and she only really discovered her Jewishness when the Nazis came into power. Both my parents identified deeply with being Jewish without being members of any organized branch of Judaism.

Along with Hebrew studies, my parents also encouraged piano lessons. I did not practice very much, though, and I kept changing teachers until I found an older Russian woman, Mrs. Borisoff, who had studied in Berlin and then moved to the United States. In Berlin, she had begun a career as a performer, but that ended abruptly when she fled to the United States. She had brought two Bechstein grand pianos with her. They had been wonderful in Berlin but did not adapt well to the Southern California climate. I really loved both Mrs. Borisoff and my piano lessons, and between her and my parents' influence, I have developed a lifelong love of classical music.

My parents' Jungian background shaped our early days in Los Angeles. For one thing, having their practices at our home meant that I met a lot of the patients, who used the dining room as the waiting room. This was such an early time in the development of Jung's psychology that many of the patients became personal friends. In fact, my parents' social group was made up almost exclusively of their patients, so that, as a young boy growing up, I had little idea of the difference between patients and friends.

The first thing that I did when I came home from school was knock on my mother's door, and she would come out and make me a peanut butter and jelly sandwich. To a child, it seemed an entirely normal routine, and if her patients minded this, I never heard about it. What I did hear many years later, when I was already a Jungian analyst, was how many people remembered my knocking at the door and coming in and disturbing their session while my mother went out to make a sandwich for me, although when they told these stories later, it was always in the context of something humorous. When I was a young analyst, though, I would feel quite embarrassed when I was reminded about these interruptions, and I often found myself wondering what my mother said about me to her patients. It was obviously positive, because they would say extremely complimentary things to me, but nonetheless, it made me very uncomfortable. From a contemporary perspective regarding boundary and frame issues of psychotherapy and transference and counter-transference, interruptions of this sort would be absolutely verboten and could quite possibly lead to an ethics charge. Oddly, the individuals whose therapy or analysis I interrupted never consciously expressed hostility or other negative reactions to it, except for Michael Fordham, who saw my mother when she was still nursing me. I assume he had a negative reaction to being interrupted frequently by an infant, since his first words upon being introduced to me as an adult were, "My rival!"

Our first house in Los Angeles was really too small for our large, blended family. Space was a real problem, and my "room" was in the closet off the master bedroom. It was a large closet, though, big enough for both a small bed and a chair, and for the first few months I still suffered the residual effects of the London bombings and was afraid of both sudden noises and sleeping in a bed. Initially I slept in the chair, then gradually moved over to the bed. My mother and father slept in separate bedrooms, and my mother had the master bedroom with the large closet. This increased my emotional closeness to her, which persisted all through my childhood. I had a host of nighttime fears that my mother could allay, and I would tell her dreams that she remembered and I have never been able to recall. I remained in that closet for almost four years, until we moved two blocks away to the first house that my parents bought.

In 1941 Max and Lore Zeller and their son Dan arrived in Los Angeles. They lived with us for several months until they found their own small house. Max had been certified as a Jungian analyst in Germany in 1938 by Gustav Richard Heyer, a leading student of Jung's in prewar Germany. However, because of the German work laws against Jews, Max had never been able to practice in Germany and only began being an analyst in Los Angeles. Max and my mother had almost daily contact with one another, and I believe that she informally acted as his supervisor and quasi-therapist. Lore, ten years younger than Max, was busy making the transition to Los Angeles and was just beginning to learn about Jung's psychology. Max and my father saw each other frequently, but there was never any real intimacy between the two. For the remainder of their lives they continued to use the formal *Sie*, never the personal *Du*. My father and Lore also saw a lot of each other, but the two of them never had a comfortable relationship. Lore was in analysis with my father, and I don't think that was a rousing success. Years later, after both my mother and Max died, Lore attempted to get closer to my father, but my father resisted her efforts. A steady hostility simmered between the two, though it was seldom directly expressed.

In 1941 my father made the acquaintance of Bruno Klopfer, another German Jewish refugee living in Los Angeles, who was instrumental in development of the Rorschach ink blot test, which was very well-known in the United States. He was a professor of psychology at Columbia University and at UCLA, as well as a brilliant interpreter of the Rorschach. My father studied with Klopfer after he came to Los Angeles, and he also made the acquaintance of Mary Crile, a recently widowed, rather introverted English woman who had just moved to Altadena, California. The Rorschach seminars were held at her house, and I was often taken there while my father participated in the seminars. Although I remember taking the Rorschach test, I'm not sure how often I took it, and I don't remember ever receiving any interpretation of the tests I did take. But I do remember the drives to Altadena with my father during the war years, when gasoline was rationed, and how he had to save his coupons in order to make the trip. Part of the drive to Altadena was via the Arroyo Seco, which at that time was the only freeway in Los Angeles, stretching between downtown Los Angeles and Pasadena. Angelenos were just becoming familiar with the freeway concept, while today it is hard to imagine Los Angeles before it was laced with freeways!

Beginning in 1942, my father began to give evening seminars on untranslated works of Jung or on various themes from the Old Testament. Some of his patients at that time were well-known movie stars, and when I was a young boy, it was a thrill for me to meet some of these well-known personalities that I had seen on the movie screen. One in particular was a well-known Jewish comedian who would absolutely have me in stitches with his hilarious routine. Neither of my parents really had much of a sense of humor, and I think that I enjoyed him so much because he brought humor into the house. During my own analysis he came up in several dreams, and in the dream context generally represented compensatory humor, which I realized I needed to connect with. When I brought home friends from school, they would be shocked to see a famous movie star in the house. Unfortunately, having such recognizable movie stars as patients seemed to inflate my father and gave me a false sense of importance as well. These were the halcyon days of the Hollywood movie industry, when everyone went to the movies for entertainment, and in Los Angeles, living in proximity to such celebrity could be heady stuff. In my case, the transition from hiding underground in fear of our lives to being on the edge of fame was very abrupt for one so young. I still do not like to think of myself during that era, because I realize my inflation made me rather difficult.

During the war Kate Marcus made her way to the United States from Berlin, finally arriving in Beverly Hills by Greyhound bus. She had studied with Julius Spier, a psychochirologist who had been in analysis with Jung. Chirology interested Jung as it seemed an auxiliary method of approaching the unconscious, and Jung had written an introduction to Spier's book, *The Hands of Children*. Spier fled to the Netherlands just before World War II and developed a group studying psychology and chirology in Amsterdam. He died in September, 1942, during the Nazi occupation of Holland. Kate escaped and became one of the early analysts in Los Angeles. She did a handprint of me at age nine which I still have, but I do not remember being given any interpretation of it.

While my mother lacked any formal education beyond high school, my father had graduated from medical school in Heidelberg. However, he was not able to use his medical degree in Los Angeles since he had not gone through an American internship, which was a requirement to obtain a medical license in California, a requirement adopted, I suspect, as a convenient method for keeping foreign doctors out of the state. The state of New York was more lenient and did not have an American internship requirement. My father was anxious to gain a US medical license, and he moved to New York City in 1943 and studied intensively for seven months in order to pass the New York state medical licensing exam. He brought Mary Crile, who had been a patient of his, with him, and they lived together in a simple New York hotel. These were the war years, and travel was not easy. My mother continued to see patients in Los Angeles and never went to visit my father in New York. I am sure that my mother knew of the relationship, and when my father and Mary came back, all three remained very close friends. Mary moved to Carmel in 1947 and later went on to Big Sur, but she remained close to our family. As a child I did not know that Mary was living with my father in New York, something I only learned in my adult years. Of course, if this sort of sexual relationship with a former patient occurred today, it would be considered a serious ethical violation, but neither of my parents apparently viewed it as an ethical breach.

Although obtaining a New York medical license made my father feel he had reclaimed something the Nazis took from him, on a professional level, it didn't really help him to have a medical license from one state and practice in another. In spite of his New York licensure, he remained separate from the larger psychotherapeutic and growing psychoanalytic community in Los Angeles. From time to time he entertained fantasies of moving to New York, where his medical license would be recognized, but the idea never moved beyond fantasy. He also briefly considered doing an internship in Los Angeles. He was in a study group at the Cedars of Lebanon Hospital with Otto Fenichel, though the group barely tolerated his participation. Fenichel died during his internship at Cedars, and this heavily influenced my father not to do an internship himself. He was older than the other interns and was literally afraid of dying from all the overwork that interns did in those days. Unfortunately, his decision not to do an American internship barred him from ever joining the medical psychiatric community of Los Angeles. He made a few brief attempts to become part of the community, but on one occasion, when he gave a lecture at a conference, psychoanalysts in the audience got up and left in protest. After that my father gave up, but giving up meant that he was marginalized for his entire career, both because he was a Jungian and because he did not have the proper license to practice in California.

In 1944, my parents bought the two-story house on Barrows Drive, which at the time cost $13,000, and from that time on I had my own bedroom. The house was only two blocks away from our first home, close enough that none of the children had to change schools, which was part of the rationale for moving so close by. I appreciated having a real bedroom, but many things changed after we moved. My sister Ruth eloped with a Merchant Marine and got married in Las Vegas, Nevada. My father was absolutely furious, but it didn't change our lives much at first. She continued to live at home and go to high school while her husband was at sea. Two years later, she had a daughter, Kathy, and the two of them lived with us until her husband Doug came back from the war.

The change was less dramatic for my brothers. My brother Jim had graduated from Berkeley and was getting a master's degree in biochemistry, with hopes of entering medical school at the University of Southern California. Jerry was having a difficult time in high school, and he was getting ready to enter the Army. Meanwhile, I did well in school, became a "teacher's pet," and was advanced a full grade. I enjoyed the academic challenge, but on a social level it always left me the youngest in the class. After starting school I'd assumed a leadership role in class, but after moving ahead, I shunned the limelight until my junior year in high school. Later, relationships with girls were difficult. Whatever academic advantage acceleration provided, it wasn't worth the social difficulties that I encountered afterward, although it did create a precedent in my life. I became a Jungian analyst at age thirty-two, was president of our Institute at age forty, and was much younger than other presidents of the IAAP. In retrospect, I entered Jungian training a year or two too early, and I would have gotten more out of the training if I had waited a year or two. This rush to achieve was part of both a conscious and unconscious push by my parents to succeed in this new cultural setting which was such a mystery to them. It is typical of immigrants who push their children to achieve and establish themselves in the new country. It was not until I was midway in my Jungian analytic training that I was temporarily stopped by Jo Wheelwright and told to slow down. What was the rush? His putting the brakes on me was one of the best things that he could have done. Of course I was disappointed at the time, as I thought I was ready to advance, but he did me a real favor.

After the war ended, normal travel resumed, and the world once again became accessible. My parents had felt isolated during the war years, so in the summer of 1946, my father and I flew from Los Angeles to Mexico City, continuing on to Guatemala City, to visit his aging mother and other relatives who had escaped from Nazi Germany. That was my first flight of many to follow, and it was an extremely turbulent one at that. We had to fly around the two volcanoes outside of Mexico City instead of above them, as airplanes did not yet have pressurized cabins. I and many of the other passengers became extremely airsick.

Upon arrival in Mexico City, we spent three days with a childhood friend of my father's from Germany. My father's friend, Bartholomeus, had an important position with Ford in Mexico. Bartholomeus and my father spoke only German to one another, and that really upset me. I complained bitterly, and temporarily they would speak English, but they would always fall back into German. Generally, I did not like hearing German growing up, and I would be rather insistent that people around me change to English. However, we had many relatives and friends who spoke German, so, in spite of my objections, I heard the language often, but my experience in Mexico City with my father's childhood friend focused my resistance to the language. Of course I am sorry now that I did not take the opportunity to become bilingual, and I have regretted it ever since. However, during the war it was not a good idea to speak German in the United States. In England it was even worse, as German refugees were often sent to special detention centers as suspected spies. In any event, it was extremely important to my family that I become fully Americanized, something I seemed to sense and tried to ensure in my insistence on speaking English.

I still believe my resistance to learning German was part of my American assimilation process. Growing up I never felt completely American and frequently felt different from the other children in school. It began in kindergarten, where my British accent was the subject of much ridicule, and it didn't take long for me to completely lose my British English and adapt to American pronunciation. I felt quite humiliated that I was different from all the others in the class, in spite of the fact that my classmates at school from kindergarten through twelfth grade were almost entirely Caucasian and predominantly Jewish. In high school we had one black and one Hispanic student, and the Hispanic residents in Los Angeles at that time had been there for several generations.

After Mexico City, we went to visit my relatives in Guatemala. My father took me to famous tourist sites, like Lake Atitlán, Chichicastenango, and Antigua, which I remember to this day. I took many photographs that I put into an album and used for a class project the following year. The principal, Ms. Dorothy Troeger, heard about my trip, and I was invited down to her office. She was so interested in the trip that she invited my parents to school, and then she came to our house for dinner one night. I found this highly unusual, because generally being called to the principal's office meant trouble!

My parents also didn't waste much time in traveling back to Europe after the war. My father went back to see Jung in 1947, and my mother in 1949 and again in 1950. Later in 1950, though, cracks appeared in the very foundation of our family. I had just graduated from junior high school and was preparing to leave for a boy's summer camp in the San Jacinto Mountains near Los Angeles for nine weeks. Just before leaving for camp, my father told me that he and my mother were going to get a divorce and that he was going to marry a much younger patient, a woman I knew whose husband had taught me how to swim. I was extremely upset and angry and pretty disgusted with my father, and I really let him know it. He listened respectfully, and then I went away to camp for nine weeks in much turmoil about what was going to happen with my parents. Midway through the summer session, I received a note from both my mother and father saying that they were not going to get a divorce and that they had reconciled. I was greatly relieved at the time, and my mood at camp improved markedly. My camp experience changed from my being in the doldrums to receiving an award for being the best all-around camper in the upper division.

My parents, but especially my mother, wanted me to fit into the American way of life, although she had very little idea what it meant to be "American." Whatever being American was, though, she wanted me to fit in with it, and she relied on my older brother Jerry to guide her about what were appropriate activities for me and what were not. Of course, she also wanted to preserve my connection to my European and Jewish roots. Hence, the structure of my extracurricular activities was diverse. She encouraged me in sports, but I also studied piano for ten years and went to Hebrew school for almost as long. I became a good tennis player, playing in numerous junior tournaments in Southern California. In those days most of the top players in the country came out of Southern California, and I was playing against players who later became members of the Davis cup team. Needless to say, I was trounced on several occasions. I became so engrossed in tennis that I practiced and played for three hours every day after school, as well as most of the day on Saturday and Sunday.

Professional sports were family favorites. We had season tickets to the Los Angeles Rams professional football games from 1947 through 1953, and my mother fell in love with the Rams quarterback, Bob Waterfield, who was married to Jane Russell, a very sexy movie star of that era. My brother Jerry also frequently went to the games, and we had wonderful times together.

Eventually, though, my parents began to worry that I was not spending enough time on my studies. In 1951 they sent my horoscope to Ernst Bernhard in Rome. Bernhard was a cousin of Max Zeller and a friend of theirs from their Berlin days. He had become the founder of the Jungians in Italy, having emigrated there in 1935. After studying the horoscope, he told them they should not worry about me and that my interest in sports was a positive thing.

I enjoyed piano and Hebrew classes when I had good teachers, but I found that I lost interest when I was forced to change instructors. However, classical music itself always caught my interest. My parents bought classical records for me and took me to symphony concerts from about the age of five. One of their first purchases when we came to the US was a record player that I had until I went away to college. The symphonies, records, and my parents' enthusiasm instilled a love of classical music that has never faded.

With the development of international air travel in the aftermath of World War II, my parents began to invite analysts from Zürich and London to come to Los Angeles. They were eager to reconnect with friends and colleagues from Switzerland and England since they felt professionally isolated in Los Angeles. Many of Jung's closest associates came to visit, and my parents were so happy to have them around. They often stayed with us, and my parents took terrific care of them. The three that I remember best were Marie-Louise von Franz, who seemed like a frumpy schoolteacher, Rivka Schaerf, an extremely scholarly woman who at the time seemed more intellectual than von Franz, and Michael Fordham from London. At the time Marie-Louise von Franz helped Jung with Latin translations and was also an analyst. Over time she became a major spokesperson for Jung's psychology. Rivka Schaerf was a Swiss Jew and a biblical scholar Jung liked and published. She later married Yechezkel Kluger, and they moved to Israel. Michael Fordham, my mother's first patient, was becoming a leading Jungian analyst in Britain. He worked as a child psychiatrist, which was not common at the time. These three were the first Zürich and London Jungians I was to meet.

I went to Fairfax High School, which at the time was over 90 percent Jewish. Many of the students had older relatives from New York or Eastern Europe living with them, and I learned a lot of Yiddish expressions. Neither of my parents spoke Yiddish, only German. There were several private clubs or fraternities and sororities at the high-school level. I wasn't sure whether I wanted to join one, and my mother didn't know what to think about it. She asked my older brother Jerry to find out about the fraternities, and he gave his approval. So in the tenth grade I pledged the Lochinvars, where most of the members were good students who were interested in school politics and not terribly "macho." It was a good fit for me, and it helped me to make the adjustment to the high school social scene.

My cousin Peter, the son of my mother's brother in London, came to stay with us in January, 1950, and lived with us until he started Cambridge University that fall. He was three years older than me and in many ways became more like a brother than my own half brothers were. He was already a brilliant mathematician and scientist, and we had a competitive relationship in sports and academics and in our social lives. He tutored me in math and Latin, and I did very well. My parents became second parents to him for many years, as his parents were for me when I began traveling to Europe.

Fairfax High School was located close to Hollywood and Beverly Hills, and many of the students had parents associated with the entertainment business, while others became well-known in the entertainment business in their own right. One event stands out among my memories of living along the edges of film culture. I was taking an advanced Latin class, and we were supposed to be reading Ovid and Lucretius, but our teacher, Mr. McGrath, was more interested in talking about Zsa Zsa Gabor, who was the rage at the time. A girl in the class named Cynthia, whose father worked in the movie industry, said she could arrange for Zsa Zsa to visit the class if the group could skip the planned final exam. Mr. McGrath agreed, and we waited to see whether our classmate would be able to pull this off. Incredibly enough, she did, and Zsa Zsa paid the Fairfax advanced Latin class a visit. It was quite an event, not only at Fairfax, but in the media as well. A photo of her visiting the school even made it into one of the national magazines, *Time* or *Newsweek*. And advanced Latin did not have a final exam that year.

After the threat of my parents' divorce was averted, they wanted to take a sabbatical year in Zürich. I did not want my high school social life disrupted and refused to consider it. Eventually, my parents decided against going for the year and instead made consecutive trips to Zürich the following spring.

As my high school years progressed, I became more focused. I studied more, but also played on the tennis team and ran for class president. I lost to the captain of the football team, but it was a close election. I remained active in student government, though, and by the time of my senior year was a well-rounded student. I also had my first semi-serious girlfriend, and I considered attending college somewhere close to Los Angeles so that we could continue to see each other. Eighty-five percent of our class of five hundred went on to college, many of them to UCLA. In some ways it seemed a logical choice, but something inside said that I did not want to do that. I realized that I needed to get away from Los Angeles and the environment I was immersed in. I wanted to experience the world outside of Hollywood and the movie industry and outside of the strongly Jewish environment of my neighborhood and school.

My parents, and especially my mother, continued to take an active interest in my dream life. I had an early repetitive dream in which I was at the beach and big waves came up and threatened to overwhelm me. I always awakened before the waves took me under. I told this dream and many others to my mother, who always had some unsettling but accurate remark about the meaning of the dream in relationship to my life. When growing up I often had the feeling that my mother could anticipate my needs. This was both a blessing and a curse because, while her insights amazed me, they also imbued her with tremendous power. I found myself asking for her opinion on a host of subjects, some of them quite intimate, and most of the time, she was correct. As an example, at about the age of thirteen I decided I needed to get in shape and began going to the gym to work out with weights. She told me I might meet unsavory characters there and spoke to me about homosexuality and other sexual pressures. While I had no problems at the gym, she was definitely watching out for me. She was correct so often that I had great difficulty going against her opinion. I would go to her for advice about problems with my high school girlfriend and even later in life, which I suspect had a negative effect on my first marriage. It was not until I left home for college and later entered analysis that I began to have some perspective on the shadow aspects of such intimacy and how her intrusive nature was inhibiting my masculine development. On the positive side, though, her abilities to seemingly look into my soul gave me a very positive attitude toward the unconscious and its wisdom, the power it had in my daily life and how it revealed feelings and emotions.

Looking back now on my relationship with my mother during my school years, I realize how much she looked at me as a little husband. She gave me a lot, but was far too involved in my emotional life. It took me many years of analysis with Joe Henderson to really see the dangers of having such strong positive feelings toward one's mother. With the help of analysis I was able to pull back from the relationship without having to break off with her completely. I know that it was hard for her to lose our sense of intimacy, but her background as a Jungian analyst helped her accept it, although I'm sure she felt that I had moved too far away emotionally, while I was comfortable with our rebalanced relationship. I don't think that we ever fully resolved that tension, but when she was dying of pancreatic cancer I visited her often, and we had a positive relationship at the end of her life.

My father's comments about Jung did not touch my soul in the way my mother's did. I barely tolerated many of his interests, and I'm sure he was bitterly disappointed that I was not reading Kant, Schopenhauer, and Goethe and focusing on intellectual subjects rather than playing tennis. I'm sure, too, that he had difficulty with my closeness to my mother. But one side effect of my father's affair the summer before I entered high school was that his opinion lost weight in my estimation, and I didn't pay much attention to his wishes.

Jung's name was often mentioned around the dinner table, and I usually listened with respect, but my siblings felt that Jung came ahead of them and responded negatively to his being mentioned. Many Jungian terms worked their way into conversations, and so I learned about the various archetypes without really knowing what they meant. Living in Los Angeles right after the war was a difficult time to be a Jungian. All the information about the full extent of the Holocaust was coming out, and psychoanalysis in Los Angeles was heavily dominated by Jews, some of the most prominent ones having fled from Europe as my parents had. The fact that my father was both Jewish and a Jungian was anathema to the psychoanalysts, and my parents and Max Zeller reciprocated the negative feelings. My father had several negative encounters with psychoanalysts, and increasingly I learned that Freudians were evil.

My friends seemed to like to come over to the house, and my mother was always very welcoming. My father was welcoming, too, but could never remember any of their names. I gave him a very hard time about this. The only person I remember who was not comfortable coming to our house was my first girlfriend. Her parents were Jewish business people and did not like the fact that my parents were interested in dreams. So, although she lived almost directly across the street, she wasn't allowed to come to our house. However, I was allowed to take her to San Diego to visit a patient of my parents I had visited many times before. Her husband, who was not a patient, was the harbor pilot for San Diego, and we had an absolutely lovely day on San Diego Bay.

I began to plan for college. I intended to be a premed student, then go to medical school and perhaps become a psychiatrist. I did not want to endure the hassles my father had because he wasn't recognized as a doctor in California. Applying to colleges and universities then was much different from what it is now. Harvard was looking for students from the West Coast, and I was invited to apply, but I was not interested in going so far away from my home, family, and girlfriend. I looked at Pomona College to the east of Los Angeles but felt that was too close to home. I ended up applying to the University of California Berkeley and Reed College in Portland, Oregon. A long article in the *Saturday Evening Post* had extolled the virtues of Reed College, its small classes, individual attention, and lack of emphasis on grades. All this appealed to me. I visited Berkeley and liked it very much, but I could not make up my mind for months. My mother was completely exasperated with my indecision. In desperation she pulled the *I Ching* off her shelf and said that, when one cannot make a decision, one can ask the *I Ching*, and the answer will be there in the *I Ching's* symbolic language. I threw the coins and came up with a hexagram that I cannot remember now. After much discussion she decided that the *I Ching* was saying that I needed to go to a small college where I would have more individual attention, rather than a large university like the University of California. That decided it, and I was going to Reed College. I did not know anyone in Portland and never had visited Reed, but the *I Ching* had spoken! This was my first experience of trusting the unconscious through using the *I Ching* to gain a deeper understanding of a problem.

As my senior year drew to a close, my mother offered to take me to Europe with them as a high school graduation present. At first I was indifferent to the idea, but as graduation approached, I grew more interested. Late in the spring my mother went back to Zürich to see C.A. Meier in analysis. She was still feeling the reverberations of the near divorce a couple of years earlier. My father called on his family for help, and my cousin, Bea, his sister's daughter, came to take care of both my father and me. She was a little older than I was and had just graduated from Goddard College. I got a very bad case of herpes in the mouth and could not eat for several weeks. It was just too painful. I lost about twenty pounds, and my mother in Zürich was quite worried. I missed my high school graduation ceremony and all the ritual associated with it. I did recover from herpes, and my father and I traveled to Europe alone, where we visited London and Paris before meeting up with my mother in Zürich. And so my focus expanded as I stepped outside of Los Angeles and California.

3

RETURN TO EUROPE

The transition from high school to college was one of the biggest transitions of my life, not only because I left home for the first time, but also because of the European summer trip I took with my parents after graduation, which was an introduction to the continent and the worldview that had shaped my family.

In many ways, being opened up in this way caught me by surprise. From age four to seventeen, I had done everything to adapt to my new home in the United States, but in spite of this, there were aspects of my life that set it aside from the typical American childhood. Beneath the surface, I felt a restlessness and unease that my experiences growing up in the Jewish section of Los Angeles from 1940 through 1953 could not explain or resolve. My family was not like the other families in our neighborhood. My parents had a strange profession that placed a powerful emphasis on dreams, every wall of our house seemed covered with books, and classical music was a mainstay of our home. In school, on the other hand, the emphasis was on social life and on sports. My parents, especially my father, did not understand or accept these priorities. Hence, there was much tension between the values that I was exposed to at school and those which I was receiving through my family, although, of course, my parents wanted me to succeed in school all the same.

By the time that I had graduated from high school, my adaptation to American culture was pretty complete. I had done well enough academically, was involved in competitive sports through tennis and basketball, run for school office, and been part of a high school fraternity. I had also had my first serious girlfriend, and so on one level, I appeared well adapted. At least, that was the general impression I gave to others. At a deeper level, I was aware of a level of anxiety that I did not know what to do with.

24

When I graduated from high school in 1953, post-war travel to Europe was just beginning. It still was an unusual thing to do, but my parents had made going to Europe the highest priority, although the continent they returned to was hardly the continent they knew before the war. War-time rationing was still in effect for meat and butter in England, and the rest of Europe was just recovering from the devastation of World War II.

After school was out, my father and I traveled to London and Paris alone and then went on to Zürich to join my mother. We traveled by air from Los Angeles, with an intermediate stop in New York, arriving in Prestwick, Scotland, on a Sunday afternoon when everything was closed. Scotland was bleak and empty, and London was still full of rubble that had not yet been removed. However, the coronation of Queen Elizabeth II had just taken place, and London was as spruced up as it could be considering the overall level of devastation. There were not many Americans there, and I stood out like a sore thumb with my California clothing of light blue denim pants and an Eisenhower jacket. My cousin Peter Kirstein and I queued to see the crown jewels at Westminster Abbey, and he could not stand the long wait, so he went up the side pew. I followed him, but an English policeman apprehended us. I was easily recognizable as an American and received a severe scolding from him in front of that large crowd, while my English cousin quietly slipped back into the line. The ease with which he vanished into the crowd, while I earned a reprimand, has stayed with me all these years, an example that illustrates both the friendliness and competitiveness of our relationship.

Having felt so Americanized at the time of my departure, I was surprised that being back in London brought back a flood of memories of my life prior to leaving for California. I was suddenly overwhelmed with images of sleeping on a chair in the shelter and all the antiaircraft guns on Hampstead Heath. Even more overwhelming was remembering the traumatic effect of so many bombs falling close to our London home, the terror that I felt walking on the streets of Golders Green, and the fear I could see in my mother's eyes when we went shopping. We never went out without wondering if suddenly there would be an air raid and where we would go for safety if one did begin. Of course that did happen, and my mother was quick to pull me off the street and under cover. Once I was on the third floor of our house, and an air raid began. I was quickly whisked to the basement, which was considered the safest place if an air raid occurred while we were at home. I remember my mother's panic at the time and how infectious it was. Another night my father had dug up an incendiary bomb, which could have destroyed our house and everyone in it, from the middle of our backyard. A fear of sudden loud noises or pops has remained with me till this day. Even opening a bottle of champagne can make my heart race. After putting these slumbering memories aside for so many years, it was difficult to confront them that summer, but even then I realized that it was important to face them and work through them. In my adult life I have often thought of spending some time in London with a Society of Analytical Psychology analyst and doing a regressive analysis of my early infancy in London. At times that urge has been fairly strong, but it never seemed quite urgent enough to actually follow through with it. Still, in looking back, returning to London that summer before college seems like a significant bridge between my early childhood and adulthood, something that was crucial for my overall development and that played an important role in my relations to the Jungian community in London later on.

The next stop that my father and I made was in Paris. The doctor who had helped my father pass the medical exam in New York during the war, whose name was Tuchman, had retired there. Of course they spoke German to one another, while all around me all I heard was French. I felt completely helpless in Paris, and I decided immediately that learning French would become a high priority for me in college. French was the *lingua franca* of the times, and I still was not ready to learn German formally. My father was interested in showing me all the Paris museums, and as a seventeen-year-old I was more interested in the nightlife. We did do both, but I became exhausted by the foreignness of everything there and by not understanding a single word of the language. We left Paris by train to go on to Zürich to meet my mother. Given all the destruction from the war, I found both London and Paris quite drab, and it was only when we arrived in Zürich that I really came alive.

Arriving in Switzerland was like being on another planet. The Swiss had not succumbed to the Nazis, and Switzerland had barely been touched by the war. There was no evidence of destruction. The streets were clean, and everything worked. I was charmed by the old world architecture, churches, and natural scenery. My parents stayed at the Hotel Sonnenberg, a lovely setting with excellent food. The hotel became their and my home in Zürich for the next ten years. The owners, Mr. and Mrs. Rudi Wismer, made many special accommodations to my parents and me, and we could always find a place to stay there even when the hotel was full. Many a time a bed was put in the bathroom, and I stayed there, though usually I only did this for one night at a time. At that time, many European hotels did not have a shower or bath in every room, so there were always bathrooms on each floor. The Hotel Sonnenberg was close to the original Jung Institute and high up on the Zürichberg, which meant that one had a fabulous view of Lake Zürich and the city from the terrasse. It was also right on the edge of a large forest where one could walk for hours in the woods and, at the same time, see the farmers bringing in the hay. Suburbia had not hit Zürich yet, and at that time the city quickly turned from city life to farmland. It was a popular place for students at the Jung Institute, and with the favorable exchange rate one could stay there for five dollars a day with three wonderful meals. However, by the mid-1960s, my father had gotten into some argument with the Wismers as he was prone to do, and so after that my parents found other hotels in Zürich. More recently the Hotel Sonnenberg has become the world headquarters for FIFA, the international soccer association, so one can no longer have dinners or hold meetings there. But I can still become quite sentimental about Hotel Sonnenberg, because it was such a wonderful place to stay.

During that stay in Zürich, which lasted for about two weeks, I met many of the first generation of Zürich analysts such as C.A. Meier, Heinrich Fierz, Aniela Jaffé, the Hurwitz family, Liliane Frey-Rohn, and Barbara Hannah. My mother thought I was conflicted about leaving Los Angeles and my girlfriend, and my parents thought it would be a good idea for me to see Meier professionally once while I was there. I did see him and explained my situation to him, and he recommended that I not have any therapy then, but that I should just go on and live my life, let my problems develop and my "neurosis grow," and enter analysis later. How right he was! I went back to Zürich with my parents in the summers of 1955 and 1956 with no thought of analysis.

There was a certain familiarity about Zürich that explained the contrast I found between my parents' values and those of my Los Angeles neighborhood. My parents' values were right at home in Zürich. Everyone here seemed to share that deep sense of culture, intellectual curiosity, introverted sensibility, charm, and disdain for ostentatiousness. People seemed aware of their roots in European traditions, yet they were not afraid to discuss shadow issues. All the values I'd absorbed, which at times made me feel so out of step in Los Angeles, made me feel right at home in Zürich. I was drawn immediately to the depth of the people I met, and their closeness to Jung made a strong positive impression as well.

I especially liked the Hurwitz family, Sigi and Lena, who had two children, Immanuel and Naomi, who were about my age and who later became my traveling companions. Sigi Hurwitz, Jung's dentist, was also a scholar of Jewish mysticism at the Jung Institute, while Lena Hurwitz was the general editor of Jung's *Collected Works* in German. Unfortunately, she died from pancreatic cancer at a fairly young age. The Hurwitz parents had deep connections both to Jung and the Jungian community and to their Judaism and Israel. I still remember their traditional Shabbat dinners.

That trip was also my first introduction to the Swiss Alps and the culture of hiking and *Wanderweg*. Hiking in the Alps is so civilized, with accurate markers telling one how long it is going to take to reach one's destination, and often that destination will have a small hotel and restaurant. One did not have to worry about poison oak or poisonous snakes along the path and could focus instead on the pristine valleys, beautiful mountain peaks, and immense glaciers without worrying about disasters on the trail. Then one could come back to the hotel and enjoy a wonderful meal. Hiking in the Alps has become a lifelong passion, and there are very few things that I enjoy more.

In that first trip to the Swiss Alps we went to Zermatt, which is at the foot of the Matterhorn. One day we took the cog railway up to ten thousand feet, where we enjoyed a panoramic view of the Alps, including the Matterhorn. The train ride was a little more than an hour, and I sat with a group of four middle-aged Americans from Southern California. Since I also was from Southern California, it was only natural that we struck up a conversation. We chatted amiably till we reached the top, and, as we were about to get off the train, the woman asked me if I knew who I had been talking to. I said I had no idea and was shocked when she told me it was Walt Disney! When we got off the train at the top, hundreds of people there wanted to get a glimpse of him. He is probably the most famous person I have ever met. Two days later I met him again walking in the village of Zermatt, and he was friendly, but I was suddenly extremely shy. Three years later Disneyland opened in Southern California, and the Matterhorn ride was one of the featured rides. I knew where he had gotten the inspiration for it.

Between meeting the Jungians in Zürich and falling in love with the Swiss Alps, Switzerland quickly became my favorite place to visit, and it has remained so for the past fifty-five years. In spite of all the changes over the course of my life, my deep love of the Swiss people and all things Swiss has remained. I have been back so many times that I cannot count the number, but it has been at least sixty!

From Switzerland my mother and I met my favorite cousin, Peter Kirstein, and the three of us traveled to Rome and Naples, where we all had a marvelous time.

From that time on the European continental influence, which I had been fighting all those years in Los Angeles, emerged in full force. I wanted to immerse myself in European culture and to study its history. I wanted to study both French and German and to be able to speak with the people I was meeting, make deeper connections with my European roots. Although I was a pre-med student at Reed College, I took only the minimum science requirements so that I could pursue my new cultural interests. Plato, Kant, and British empirical philosophers attracted my attention, along with an interest in the literature of France. Also, as part of my European immersion, I began a four-year study of French, which I continued intermittently over the next four decades. I spent a year in individual reading of *À la Recherche du Temps Perdu* by Proust, which was both fascinating and tedious at the same time. But I can always say that I did read Proust in French, and that impresses some people!

Somehow reconnecting to my European roots helped make the transition to Reed College a little bit easier. It was not an easy transition, but it was reinforced by my new interest in studying the humanities and my strong wish to become a psychiatrist. I had read Jung's *Modern Man in Search of a Soul* and Frieda Fordham's *An Introduction to Jung's Psychology*, and they had both made an enormous impression on me. Reed had a very strong humanities program, and to this day I find myself referencing readings I did at that time.

I began Reed College in September, 1953. During the first week of orientation before classes I was playing tennis when I was invited to the office of the president of the college. It turned out that president Duncan Ballantine was an avid tennis player, and they were looking for a fourth for doubles. So prior to starting classes I was out on the court playing tennis with the president of the college and calling him by his first name! This was certainly different from high school!

Reed was known as a very liberal college, and a common phrase of Oregonians was that Reed represented "communism, atheism, and free love." That was a gross exaggeration, but there was just enough truth to the saying to give it staying power. Shortly after my arrival, President Ballantine did not allow a speaker on campus who was a suspected communist. Although it was the height of the McCarthy era, the faculty council was extremely powerful and passed a motion of no confidence in the president. Shortly thereafter, President Ballantine resigned. I missed him as a tennis partner.

I had two roommates at Reed. One of them, Claudio Segre, was a close friend whose father was a Nobel prize-winning physicist at the University of California. During high school, Claudio had done what my parents had wanted me to do: he had traveled with his parents in Europe as a teenager, gone to school in Switzerland, and become fluent in French and Italian. Needless to say, I was quite envious of him at the time. Claudio later became a professor of history at the University of Texas and a leading expert on the Holocaust in Italy. Sadly, his life was cut short when, while on sabbatical in Berkeley, he suffered a heart attack while jogging and died at a fairly young age.

During the summer between our sophomore and junior years, a group of four of us made plans to travel in Europe. Claudio and I had friends and relatives in many places in Europe, so we spearheaded the effort. In those days, one could still easily get by on less than five dollars a day, so it wasn't hard for me to persuade two of my high school friends to come with us. One was Harvey Sagorsky, a close friend in high school who had a brilliant mind and was extremely introverted. He had been valedictorian of our high school class, and the summer before had spent a great deal of time with my father, who had encouraged Harvey to read all of Jung that was available in English at the time. Harvey did. I cannot remember ever discussing Jung with him, although at that time in our lives, he knew much more than I did.

At the time we scheduled the trip, Harvey was a premed student at Harvard. In May of that year, just weeks before we were to leave for our trip to Europe, I received a phone call informing me that Harvey had died of an accidental overdose from a compound in the chemistry lab. For some time it was thought to be an accidental death, but later I learned from Harvey's former roommate that suicide was likely. My father spent countless evenings with Harvey's parents trying to help them with the loss of their brilliant son.

The other high school friend was Howard Miller, who had been a close friend of Harvey's and was someone I barely knew. In spite of Harvey's death, the three of us decided to continue our plans to travel that summer, which was probably a mistake. There was a lot of bickering on the trip, and many times we were split about what we should do next. The disagreements essentially cost Claudio and me our friendship, and I did not see Howard again for fifty-four years. Only through the wonders of the internet did I locate him then, and it was great to see him. He had become a well-known lawyer in Los Angeles and at one time had served as president of the Los Angeles unified school system.

That summer, though, we met in New York and took the French ship *Liberté* to South-ampton, where we began our journey in London. I soon experienced gastrointestinal problems and could not find a physician who would agree to see me. My mother was in Zürich, so I flew there and the following day had an appendectomy under ether. I'd made plans with Claudio and Howard to meet them in Rome after my surgery. In the interim they went on to Paris, while I spent several days recuperating in Zürich.

My emergency appendectomy happened to coincide with the public celebration of Jung's eightieth birthday at the Grand Hotel Dolder at the top of the Zürichberg. There was a long receiving line to congratulate Jung, and my mother snuck me in past the authorities. I had a chance to give Jung my personal good wishes, and he was extremely warm toward me. He liked the fact that my mother had brought me into this formal affair. He absolutely charmed me, and from that moment on, I was hooked.

After a bit more recuperation in the Swiss Alps, I rejoined Claudio and Howard in Italy, and we continued our travels for the rest of the summer, although the frequent squabbles made us glad when the summer was finally over.

During spring break in 1956, my parents and Mary Whitehouse, a Jungian-oriented dance therapist, had attended the North-South meeting of Jungian analysts in Carmel. Afterward they all had driven up to Portland to visit me. I arranged for my father to give a lecture on Jung at the college, and he gave a wonderful lecture to a packed hall. The size of the audience was surprising, especially since the students were away for spring break, but Jung had been on the cover of *Time Magazine* in February, 1955, accompanied by a feature article about him, so he was becoming better known in the United States. My father's lecture at Reed transformed my relationship to him, and my appreciation for his vast knowledge of analytical psychology and related fields began to eclipse some of the problems that had clouded our relationship earlier. Some of the professors I admired most attended the lecture, and I saw my philosophy professor and my father discussing Aristotle, Plato, and Kant in relationship to Jung. It was an eye-opening moment.

The following summer my mother was a Los Angeles delegate to the newly formed International Association for Analytical Psychology, or IAAP, and my parents headed to Zürich for the August meeting. I was invited to go along with them. We started in Amsterdam and from there took a cruise down the Rhine. It was the first time that either of them had been back in Germany since the end of World War II, and the war seemed to color the entire cruise for them. They were at each other's throats the entire time, so that traveling with them was impossible. But I remember that we visited Heidelberg, where my father had gone to medical school. The average German could not understand how this American in his Beverly Hills clothes could speak such a beautiful German. When he said that he was German and had left the country in 1933, what inevitably followed was absolute silence, as if the conversation itself had fallen into a vacuum.

That same sense has colored my own efforts to speak German to Germans, in spite of my having taken a university-level course in German grammar, which, combined with the German I heard growing up, has made me fairly comfortable in the language. When I met Germans during the post-war years, I inevitably began to wonder what they did during the war and whether they were members of the Nazi party. This sort of inner dialogue plagued me for at least twenty years, especially since at that time almost no German would admit to having been a member of the Nazi party. I remember one occasion in which I was sitting on a park bench in Munich and struck up a conversation with a middle-aged man sitting at the other end. He went on about how Munich had been destroyed by allied bombing during the war and how terrible it was. I mentioned that I had been in London when the Germans had done the same thing, which surprised him, as he had never heard about German bombings. Then he admitted that he had been a Nazi, saying simply that that was what one did at the time. Incredibly, I actually found myself feeling relieved to hear him admit that, and, because of his honesty, I felt comfortable with him. He was the only German I ever met who was willing to admit an allegiance, let alone talk about it.

From Germany we went to Salzburg, where they were holding the week-long Salzburg Festival celebrating the two hundredth anniversary of Mozart's birth. My father had bought opera tickets for *The Magic Flute*, *The Marriage of Figaro*, *Così Fan Tutte*, *Don Giovanni*, and *Idomeneo*, along with tickets for several orchestral concerts. Because it was the bicentenary of Mozart's birth, it was only his music that was played that year. The greatest Mozart opera singers, some of the greatest in the world at that time, were in their prime and were singing. Singers like Elizabeth Schwarzkopf, Dietrich Fischer-Dieskau, Cesare Siepi, Walter Berry, Karl Böhm, Rita Streich, and many others were performing almost nightly. Although I had heard much Mozart prior to this week in Salzburg, I was so moved by the music that I was ready to almost change majors at college in order to engross myself in the magic of Mozart.

From Salzburg we traveled to Zürich, where my father and I had an afternoon tea with Jung. Emma Jung had died the previous November, and my father went out to pay his respects to Jung. We sat in the garden for an hour and a half, and I had a chance to ask Jung some questions. By then I had read more of his books, and I was somewhat versed in philosophy. In my most sophomoric fashion I asked Jung about his statement that everything was relative. I gently challenged him if that was not an absolute statement? He liked my lightly challenging him, and, although I cannot remember how he answered me, it clearly did not upset him. In fact, I think he liked being questioned about his ideas. I remember feeling extremely grateful to my father for the opportunity to visit Jung.

When I arrived back at Reed for my senior year, I was still full of the music of Mozart. It was what I wanted to study. On the other hand, I was a premed student, and I had signed up to do my thesis in biochemistry. However, I was also one of several selected to be a Rhodes scholar nominee from our college, and the selection process required one to write an essay on one's interests. I wrote about my experience with Mozart the previous summer. My knowledge was on a feeling level and was not an intellectual analysis of Mozart's music, and, when I was quizzed about Mozart, it was clear that there were many gaps in my knowledge. As a result, I did not do well in the interview and was not selected to be a Rhodes scholar. I'm sure that going to Oxford for two years before going to medical school in the United States would have changed the direction of my career substantially, but instead, I went ahead with my applications to medical schools in the US. As I look back on that experience, I realize that being a feeling type in Jungian terms expressed itself strongly in the Rhodes interview, that my feeling, as expressed in my love for Mozart, won out over my thinking, and that in turn hurt me in the interview. I see it now as part of my personality structure, but I would have done better at the Rhodes interview if I had stuck to my work and interest in science, where I was on much more solid ground. I suppose there is some regret about the road not taken, but it was also a blessing in many ways. At that stage in my life I was already very caught up in a pattern of overachievement and was becoming rather driven. Two years in Oxford as a Rhodes scholar would only have exacerbated that. Instead, I began to consider where I would attend medical school.

For the first time in my life, I was no longer part of a Jewish community, and over the course of my college experience I was able to reflect and contrast the world around me and the one I'd left behind. Slowly, I began to gain a certain perspective on my Jewish heritage. In many ways I had idealized the Hurwitz family in Zürich, where they all seemed to get along so well together within the context of a firm Jewish tradition, although Jewish ritual in their lives was limited to a Shabbat dinner on Friday nights. Still, they had all traveled to Israel and had a strong connection to being Jewish. Like all idealizations, though, this one did not quite hold. The family was extremely close, but Sigi was rather moody and distant, and father and son were really not that close, even though at the end of Sigi's life, he lived next door to Immanuel, his son. If I was searching for a way to integrate a sense of Jewish character into a modern, Western life as a psychiatrist, I would have to look further.

I also had the opportunity to meet Gershom Scholem at the Hurwitz home, and I found him fascinating, as well as one of the most brilliant people I have ever met. Each summer he came to lecture at the Eranos lectures, and the Eranos groups listened with rapt attention. Twelve years later I had another opportunity to have dinner with him in Los Angeles, and over dinner he described how he had faked schizophrenia to get out of the German army during World War I. He was one of those rare souls who was brilliant and quirky enough to pull that one off!

My search for a method of integrating Judaism into contemporary life was also influenced by a long-lost college friend of my father's who had visited Los Angeles. During my father's college years in Heidelberg, when he had belonged to the Zionist organization Blau-Weiss, or Blue White, he became friends with Erich Fromm and Ernst Simon. Simon had gone on to become a professor of education at the Hebrew University in Jerusalem and had become a close colleague of Martin Buber. Although my father and Simon had not seen each other in thirty years, they renewed their relationship when Simon had a sabbatical at the Hebrew University in Los Angeles. They ended up spending a lot of time together discussing religious, political, philosophical, and psychological issues. Professor Simon was convinced that Jung was anti-Semitic, and he and my father would have lively discussions on the subject. Generally someone's expressing beliefs in Jung's supposed anti-Semitism was sufficient grounds in my father's eyes for terminating a friendship, and Simon was one of the few people from whom my father was willing to tolerate a difference of opinion about Jung and Judaism. Simon was extremely liberal in his political views, and at the same time he was an observant, conservative Jew. His house in Jerusalem had been bombed because of his sympathy toward the Arab population.

My mother was particularly drawn to Professor Simon, and on some level I identified with my mother's attraction to him and to Judaism. I have always been ambivalent about being a member of a Jewish congregation, and growing up we never joined one, although my father had a positive relationship to Rabbi Sonderling, a German Jew who was my spiritual guide at the time of my bar mitzvah. On the other hand, Simon's passion for Israel, his idealism, and his acceptance of the Palestinians as potential equals drew me again closer to Judaism. This man was part of the central European, mainly German, Jewish collective who were the leaders of Zionism in the founding of Israel.

As a result of these contacts with impressive Jewish intellectuals, I decided to go to the new Albert Einstein College of Medicine in New York and enter their third class. I was looking forward to being part of this idealistic new medical school. I had also thought of going to medical school in Zürich, but I knew that there was a stigma attached to American Jews who went to medical school in Europe, as it usually meant that they were not able to get into an American medical school. I did not want that label applied to me, so I chose to go to Albert Einstein over some other American medical schools to which I was accepted.

Before heading east to medical school, there was another issue which had caused me many problems. That was my relationship to women. I had had two approximately year-long relationships with women at Reed, and I found myself pulling back from any commitment to them. In my senior year at Reed my girlfriend was three years older than me, and she wanted to live with me in New York when I went there for medical school. I did not want that, and at the same time I was not able to completely let go of her, either. The issue made me extremely anxious, and I thought that analysis might help, so I decided to turn to professional analysis for the first time in my life. I could not see anyone in Los Angeles because all the analysts there had either been in supervision or in analysis with my parents. So my parents suggested that I spend the summer in Zürich and see Professor Meier three times a week. They worked out an arrangement where I would stay in the servant's quarters of a hotel on the Zürichberg for under four dollars a day, which included three delicious meals.

A few weeks after graduating from Reed with a thesis in biochemistry, I headed to Zürich. I soon learned that Meier spent every August on the Italian coast and that nothing had interfered with this routine for probably thirty or forty years. So I had close to a month in Europe before I was to begin medical school in New York. I audited a class on the *puer aeternus* at the Jung Institute that was taught by Marie-Louise von Franz, and I played a good bit of tennis, sometimes picking up games with local Swiss who would turn up at the courts and occasionally with David Hart, who was a student at the Jung Institute in Zürich and liked to play.

I had met a family with two young children, and the parents and I decided to take a short trip to French Switzerland. When we got there, the family received a telephone call to let them know that one of the children was sick. So the wife returned to Zürich, and I was left alone with the man. I soon learned that he was basically homosexual, but a therapist in the Midwest had urged him to get married and have a family. In those days you absolutely hid any homoerotic tendencies. He broke down telling me his story, and I found myself extremely anxious. I was not interested in getting involved with him. After a very restless night, we returned to Zürich.

After that I felt even more strongly that I did not want to begin medical school without first having some analysis, notwithstanding the fact that Meier was in Italy. So I telephoned Liliane Frey-Rohn to see if I could have some hours with her. She was open to seeing me, and that is how I began to see her in addition to Meier. We worked on my dreams, and analysis greatly relieved my anxiety. However, I had only a few sessions with her that summer.

At the end of the summer I went camping in Florence with the two Hurwitz children and their mother, who stayed in a hotel. At the time Immanuel and Naomi did not speak English, so my spoken German improved markedly on the trip. It was marvelous to see Florence through their eyes. I returned to New York at the end of the summer to live near Albert Einstein, which was in the upper Bronx. My girlfriend from Reed College lived in Manhattan, where she was a nursery school teacher and student.

4

MEDICAL SCHOOL AND INTERNSHIP:
NO MAN'S LAND

Leaving the protected but anxiety-provoking atmosphere of Reed College and arriving in New York was a shock. Albert Einstein College of Medicine was in the upper Bronx, an hour and a half from Manhattan by subway, and was a new school just entering its third year of operations. I had been told that I would not need a car in New York, but I found I was well outside Manhattan, nearly as far out as Westchester County, something I had not been aware of when I applied. A dorm had been built for the medical students, but the walls were paper-thin and the rooms extremely small. Over 90 percent of the students were Jewish New Yorkers, and most seemed accustomed to studying day and night. I'd chosen Albert Einstein in large part because it was a predominantly Jewish school, but also because it had been publicized as being a medical school that, like Reed, did not emphasize grades or test scores. However, when the first class of students to take the national board medical exam had not done well, the school's philosophy changed abruptly from one of relaxed learning to one that was oriented toward tests and achievement. Weekly tests in each subject became mandatory, and the current administration pushed for good test scores from their students. In fact, the students did much better on the National Boards under this regimen of tests, but that was little comfort to me. I suddenly found myself in a school on the other side of the country from where I'd grown up, with an atmosphere that was the polar opposite of what I had wanted and expected.

That first year I seriously considered dropping out of medical school and getting a PhD in psychology instead, and I made many calls home to speak with my mother about my options. The memorization required in gross anatomy and the long hours in the lab seemed pointless to me. How was I going to use this information? Also, I was getting pressure from my girlfriend in Manhattan to see more of her. After all, she had come to New York City in order to be close to me, and I had not discouraged her from that, although I had not made any promises, either. Still, I was terribly ambivalent about her being there. There were various reasons for this. I had chosen Albert Einstein because, after four years at Reed, I wanted to be part of a Jewish collective once again, and my girlfriend was not Jewish. I was also very young, and in retrospect not ready for a committed relationship, while she was three years older than I was and was already feeling social pressures of her own, since in the 1950s women tended to marry at much younger ages. This combination of academic and romantic pressures made life pretty uncomfortable for me. I found that the analytic work which I had done that previous summer in Zürich had not been enough. I needed more professional help. At first I contacted Edward Edinger, and I saw him once. He had just finished his residency and seemed awfully young and inexperienced. In addition, he had not worked with Jung, and at the time I felt that was essential. Now, of course, I have to wonder what direction my life would have taken if I had entered a serious analysis with Edward Edinger! For one thing, I would probably have stayed on the East Coast and entered the New York Jungian training program. But I was looking for an analyst who had worked with Jung, so I again contacted C.A. Meier in Zürich. He recommended the psychologist Eugene Henley, whose primary analysis had been with Jung and who also was one of the only male Jungian analysts in New York.

I began to see Eugene Henley in March of 1958, meeting with him once weekly, and it was extremely helpful. He was a man in his early seventies and extremely vigorous and healthy. He and his wife Helena had been going to Switzerland to see Jung most summers since the late 1920s, and we immediately formed a strong bond. I wanted help in making a decision about whether to remain at Albert Einstein or attend another medical school, because transferring from one medical school to another is complex, much more difficult than transferring from one college to another. In looking at my dreams and my conscious perceptions of the situation, we could not come up with a solution. So for the second time in my life I referred the decision to the wisdom of the *I Ching*, and I came to the conclusion that I should apply to Yale Medical School. The philosophy at Yale was much more like that at Reed in that there were fewer required courses and the only exams one had to pass were the National Boards at the end of the second and fourth years. Otherwise, the emphasis was on learning medicine rather than on tests. Also, almost everyone at Yale passed the National Boards, but, although there was considerable anxiety about the exams, the situation was much better than at Albert Einstein, where test pressure was nearly constant.

That summer of 1958 I decided to return to Zürich and continue my analysis with Meier. I still found that my primary transference was to him. During the early part of the summer I again stayed at the Hotel Sonnenberg. My father was also in Zürich during part of that summer, teaching at the Jung Institute while also doing analysis with Meier, and I shared an apartment with him during some of the time that he was there. As I write this I am wondering how strange that must have been for Meier to see both a father and son in analysis concurrently! At the time it seemed perfectly natural, and neither I nor my father felt it was unusual. Our analytic hours were not back-to-back, so we never saw each other there. But such an arrangement would certainly not be acceptable today, and, looking back from fifty years later, I still wonder how it worked. I think the projection was that Meier, as Jung's crown prince, was above personal relationships, and, if Jung would have seen many members of the same family, why shouldn't Meier? It was simply assumed that he would keep the two analyses separate, and in fact I think that he did do that, and I never felt a contamination from my father. I think it would have been more difficult to maintain the separation if I tried to share Meier with my mother, rather than my father.

Over the course of the summer I seemed to get more of a grasp of myself, and I began to realize that I needed to break up with my Reed College girlfriend whether I remained at Albert Einstein or was accepted to Yale. At the beginning of August, 1958, I heard that I had been accepted as a transfer student to Yale, and I was very excited about the change. I should have applied to Yale in the first place, as it had a philosophy similar to the one at Reed College. One of the things that Meier had me do over the summer was read Kant's *Critique of Pure Reason*. He thought that for a "feeling type" it would be good for my "inferior thinking." I did read Kant's book that summer, and although it was difficult, I enjoyed the exercise very much.

One day my father was invited to visit Jung, but he had to teach at the Jung Institute at the time Jung had suggested he come. He called Aniela Jaffé, Jung's secretary, explained the situation, and asked if I could go in his place. A few minutes later she called back to say that would be fine with Professor Jung. So I now had a chance to see Jung one-on-one, and I was extremely nervous. What would I say to him? Meier suggested particular dreams, one with intersecting circles and others that connected to flying saucers, which Jung was interested in at the time. So I took the train out to Küsnacht on a Friday morning, nervous as hell, and went to see Jung. When I was ushered into his study, the first greeting was, "So you want to see the old man before he dies." I was shocked and bowled over by his response, and as a result I cannot remember a single thing that happened the rest of the hour. I am sure I told him the dreams that Meier suggested, but I don't remember anything else that either of us said. I have spoken to other people who spent an hour with Jung who have had similar experiences. Although they cannot remember specifics, they remember the positive feeling of being in the room with him, and some said it was life-transforming. My parents had passed their idealization of Jung on to me, so for me that single hour was the opportunity of a lifetime.

I left his office feeling more strongly than ever that I wanted to become a Jungian analyst. The fact that I could not remember any specifics didn't matter in the slightest. It was the third time I'd met him, and, on each of the three occasions, I had been completely taken in by his wit, intelligence, charm, and immense charisma. Over the next few years, as I began my psychiatric training, I heard others say many negative things about Jung, and it would upset me a great deal since I had had such a different personal impression of him. Even today, knowing a lot more about Jung and his shadow, I am upset when I hear negative comments about Jung which go against my experience of being with him.

Some of the American students at the Jung Institute, James Hillman, Robert Stein, and Marvin Spiegelman, played tennis on a regular basis and were looking for a fourth for doubles. At that time I was a fairly good tennis player, and I was teamed with Jim against Bob and Marvin. During the summer of 1958, we played two or three times a week and then would sit around and chat, have a drink, and talk about life in the Jungian world of Zürich. Through them I became acquainted with what was going on at the Jung Institute, which at the time was quite small. I was a decade younger than the other three, who were all finishing up at the Jung Institute and who were to remain lifelong friends. They were considered the Young Turks of the Institute, and already they were rebellious. Being with them on the tennis court and afterward provided a glimpse of another side of the Jungian picture at that time. All three of them were searching for alternative ways to view Jungian psychology without falling into the hagiography toward Jung that existed at the Jung Institute during the 1950s.

I had known Bob and Marvin in Los Angeles before, but that summer in Zürich was my first exposure to Jim. I was absolutely captivated by his brilliance and quick mind, and his ideas were very important in my early Jungian training. As with so many others, I developed a deep connection to Jim that never left me. There were many times that we found ourselves on opposite sides of an issue, but I always had a deep fondness for him, even during times when he rejected me.

The first international congress for Jungian analysts was held that summer in Zürich. I was still in analysis with Meier, but he strongly urged me not to be in Zürich at the time of the congress. He was not going to be there either because it conflicted with his annual scuba diving vacation off the coast of Italy, and he was not going to change those plans for anything! At some level I liked his irreverence and the fact that he felt he did not have to be at the first IAAP congress. That was liberating for me. I did not quite understand why he thought I should leave Zürich completely, but I certainly did not belong at the congress. Only analysts and a few candidates were there, and not even spouses of analysts were allowed in, so it would not have been right for me.

Instead I went to Henley-on-Thames, where I had been invited by my friend, Susan Hunt. Susan's father was Sir John Hunt, who had led the first ascent of Mt. Everest, when Hillary and Tenzing reached the summit. I had met Susan and her family the year before in Zermatt, where my uncle Welti and I were attending the Alpine Club celebration of the hundredth anniversary of the first ascent of the Matterhorn. Later Susan invited me to their home, and her family was gracious and welcoming. She and I did correspond for a while after that, but we were both going in other directions and drifted apart after a time.

I did go back to Zürich just as the congress was wrapping up and had dinner with my parents, Barbara Hannah, and Marie-Louise von Franz. My parents were in the habit of including me when they had dinner with colleagues, and in that way I was often privy to conversations I really should not have heard. On that evening they were all rehashing the congress, and von Franz and Hannah were wondering why Jung was so friendly with Fordham and his developing psychoanalytically informed views of analytical psychology? They felt that Fordham did not really understand Jung very well. I just listened and took in the gossip. That was my only connection to that first 1958 congress, although I heard that Jung had attended a couple of events. My parents both gave talks at the first congress, though, and my mother's talk turned out to be the only paper that she ever gave in public.

The entire Zeller family was in Zürich that summer. Max had received a generous financial settlement from Germany for all his back pay as a civil servant, and that allowed him to bring the whole family over to spend a year and a half in Zürich. I'd known them so well in Los Angeles and spent quite a bit of time with the family during my summer in Zürich. Through them I met a young woman, Eva Stern, from Los Angeles. Eva's parents were part of the Jung Club in Los Angeles, and I had met Eva briefly ten years earlier, when she babysat the younger Zeller children at Lake Tahoe and our families had shared a house together. In the summer of 1958 we were both coming out of long relationships that had not worked, and we dated briefly before going our separate ways at the end of the summer. The next year, when I was in Los Angeles, I introduced Eva to my brother Jerry. Within six months they were married, and Eva was my sister-in-law for forty-nine years! Sadly, she died in March of 2009 from the ravages of breast cancer.

That summer in Zürich changed my family's relationship to the Zellers. Prior to their move, our two families had been almost inseparable, but when they returned to Los Angeles after a year and a half in Zürich, the relationships were never the same. According to my mother, Max had sent several patients to her while he was away, but they did not want to return to Max when he came back. This produced a lot of tension which, sadly, was never really resolved.

In September, 1958, I drove the eighty miles from the Bronx to New Haven, Connecticut, a trip I was to make many times over the next three years, and began my remaining three years of medical school. I also resumed my analysis with Eugene Henley, whose wife had died suddenly over the summer while I was in Zürich.

It really was not much further from New Haven to New York than it had been from the upper Bronx. The New Haven Railroad was a fine way to get to Dr. Henley's office on the east side of New York. By this time I also owned a car, and about once a month I would be invited to the Henleys' weekend house in Ridgefield, Connecticut. It was easy for me to drive there for analysis. In fact, I would go there for analysis, have dinner with Dr. Henley and his daughter, who was an anesthesiologist in New York, stay the night, have breakfast, and then return to New Haven the next morning. It was certainly a unique way of doing analysis, and, as I look back on it, I am surprised that it worked as well as it did.

Although boundaries were looser in those days, this analytic arrangement was really stretching the limits. I saw it as a sort of privilege that arose from my circumstances. There were not many Jungian analysts in those days, they all knew each other, and, since I was the son of two of them, I sometimes received a sort of special treatment. This had plusses and minuses. On the one hand, I was able to see an analyst under special conditions; on the other, since everyone was so generous with me, I was hardly free to be critical.

In this case, though, I felt greatly supported by Eugene Henley, which is certainly what I needed at the time, because Yale was a somewhat lonely place for me. I had broken up with my Reed College girlfriend, and at the time New Haven and Yale had very few women students. I lived in the medical student dorm, which was separated from the main campus but close to the hospital. Our class had 5 women students out of 80, and 3 of them were Jewish women. After my experience at Einstein, I was again ambivalent about the once-appealing idea of being part of a Jewish community, so I tended to stay away from the Jewish women. For the single Yale medical student, social life was driving up on a Saturday afternoon to one of the women's colleges in Massachusetts or inviting a girl from one of these colleges down to New Haven. Neither of these approaches to meeting girls appealed to me. What if you did not hit it off with the woman for whatever reason? It was a captive situation for both people, and so I avoided it. I did go to the Massachusetts colleges once or twice for mixers, but otherwise I stayed away.

In the spring of 1959 I took pharmacology, one of our assigned classes. The lab portion of the class required us to break up into groups of four. One of the women in the class, Marguerite Stein, was looking for a group and asked a couple members of my group if she could join us. Since transferring to Yale, I had avoided Marguerite, and when she heard that I was the third member of the group, she expected me to object. I wanted to be more welcoming than rejecting, though, so I agreed, which turned out to be a momentous decision. We got to know each other that spring as we worked through our various lab experiments on dogs, and slowly my attitude towards her changed. I found her cultured, intelligent, and sexy with a good sense of humor, and over the course of a few months we both realized that we had fallen in love with one another. By June of that year, we were engaged.

Marguerite had been born in France to Polish Jewish parents. Her father had been a doctor in southwestern France, but during the German occupation, her parents placed her with a French Huguenot family and joined the French resistance. Near the time of the liberation, Marguerite's father died, but her mother survived and was able to retrieve her. After the war, Marguerite's mother booked passage to New York, where her brother lived, for the two of them, and Marguerite grew up there. She graduated from the Lycee France in New York and then attended Bryn Mawr for two years until, at age nineteen, she was accepted to Yale Medical School.

We both took our National Board exams in June, 1959, and then Marguerite came back to Los Angeles with me to meet my parents and to celebrate with a small engagement party. My parents were pleased with my choice of Marguerite and welcomed her into the family. However, we had each already made separate plans for the summer, so she went back to New York to work at a summer job, while I worked at a neurophysiology lab in the Veterans Hospital connected with UCLA. I had enjoyed science at Reed and in medical school, and I had been so immersed in Jungian analytic thought throughout my life that the idea of doing research in physiological psychiatry and being a part of medical psychiatry appealed to me. I worked as a research assistant on a project locating the pleasure centers in the rat brain. The project involved doing neurotaxic surgery on rats and seeing how they reacted to electrical stimulation, depending upon placement of the surgical implants. I used the data I obtained that summer for my medical school thesis from Yale, and later it helped secure a position at the National Institute of Mental Health.

That summer was very satisfying because I also returned to studying the piano with my old teacher. Oddly enough, the combination of doing research and playing the piano was both soothing and fulfilling, and at the end of the summer I found myself thinking that it would be nice to come back to Los Angeles again with Marguerite and continue my piano studies for a year.

When I returned to New Haven and mentioned the idea of returning to Los Angeles, however, the beginning of our problems came to the surface. Although Marguerite was fine with our returning to California for internship and residency, she adamantly refused to consider spending a year in Los Angeles. That was too close to my family, and she would have none of that. Northern California was the only part of California that was acceptable to her. She had already surmised that I was too close to my mother and that this sort of proximity would not be good for us. So in the fall of 1959 our engagement was almost broken off, and we both began to realize that we needed to go back into analysis.

My distress spilled over into my studies, and I did not do well in my clinical clerkship in pediatrics. The professor of pediatrics, Milton Senn, a prominent child psychiatrist, head of the Yale Study Center, and chairman of the department of pediatrics, called me into his office and wanted to know what was going on with me. He obviously took a genuine concern in my well-being, and the summons was a wake-up call to focus on my studies. I began to pull myself together, and I survived the pediatrics rotation. The next rotation was internal medicine, where I had Howard Spiro as my attending. I had seen him professionally for a "nervous stomach" the year before, so we knew each other. We got along very well, and, of all the faculty at Yale, he was the most interested in Jung's psychology, even though he was a gastroenterologist. Over the years his interest in the humanities has grown, and he has become a leader in integrating medicine with the humanities. I met Howard again last year for the first time in almost fifty years, and it was a real homecoming for me. He was still doing some clinical gastroenterology, but clearly his focus was the connection between soma and psyche. One of his sons had become a psychiatrist, and Howard was still interested in Jung. It was a real stroke of good fortune to have met both Milton Senn and Howard Spiro in medical school. Later I would meet Stephen Fleck, a psychiatrist and member of the Yale medical faculty who would launch me in my career as a psychiatrist.

Although Marguerite and I realized we needed analysis to work through the issues in our relationship, we could not return to my former analyst, Eugene Henley, because he had suffered a subdural hematoma, effectively the equivalent of a stroke, when a tree that he was cutting down had fallen on him. He was lucky to have survived at all, but he was never the same again. So we then contacted Esther Harding, a physician and Jungian analyst in New York, and she recommended another analyst and physician, Eleanor Bertine, who in turn recommended a woman analyst living in Connecticut. I am not going to name the Connecticut analyst, because she acted in an unprofessional manner towards me. Marguerite started seeing her individually, and when Eugene Henley was not available for me, I also went to see her. The Connecticut analyst clearly took the side of Marguerite, and I was not strong enough at the time to protest effectively. The Connecticut analyst had also known my parents and told me negative stories about their histories that I had never heard before. At first the revelations shocked me, then later they made me feel extremely vulnerable and defensive. I could see that she clearly did not like my parents, and at some level I knew that it was unprofessional of her to tell me shadowy stories about them, but I did not have the strength at that time to counteract her attacks. Instead, I kept returning because I was desperate for help. However, in spite of her unprofessional behavior, she was able to calm us down enough so that the marriage took place in June, 1960, in New York. It was a fairly traditional Jewish wedding, with lots of family and friends in attendance.

My parents gave us a long summer trip to Europe as a wedding gift. The American dollar still went very far, and we were able to stretch the trip out for a couple of months. We started in Vienna, but with Marguerite's background with the Nazis in France, Austria was not a good choice to kick off the trip. The Austrians were too similar to the Germans, especially at that time since Austria had just become an independent country. It was still recovering from the war, and the populace was still steeped in the wartime mindset. In spite of Freud's world-wide renown, for example, Austria had seemingly not yet recognized that the famous Jewish physician was Viennese.

My parents had an Austrian patient who had returned to Vienna, and the patient selected the hotel and made travel arrangements in Austria. A big mistake! Every time Marguerite saw a customs official or another Austrian in uniform, she would absolutely freak out. I rued allowing my parents to plan this phase of the trip, because the outcome could hardly have been worse. We spent two ghastly weeks in Austria and then went on to Switzerland to meet family friends in Zürich and to spend some time in the Alps. By this point the tension between us was so great that a planned trip to Palma de Mallorca was canceled, and instead we both went to see C.A. Meier and Liliane Frey-Rohn in analysis for three weeks. That helped considerably, and from Zürich we went on to visit friends who had hidden Marguerite and her family in southwestern France during the war. The friends lived near Cognac, and we were lavishly wined and dined and presented with several bottles of cognac. It was an extraordinary time with four- and five-hour lunches, French country cooking and drinking at its finest. From France we went to London to visit my family there, and we spent the last week at the Edinburgh Festival, hearing Joan Sutherland, who was still relatively unknown at that time, and others in wonderful opera and chamber music. Most of the experiences on that trip were actually quite wonderful, but many problems that continued to plague us arose. We returned to New Haven to live in the married quarters of the dorm and finish our last year of medical school. We both individually went to see the analyst in Connecticut, but not on a regular basis.

I had a rewarding six-week rotation as a medical student at the Yale Psychiatric Institute, where I was able to interview long-term patients in a psychiatric inpatient setting that was psychoanalytically oriented. Most of the patients were on tranquilizers, which at the time was a fairly recent development for psychotic patients. Stephen Fleck was the clinic director, and he ended up writing a strong letter of recommendation for me for both my internship and psychiatric residency. With it I had my choice of psychiatric residencies. The department at Yale wanted me, but a subsequent experience made me realize that I should return to the West Coast.

That year Jo Wheelwright, by far the most significant Jungian in American academic psychiatric life at that time, came to lecture at the student health center at Yale University. I arranged to have a personal meeting with him, as I had heard a lot about him from my parents. Wheelwright was one of the cofounders of The C.G. Jung Institute of San Francisco, along with Joe Henderson, and was a significant figure in studying the mental health of college students. He was the only Jungian known to any of my professors either at Albert

Einstein or at Yale. Like so many others both before and after me, I was absolutely captivated by him, and I realized that I wanted to go to San Francisco for both psychiatric and Jungian training. Although I wavered at times, I knew that with Marguerite's allergy to Los Angeles and my desire to get out of the Northeast, the Bay Area of California was the logical place for me, and Marguerite concurred.

In the 1960s the draft was still in place, and most medical students signed up for a plan that allowed them to finish their residencies and then go into military service. I signed up for the program as well so as not to have my residency training interrupted. There were two or three slots available at the National Institute of Mental Health in Bethesda, Maryland, where one could both do academic research and at the same time get credit for being in the US Public Health Service. If I were to get this position, it seemed like an ideal way to satisfy my military service. So, in the spring of 1961, I went to Bethesda and spent two days being interviewed by researchers there. I also met David Hamburg, a psychiatrist who was currently the head of one of the research sections but who was leaving that July to become the head of the department of psychiatry at Stanford. In addition to being interviewed for the National Institute of Mental Health, we also discussed the possibility of my becoming a psychiatric resident at Stanford. I left Bethesda in May, 1961, feeling fairly certain about my career path for the next six years. I would spend three years in a psychiatric residency at Stanford, then go back to the National Institute of Mental Health for two years, and then my career would be set. Positions at the National Institute of Mental Health were considered plum positions and were extremely competitive, so I was pleased with this outcome, but I still found myself thinking, "How can one be so sure that all these plans will work out? So many things could happen in between." And they did.

With my sights now oriented toward San Francisco, my relationship with Marguerite improved. I still wanted to spend my internship year in Los Angeles, but that was a source of great conflict and, I realized, nonnegotiable. Instead we applied for internships in Boston, Seattle, San Francisco, and Portland, Oregon, and, since we both had to be accepted in the same city, we ended up spending the year in Boston. I was a medical intern at the New England Medical Center, where I learned how patients who present with difficult problems get worked up. The New England Center had world-class experts in cardiology, hematology, infectious diseases, and internal medicine, so we saw many complicated medical problems. However, many of the patients ended up with psychiatric diagnoses and were given Dexedrine and Amytal as their treatment. I still look back in dismay at how these patients were treated.

Marguerite was a pediatrics intern at the Boston City Hospital. We were both working thirty-six-hour shifts and then were off for twelve, so there was relatively little time to do anything else but work and sleep. It was a physically exhausting year, and we did well just to maintain our equilibrium.

We still planned to arrive in San Francisco the following year, and we had been given Joe Henderson's name by C.A. Meier. Our Connecticut analyst had concurred that he would be a good analyst for the two of us. I wrote to him in San Francisco to tell him of our plans and our histories with our Connecticut analyst and with C.A. Meier in Zürich, saying that both Marguerite and I wanted to see him in analysis twice a week. Joe Henderson was an introvert, and in many ways he was the US analyst who most resembled Jung. He wrote back that, given our situation, he would begin by seeing both of us twice a week, but he made it clear that at some point we should each have our own individual analyst and that I would be his primary patient. Marguerite would eventually have to find another analyst. He said that in principle he did not see couples, but, given our previous situation, he would begin that way with us, providing that as soon as possible Marguerite should seek out her own analyst. Marguerite and I agreed to these conditions, and so, a year in advance of our anticipated July, 1962, arrival, we had already made our San Francisco analytic arrangements.

Prior to moving to San Francisco, my analysis had been highly unorthodox. At one time I saw the same analyst as my father, at another time the same analyst as my wife, and with a third analyst I regularly stayed overnight at his house in the country. In none of these analytic situations did I have the luxury of seeing someone on a regular basis. Up until that point, while I had received special treatment in some ways, in other ways my analysis had been deficient. Analysis always had to be squeezed in around school and other commitments, and I had to travel some distance to see the analyst. I was not aware of it at the time, but I was looking forward to really settling into analysis and working consistently on my problems. Only in retrospect did I realize how unorthodox my prior analytic experience had been.

5

PSYCHIATRIC RESIDENCY AND NATIONAL INSTITUTE OF MENTAL HEALTH

Arriving in Palo Alto to begin my training in psychiatry was a major turning point in my life. I'd sampled life in the Northeast and in Europe, and now I was returning "home" to California. I would have liked to spend one year in Los Angeles, of course, but Palo Alto was distinctly California, and it felt very comfortable and familiar, even though I had never lived or spent much time there. For me it meant beginning my formal training in psychiatry, which would move me closer toward my goal of becoming a psychiatrist and a Jungian analyst. Now for the first time I could be involved in Jungian analysis on a regular basis and not feel that it had to be squeezed in among a host of other activities. My new analyst, Joe Henderson, knew my parents, but he had a rather distant relationship to them. I did not have to worry about him telling my parents things or having him tell me gossip about my parents. Marguerite seeing him at the same time did not disturb me; in fact, I thought it could help our relationship. I was right about that, because three years later, when Marguerite began analysis with someone else, our relationship quickly began to fall apart.

I was relieved to be out of the Northeast, because I had had enough of the Ivy League and enough of New York. And I had had more than enough of East Coast winters. Being four hundred miles away from my family and even further from Marguerite's mother helped us keep the focus on our own relationship. We were both at a new medical facility, which was very different from our experiences in New Haven and Boston, where we had trained in old, established hospital settings. Everything in California was new and relatively young, and the hospital setting and the Bay Area environment were in flux. Although Palo Alto was a pretty quiet place when we arrived there, it was not to remain that way for long. Research with LSD, Esalen, student protests at Cal, and the hippie revolution were just around the corner.

The medical school at Stanford had moved from San Francisco to Palo Alto in 1959. David Hamburg had become the chair of the department of psychiatry, and he was in the process of building up a research-oriented department. At that time the Stanford department of psychiatry was heavily psychoanalytic, as were most psychiatry departments in the US. David Hamburg brought in many young psychiatrists, psychologists, and researchers in various scientific fields in the hope they would facilitate department-wide change.

There were holdover faculty members from San Francisco, and in addition there had been a residency at the Menlo Park Veterans Affairs hospital headed by Henry von Witzleben, a psychiatrist and a member of the well-known Prussian family who had come from Berlin to have analysis with Frieda Fromm-Reichmann in Washington, DC. He had run the VA residency program in Menlo Park for many years, and it was considered an excellent training in psychotherapy and psychoanalysis. Von Witzleben was intrigued by my family background, and I saw behind his formal German persona a very gentle man. There is a Witzlebenplatz in Berlin, and General von Witzleben, a cousin, was responsible for protecting Berlin until he was part of the plot to overthrow Hitler in 1944, which was recently made into a movie entitled "Valkyrie." When my father came to lecture at Stanford, von Witzleben cordially invited us over after the lecture. He lived to be close to one hundred years, and I would see him and his wife walking around Palo Alto for many years thereafter.

Henry von Witzleben had a yearly Frieda Fromm-Reichmann memorial lecture, and I think 1963 was probably the last year it took place. The lecturer in 1963 was our own Joseph Wheelwright, who had been a good friend of Frieda's. Jo was much better at speaking spontaneously than he was at giving a prepared lecture, so I cannot really remember much of the content of that lecture. What I do remember was that two of Jo's best friends, Erik Erikson and Gregory Bateson, were in attendance. At the time they were considered two of the most prominent and influential people in the field of psychiatry and psychoanalysis. With Jung being as marginal as he was at the time, it made a big impression on me that these two influential thinkers had come to hear Jo.

Another senior psychiatrist in the department was Harry Wilmer, at the time a Freudian. Harry Wilmer had been instrumental in bringing community psychiatry and the open ward policy to inpatient psychiatric units in the United States. He was a prominent psychiatrist in the United States, and his special field of research was studying disadvantaged patients who were not being treated properly. In the early 1960s he was studying prisoners at San Quentin prison. He became a consultant when I was a resident at the San Mateo County inpatient unit, which was part of the Stanford program. He was the most impressive clinician in the department of psychiatry, and I developed a strong idealizing transference towards him. Little did I know that he would become an important Jungian and a friend in the future.

When I arrived at Stanford the curriculum for the residents was in flux. As a result I was able to bring the medical doctor William Alex to teach Jung. He had just moved north from Los Angeles and was willing to make the weekly trip from San Francisco to Palo Alto. There had been such a course in San Francisco given by Joseph Henderson, but William Alex was the first Jungian presence in the new setting. My fellow residents were quite intrigued by his presentations, and several of them considered going into Jungian analysis. Not many of them did, however, because at that time becoming a Jungian meant risking marginalization as a psychiatrist. Young residents with growing families could not take that chance. With my family background to support me, I knew that it was not as bad as the others feared.

Our first rotation was seeing outpatients at the Stanford clinic, but after six months we were all transferred to the VA hospital to work on an inpatient unit. My inpatient supervisor and co-ward chief was the young Irv Yalom. Irv and I got along well, and we ended up playing tennis regularly and running a group therapy for schizophrenic patients. Irv was extremely quiet and seemed to be eclipsed by some of the other psychiatrists David Hamburg had brought in. Irv's co-ward chief was the flamboyant George Solomon, whose parents were noteworthy, his father a psychoanalyst in San Francisco and his mother a published novelist. George seemed destined to go far, whereas Irv appeared reserved and not ambitious. Was I wrong on that account! As a young psychiatrist Irv was extremely proper, expecting all of us to wear a tie to work every day. He also suggested that my going into Jungian analysis was potentially throwing away a promising career in academic psychiatry, since a Jungian analysis would not be looked upon favorably in academia. How his views have changed today! Irv and I have remained friends all these years, and I have a great deal of respect for the work and writing that he has done, while he has been extremely supportive of my own creative efforts.

During this period Marguerite and I were driving in separately to see Joe Henderson. Our life in California was beginning to take shape, and the family issues with our respective parents were becoming less problematic. In August of 1962, after about a month in analysis, we received a call late one Sunday night from Joe Henderson's wife, Helena, who told us that Joe had had some kind of cardiac arrhythmia, and that he was hospitalized and would not be coming to the office. Since the two of them were to leave shortly for Europe and an IAAP congress in Zürich, we did not see Joe Henderson again until the beginning of November of that year. Here we had made preparations to see him in analysis far in advance, and now we wondered if he would be healthy enough to continue his analytic practice? He was fifty-nine years old at the time, although he looked older than his age. Fortunately he was able to continue his analytic practice, and his appearance changed very little over the next 35 years, so that when he was close to 100 years old, he looked no more than 80. Little did I know that we would have a relationship for the next forty-five years!

One of the high points of my residency was bringing in Jim Hillman to speak at the VA hospital in 1963. After graduating from the Jung Institute in Zürich, Jim had become the director of studies there, and now he and Adolf Guggenbühl-Craig were making a trip across the US, speaking at various places. At first he was not planning to come to the Bay Area, but I wrote him and was able to change his mind. This speaking trip was also the first time I met young Adolf Guggenbühl-Craig, although we were not to get to know each other for another fourteen years.

During this visit to the Bay Area, Jim spoke at the VA hospital, The Analytical Psychology Club of San Francisco, and in Berkeley. He gave two lectures, both of which were brilliant. One was on the theory of emotion, which had been his PhD thesis from Zürich and had become a book, and the other was a lecture on suicide. He was in the middle of writing his book *Suicide and the Soul,* which to me is still is one of the most profound books in Jungian literature. I found it deeply moving, and in 1966, not long after Jim's book came out, I gave a lecture on it to the Analytical Psychology Club of Los Angeles, which I then had published in the *Journal of Existential Psychiatry.* In *Suicide and the Soul,* Jim differentiates between the depth psychology approach to suicide and the approaches of other disciplines, arguing that, while medicine, sociology, and theology all have an absolute taboo against suicide, analytical psychology with its archetypal base must move beyond the taboo. Jim understood Jung's archetype of death and rebirth, and he realized that death needs to be lived and experienced before rebirth can occur, that one cannot circumvent the death experience and just expect renewal. To the contrary, according to Hillman, circumventing the death experience can actually make suicide more alluring. However, he also acknowledged the risks implicit in taking this stance in that the death experience can lead to literal suicide.

Midway through my first year of residency, I decided to apply for the Jung institute training program. At that time the application was only one page long and just asked for personal identifying data and how many hours of Jungian analysis one had. The minimum requirement was one hundred, and between my work in Zürich, New York, Connecticut, and San Francisco, I had well over a hundred hours. When applying as a doctor, the requirement was one year of psychiatric residency, which I was in the midst of fulfilling. One did not have to write an essay or obtain references, a far cry from the application process today, where the application form is so long that it takes weeks to fill out. The process was not particularly stressful, and I began training in the fall of 1963.

In 1964 Dieter Baumann, Jung's grandson and a psychiatrist, made a visit to the Bay Area. He was the first member of the Jung family to visit the Bay Area, and he drew large audiences at Stanford, San Mateo Medical Center, and The Analytical Psychology Club of

San Francisco. He spoke on the "Spheros Empedocles," which is an amplification of the Self which exists when earth, fire, air, and water are held together in an inert position by love and strife. The concept was Greek to both general psychological audiences and Jungian audiences. Baumann had studied the extant literature on the pre-Socratic philosopher Empedocles, but the lecture left audiences, especially general ones, stupefied by what all this had to with psychology. Unfortunately, although Baumann was an extremely affable and charming man, the talks reinforced the idea that Jungians study very esoteric subjects, which did not enhance the Jungian position in the Bay Area.

Mary Crile, who had been on such intimate terms with my father in New York in 1943, had moved first to Carmel and then to Big Sur. She had a small A-frame house on the edge of Pfeiffer State Park in Big Sur, and one could walk out of her house directly into the State Park. It was a magnificent setting overlooking the Pacific Ocean through the forest. The Big Sur Hot Springs had just been renamed Esalen, and the public programs at Esalen, which quickly became so popular, were just beginning. Both Marguerite and I enjoyed going down to Big Sur and spending free weekends with Mary. One memorable visit occurred when Gregory Bateson gave a workshop at Esalen and then came over to Mary's house for lunch. He talked about the experience he had with marijuana and the thoughts and feelings he experienced under its influence. It was fascinating to hear this giant intellectual talk about the different ideas and theories that came to him under the influence of marijuana, although he also said that even while he was still experiencing the effects he realized that the ideas had no lasting value. Mary was also good friends with Maud Oakes and Elizabeth Osterman, who were in a relationship at the time. I had never experienced anything like the Big Sur community before, and it was fascinating. Mary drove the first Toyota I saw in Northern California, which she bought when the brand was first introduced in the US. Mary was a modest person, but she had ideas far in advance of her time. By the time I finished my residency, she had had the first of several strokes, and she died in 1968.

As my analysis deepened and I became more involved with the Jungian training program, the idea of going back east and taking that prestigious position with the National Institute of Mental Health lost its luster for me. By then we had also decided to start a family, and our son David was born on election day in 1964 as Lyndon Johnson won election in a landslide. I wanted to stay in the Bay Area and continue my analysis and the Jungian training. A National Institute of Mental Health position came open in San Francisco, which was the regional office for the nine Western states and had responsibility for the mental health grants which were distributed in the region. I made more telephone calls than I can count and couldn't find anyone in the inner sanctum of NIMH who could help in securing a transfer to San Francisco. It was a truly Kafkaesque experience trying to get inside the "castle," and I was told that it was impossible to change my position. I finally reached the associate director of the National

Institute of Mental Health, Stanley Yolles, and arranged to fly back to Washington to meet with him. When I got there, Stanley Yolles was between Congressional budget hearings and did not have much time. The meeting lasted for one and a half minutes at the most, but he said that he would change my position from the NIMH Research Center in Bethesda, Maryland, to the Region Nine office in San Francisco. After all I'd been through trying to make the switch, it seemed miraculous and hard to believe, but then, while I was still a psychiatric resident, he made a visit to San Francisco and that made it real. I met the Regional Office staff over lunch at the Whitcomb Hotel on Market Street, the former residence of my two unmarried great uncles who had lived there for many years and where we had stayed as a family in 1943 in my first visit to the Bay Area. It was a momentous occasion for me and a great relief, because it meant that we would stay in the Bay Area. We promptly bought our first house, a small California ranch house in Palo Alto, for under thirty thousand dollars. Life seemed to be looking up.

In July, 1965, I began work at the National Institute of Mental Health Regional Office in San Francisco. I immediately began wondering what I had gotten myself into. The work was largely administrative, and I found myself performing organizational tasks on mental health projects with lifetime civil servants, when I wanted to be a Jungian analyst and practice analysis. How was learning about how our government functions going to make me a better Jungian analyst? I had no idea that the administrative experience that I obtained here would be extremely valuable in my later jobs.

The first year I spent two days a week at the US public health hospital treating Coast Guard personnel and Merchant Marines. I was the only psychiatrist on the National Institute of Mental Health staff, and the others were either psychologists, social workers, or nurses. Even though I was a psychiatrist, the fact that I was by far the youngest and that I was only going to be there for two years left me as the most junior person on the staff. That sometimes got under my skin, but in general I took it in stride. The job required a lot of travel to oversee different grants that Congress had passed. The Community Mental Health Act of 1963, one of the last pieces of legislation enacted before Kennedy was assassinated, was one of the principal foci of our work. We also oversaw a number of research projects in our region and were involved with grants to the state mental health hospitals.

One project which the NIMH supported heavily was the newly formed Suicide Prevention Center in Los Angeles, which had been founded by Ed Shneidman, Norman Farberow, and Robert Litman. It was the first of its kind and at the time received national recognition. Jim Hillman spoke there, and his position on suicide was extremely controversial. I did not attend that meeting, but I heard it was explosive, because Hillman's approach, as expounded in *Suicide and the Soul*, was so different from the "prevention first" attitude of suicidology. Later on the NIMH was to form a Center for Suicidology, where the aging Henry Murray was an adviser. Henry Murray was one of America's most famous psychologists, having started the Mental Health Clinic at Harvard and developed the Thematic Apperception Test, a standard psychological test. He also had had a long-standing working relationship with Jung. It was a privilege and a pleasure to meet Henry Murray, and he was treated with great reverence by all the others. I found out later, after my father's death, that Henry Murray and my father had corresponded about Melville, a subject of passionate interest to them both. In one of the letters to my father that I read many years later, Murray mentioned meeting me at the Center for Suicidology shortly after it opened.

My one year at the US public health hospital was interesting both in terms of the interns I supervised and the kinds of patients I saw. Many of the patients were Merchant Marines, who were very different from Stanford students and faculty. I also supervised the interns going through the US Public Health Service training program. One intern I met then, John Beebe, has remained a lifelong friend. John knew a fair amount about Jung before he became a doctor, and during supervisory sessions with John I realized that he was seeking analysis. I did something I've never done for anyone before or since: I actually telephoned John Perry and then handed the phone to John Beebe to make the appointment. John has been one of the outstanding figures in the Jungian world for many years.

In my second year at the NIMH regional office, I took an eleven-day trip to Alaska to survey the state's mental health needs. The survey group included people from Washington, DC, and the NIMH central office, and I was the only person from our regional office. This was prior to the Trans-Alaska Pipeline, and Alaska was still a sparsely populated state. The mental health facilities were marginal to say the least. The state mental health director was an aging Karl Bowman, who had founded the Langley Porter Psychiatric Institute in San Francisco in 1941. At the time he was eighty-five years old, yet he was traveling around with us to various Eskimo and Indian sites. As members of the federal government, we were shown facilities and introduced to people we would never have seen if we had been tourists. It was a remarkable trip, and I fell in love with Alaska.

I was sent to Alaska because I was also handling the federal mental health grants for the state of Nevada, and it was thought that the two states had comparable problems: very few resources and practitioners who were not of the highest caliber. That was certainly the case in Nevada at that time, and the situation in Alaska when we visited was even more severe. When the pipeline came in a few years later, it brought many competent mental health professionals to Alaska, and the situation changed markedly.

While I was working for the NIMH, Marguerite had shifted her analysis from Joe Henderson to Elizabeth Osterman. Elizabeth had first gotten a PhD in microbiology and then had become a medical doctor, and after that a Jungian analyst. She was one of the senior analysts in San Francisco and carried much charisma. She had white hair and intense eyes, and she listened to people so intently. She was extremely popular as an analyst, and she spoke with a deep voice and much authority. She was also emotionally volatile, but if she overreacted would often come back and acknowledge her mistake. I now saw Joe Henderson, and Marguerite no longer did. This changed my relationship to Joe as well as my relationship to Marguerite. She had finished her pediatric residency but did not want to take a clinical position in pediatrics because that would have meant night call, and we had David at home. Instead she decided to work in the laboratory of a well-known researcher.

I was traveling weekly to Nevada and frequently to Washington, DC, as well. I also had opened up a small private practice in Menlo Park and saw patients on Saturdays. My stint at the NIMH would run for six more months before I could set up a full-time office in Menlo Park. My absences were extensive, and many of the parental issues Marguerite and I had experienced earlier suddenly resurfaced, issues that I thought had been put behind us. We got into constant fights about where to live and where to spend time. Her mother wanted us to spend time with her in New York, and my parents wanted us to visit them more often. Decisions about where to visit and when became major issues which apparently never were settled.

Eventually, we realized that we had to separate, which we did in February of 1967. Initially we did not tell friends and family that we had done this. We wanted to try to work our problems out without involving others. I lived alone that spring for the first time, which at first was very difficult. The fissure in my young family almost undid me, and the task of maintaining a sort of veneer of normalcy made the burden heavier. As the months passed, however, I found living alone to be an extremely important experience analytically. It helped me separate both from Marguerite and my parents. In the language of initiation, this seemed like my necessary "ordeal." I did not know how long it would last. At times I felt as depressed and lonely as I ever have in my life, and the archetype of rebirth that Hillman had explored in his book, *Suicide and the Soul,* helped me ride out the night sea journey and hold out for a new day. Many painful confrontations between Marguerite and me occurred, though the intervening years have softened the memory. But at the time, I was in limbo, and I remained there for almost a year, at which point Marguerite and I made the separation public and quickly thereafter began divorce proceedings. By the end of that year, since this painful situation was not resolving itself, I realized I needed to remove myself from the marriage, and I wanted out. My analysis was crucial during this period of my life, and many of my life's most important analytic changes occurred during this phase of the work.

I still look back on July 1, 1967, as a day of transition, when three concurrent events set my life on a new course. First, I finished my tour of duty with the National Institute of Mental Health and the United States Public Health Service; second; I opened my first full-time office in Menlo Park so I could practice as a psychiatrist (and hopefully later as a Jungian analyst); and third, Marguerite and I separated for the third time. That turned out to be the final separation, but we did not know that at the time.

July of 1967 was a good time to begin a psychiatric practice. Not being selective in the kind of patients that I took, within a period of a couple of months I had a pretty full-time load. Very few of the patients were appropriate for Jungian analytic treatment, but I enjoyed the wide variety of both inpatients and outpatients that I saw. I also began to supervise residents at Stanford in their psychotherapy work, and I found the work very satisfying.

One of the residents that I was supervising was a close friend of John Beebe, and our relationship was a comfortable one. In October of 1967 my resident was supervising a medical student just prior to his supervisory hour with me, and he asked if I would mind if she stayed for his supervisory hour. I did not. The next week she came again, and this time they pretended to be having an affair, knowing that this would tweak me, as I knew the resident was married. I supervised the resident, but I was quite attracted to the medical student, who was poised, intelligent, and very attractive. I just filed her name away thinking that if and when Marguerite and I publicly broke up, I would ask her out. When Marguerite and I openly split up a couple of months later, I began to see Jean Penelope Ruggles. She had come to California from Alaska to go to medical school at Stanford, and I had just recently enjoyed that wonderful trip to Alaska with the NIMH. We had an instant connection through our mutual love of Alaska, but in many other ways we were so different. Jean was basically a Midwesterner who wanted to be a surgeon and was not particularly interested in psychiatry. But opposites attract, and the mutual attraction was extremely strong. I did not think that I would want to marry again so soon after my divorce, but Jean in her own way was looking for a long-term relationship. So, throwing caution to the winds, we decided to marry eight months later.

Our differences persist, of course. We are different psychological types, Jean being an introverted sensation thinking type while I am an extraverted intuitive feeling type, and we also come from very different cultural and family backgrounds. Although we have often clashed, we have both grown through our mutual struggles and are still married now, over forty-six years later.

6

JUNGIAN TRAINING

Since I applied for the Jungian training program midway through my first year of psychiatric residency, the two training programs overlapped to a large extent. And, as I'd entered the training program as soon as I was eligible, I was the youngest candidate in the group by ten years, but since I'd been the youngest since grammar school, that felt like the normal state of affairs.

At that time there were only three American Jungian institutes, and the requirements for entrance varied from one institute to another. There were relatively few Jungian training programs in the world in the 1960s, and most of them were dominated by influential women, usually women who were not medical doctors. Even in cases where the leaders were female physicians, such as Esther Harding or Eleanor Bertine, the institutes tended to resemble theological organizations rather than medical schools and hospitals. The San Francisco Jung institute was outside this norm in that it was dominated by male medical doctors, and given how much of my life had been focused on the study of medicine, I thought I'd probably feel more at home there.

After filling out and sending in the brief application form, I met individually with the members of the evaluation committee, which handled all the candidates from admission through certification. Today there are different committees for admission, review during training, and certification. The interviews were informal and not particularly probing. I was accepted as a preliminary candidate to begin in fall of 1963.

Being a preliminary candidate meant that the first year was provisional for both the candidate and the organization, and that after one year both the professional society and the candidate decided if he or she should move on to full candidate status. I was one of five people chosen as a provisional candidate in 1963, and we combined those five with the previous year's candidates to form a combined seminar group. At that time we were not yet officially an institute but still a professional society.

I distinctly remember the first seminar. Joe Henderson used one of the seminars from the ETH, the Swiss Federal Technical Institute of Technology, where Jung was a professor and where he lectured to the engineering students on psychology. Those lectures are still not published today, but they are included in the material that the Philemon Foundation is trying to gather and publish in the near future. In the ETH lectures, Jung displays his wide range of erudition while at the same time describing his psychology in a less intellectual tone using language better suited to students with a minimal background in psychology. Joe Henderson used one of the lectures to show how Jung's psychology was an open system, in contrast to Freud's psychoanalysis, which he described as a closed system. That description of Jung's psychology marked me, and I hold on to that principle even today as I hear about new developments in analytical psychology. Other topics from that first year included the theory of archetypes presented by John Perry, psychological types presented by Mel Kettner, dream theory and practice presented by Douglass Cartwright, Elizabeth Osterman on the great mother archetype, and an introduction to sandplay, which was just being introduced to California by Dora Kalff.

Our seminar group was made up of nine people, one woman psychologist and eight male psychiatrists, all between 27 and 55 years of age. As the youngest in the group, I was the only seminar member not in private practice. In fact, that whole year I was a resident in inpatient psychiatry, and so I did not have much time to do the reading. I only realized later that the others were not doing much reading, either. This reflected the philosophy of Jo Wheelwright, who considered personal development far more important than academic excellence. As a result, the written texts were more suggested than required, and the emphasis was almost entirely on personal development and growth in a fairly informal setting. Generally, the instructors treated us as colleagues. Nonetheless, the seminars often brought up personal complexes for each of the participants. Initially it was difficult for me to have Joe Henderson, with whom I was working out important family matters in my analysis, speak about mother and father complexes as well as using clinical examples. In hearing his lectures, I always felt that he was speaking directly to me. This became important grist for the mill in my personal analysis. Many years later, having seen many other candidates become similarly vulnerable in the seminar format, the requirement for personal analysis before applying for candidacy was changed from 100 to 200 hours of analysis. The hope was that, with additional analysis, candidates would have resolved more of their personal issues before entering training. That rationale made sense, but obviously, it did not really solve the problem. Complexes are always present and are evoked in the seminars, so whether one goes to seminars that are given by one's analyst is something that is negotiated between analysand and analyst.

After the first year of seminars, I was casually moved from preliminary candidacy to full candidacy. I do not remember any interview or rite of passage to the next stage. We did make a physical change, as the society of Jungian analysts bought a building around the corner from Jo Wheelwright's office building and became incorporated as an institute, The C.G. Jung Institute of San Francisco. A three-story Victorian house on Clay Street became the center of all Jungian training activities.

The second year of seminars began in the new facility with eight two-hour sessions on complex theory by John Perry. They were probably the best and most comprehensive basic seminars on analytical psychology that I have ever heard. Included in the seminar was John's own interpretation of the meaning of the word *archetype* and a pragmatic clinical approach to the use of archetypes. He called them "affect images," and he made the point that in the analytic session one should always look for where the emotion was. It was in the affect that one would find the archetypal image, hopefully through a dream or active imagination. This has been a cornerstone of my analytic work ever since. John was a fabulous teacher and probably the most popular analyst of that period. Unfortunately, in spite of his understanding of complex theory, he nonetheless became a victim of his own complexes, leading to his indefinite suspension in 1981.

The seminars during the third and fourth years were equally profound. Joe Henderson gave a series of eight sessions on Jung's "Psychology of the Transference," and that essay has become a cornerstone of my thinking about the analytic process, as well as informing me about all personal relationships, analytic or otherwise. Using a series of alchemical drawings, Jung described the processes which take place in all human relationships to one extent or another. Elizabeth Osterman gave a seminar on the mother archetype and the Villa of the Mysteries, a series of paintings on the walls of Pompeii that describe women's initiation.

By this time Dora Kalff was making yearly trips to California, and many analysts were using sand tray. I had already met Dora Kalff a decade earlier when my parents and I visited her twelfth-century house outside of Zürich. My mother especially was close to Dora, and when Dora came to Los Angeles, she would stay with my family for weeks on end. The only problem was that Dora would not tell my mother the exact date of her arrival until a couple of days before she was due to arrive. Dora was a very special person, as intuitive as anyone I have known, as well as a diva and a wonderful musician. She was a true healer, with strong interest in Eastern religions and a good connection with the Dalai Lama.

For the first couple of years of Jungian training, I was just sailing along in my yearly interviews with the certifying committee. Then, when it was time for me to begin seeing analysands under supervision as part of the training program, I met with Jo Wheelwright. I thought that I would just progress to that stage of training as easily as I had breezed through other milestones. However, Jo said that I was too young and that I had not yet had enough experience with long-term analytic patients to handle control cases. He recommended that I wait a year to begin doing control work. I argued my case to him, but I lost. I was deeply disappointed that my training had been delayed. That had never happened to me before. However, there was nothing to be done about the delay except to accept it, so I waited for a year before I began control supervision. I chose John Perry as my control analyst because he had been such a good teacher, but even then I had an intuition about his problematic relationship to women patients, and I only spoke to him about male analysands.

The control stage experience used the supervisor, in my case John Perry, as the overall consultant to the individual's practice. I did not specifically speak about one patient but about several, and I would focus on one or two at each session, depending upon the material which interested me the most at the time. So in a sense, I was following three or four different cases and presenting the most pressing clinical material from any one of these cases. I found this sort of supervision to be extremely valuable. I was in no rush to finish my candidacy, as I was working for the National Institute of Mental Health during most of the time that I was in control supervision. Then, after about one year of control work, my marriage began to fall apart. So I stopped doing supervision at all for almost a year and concentrated instead on my personal situation. After about a year I felt that I had regrouped enough to resume control work. Then basically I did another year of control work with John Perry, which was double the requirement at the time. Today one hundred hours is the requirement. I never regretted doing the extra year of supervision, because it was extremely valuable for my clinical training. During that second year of control work, I was already in full-time private practice, and John helped me sort out my practice. In the summer of 1968, John thought I was ready to write up a case, and so I did. John did not recommend a case or insist that I write up any particular one, but allowed me to take the case which interested me the most. The case I picked was a male approximately my own age who had just gotten divorced and was having difficulty finding his way after the divorce. He missed his children and was lonely. There were obvious similarities between his situation and my own, so that transference and countertransference issues were paramount throughout the therapy. What I also liked about this case was that the man had not come to me as a Jungian but sought me out as a general therapist. He did not know that I was Jungian until many years into the treatment. He began to remember his dreams as part of the therapy, and I could see the archetypal images at work without having to resort to Jungian labels. We dealt directly with the images and their possible meanings. His story appealed to me on many levels. After writing up the case report, I showed it to John Perry. He approved of the report, and in October of 1968, I went up before the joint Northern and Southern California boards. I did not have to meet with the Northern California Board before meeting with the joint board.

This was so different from the way training is handled today. First, I wrote up a case that I wanted to write up, and I did the write-up on my own without much supervision, establishing my own method of working without a heavy hand of authority correcting me and telling me how I should write it. I did not have to meet the Northern California board separately before I went before the joint Northern and Southern California boards. There were far fewer hoops to go through than there would be today, where everything along the way is so structured. Personally, I wish the training process had not become quite as structured as it has, because imposing structure takes some of the spontaneity and creativity out of the whole experience.

Up until now everything about the training process had gone smoothly. Jean and I had gotten married midway through my second year of supervision, and she was finishing her last year of medical school and was spending time on obstetrics while I was preparing to present before the combined board. To prepare to present, I read Gerhard Adler's *The Living Symbol*, which was the only long-term Jungian case I knew of at the time. Jung and most of his followers had never written up an extensive clinical case. They were more interested in amplification of specific archetypal symbols which came up in their analysand's dreams, rather than in presenting a long-term series. Hence, I had only a limited framework to use as guidance, which added to my anxiety level. As my anticipation of meeting with the joint board grew, I became even more anxious and began to have difficulty sleeping. The meeting was to be in Los Angeles in a neighborhood I knew well, one full of childhood memories. Of course, this only increased my apprehension.

The joint board included Lou Stewart, Douglass Cartwright, and Joe Henderson from San Francisco, as well as Max Zeller, Malcolm Dana, and Yechezkel Kluger from Los Angeles. Doug Cartwright was the chair of the committee, and Joe Henderson and I had discussed whether or not he should be there. We thought it seemed acceptable for him to be there, and no one suggested that he not be. In today's world, Joe's presence would be considered a boundary violation and would not be allowed. Cartwright and Stewart were not well-known to me, but the three from Los Angeles were all extremely close personal friends of the family. The Los Angeles Jungians handled themselves very well, and I received most of my questions from Cartwright and Stewart. They both asked perceptive and probing clinical questions about how I worked, and they challenged me on transference and countertransference issues. I left the one and one-half hour meeting feeling that I had handled the situation well enough. I was informed that I had passed some minutes later, which was a tremendous relief. I was drenched in sweat, and this whole experience had touched me much more deeply than I had realized, in part, I'm sure, because I knew it would be my last formal exam as a student.

The Jungian training had taken five and a half years, which was a little on the fast side but close to average. I was thirty-two years old and was the twenty-second person to become an analyst in San Francisco. It still was to take me several years to really feel like a Jungian analyst, but the formal training was completed, although being a part of this august Jungian group, where most of the members were much older than me, still overwhelmed me.

In reflecting back on my training experience, I began Jungian training too early in my professional career. It would have been better to wait until I was a more seasoned psychiatrist, but I'd wanted to be a Jungian analyst for as long as I could remember, and the notion of slowing down my efforts because I would be the youngest person in the group never occurred to me. I imagine that idea did occur to the members of the evaluation committee at the institute, but it was a time when few people applied, and under those circumstances, it would have been difficult to refuse my application.

The training program had been extremely satisfying throughout, though, just informal enough to feel relaxed and yet structured enough so that it seemed an optimal learning environment. I would have preferred more assigned reading, but I was sufficiently self-motivated to read much of the Jungian literature that was available at the time. In the 1960s it wasn't hard to keep up with all the available Jungian literature that was published in English, because there just wasn't that much of it. Today there are so many new Jungian books published that it is virtually impossible to keep up with all that is published in English.

Thinking back to my father's early experiences as a German psychiatrist and Jungian analyst in Los Angeles, I realized both how the slights to his abilities must have stung and how fortunate I was to be in San Francisco. The C.G. Jung Institute of San Francisco had a collegial relationship with the San Francisco Psychoanalytic Institute, and I truly valued the fact that I did not feel marginalized simply because I was a Jungian. The situation in San Francisco was unique in that regard. At that time both the Los Angeles and New York Jung institutes were excluded from those cities' larger psychotherapeutic and psychiatric communities, while the San Francisco Jung institute was definitely a part of the overall therapeutic community in the Bay Area. Yet the lack of rigidity that I experienced in my training was in marked contrast to what I was hearing from psychoanalytic colleagues. The San Francisco Jung institute didn't have designated training analysts, so one could see any recognized analyst for analysis. All the evaluative committees rotated on a yearly basis, and the control analyst could be any analyst who had been in good standing for five years. The authority of individual analysts was based upon psychological acuity, not perceived positions of power. I felt lucky to have had the experiences I had both with those seminar leaders and also with supervisory work with John Perry. When I see some of the power and authority struggles that go on today with candidates and the tensions that are often aroused between candidates and the various committees, I am even more grateful for my own training. In that regard, it did happen at the right time.

7

BEGINNING PRIVATE PRACTICE

The major transition that occurred in my life on July 1, 1967—the end of my tour with the National Institute of Mental Health, the opening of my first full-time psychiatry office in Menlo Park, and my permanent separation from Marguerite—meant that I had a lot of free time to devote to building up my private practice. Palo Alto and the mid-peninsula were changing rapidly in the 1960s, and the psychiatric community changed along with it. When the Stanford medical school had first moved to Palo Alto in 1959, there were fewer than ten psychiatrists in private practice in the area. By 1967, several classes of psychiatric residents had graduated from Stanford and had opened private offices in the region. The medical school had also attracted young psychiatrists from other parts of the country. The mid-peninsula area was a fast-growing community, and all the new people quickly found themselves busy. In addition to Stanford, large computer companies like HP, IBM, Varians, Xerox Park, and later Apple all had excellent medical insurance plans that covered long-term psychotherapy, so that money was not a factor for most patients.

Initially only one person in Palo Alto was openly identified as a Jungian analyst, and that was George Hogle. He did not practice full-time but did some analysis and some individual supervision with residents, although he did not give formal lectures on Jung.

However, a petite but extremely charismatic preschool teacher, Besse Bolton, had introduced Jungian thought into her group meetings for preschool families. She was also quite influential in the Palo Alto school district, and after her death, a day-care center was named in her honor. Besse and her husband Wilbur had moved from Idaho to the mid-peninsula in the early 1920s, and she had started out as a teacher before she began her innovative classes for the parents of preschool children. Besse had analyzed with Joe Henderson in San Francisco and in the early 1950s had spent the better part of a year in Zürich studying at the Jung Institute. Her experience had led her to believe that most people would be helped by Jungian analysis, and for some time she had tried to get a Jungian from San Francisco to come down to Palo Alto. However, no one was willing to make the one-hour trip on a regular basis.

Besse had a fiery personality and always seemed to influence people to do what she wanted them to do. Literally decades of parents had been influenced by her. By the time I opened up my practice in 1967, she had retired from the school district, but she was still able to introduce me to important people in Palo Alto. She seemed to know everyone.

With my connections from Stanford and Besse Bolton's backing, I was able to build up a combined psychiatric and Jungian practice rather quickly. At the end of two months, I already had a fairly steady clientele of thirty hours a week. I was seeing all kinds of patients, including inpatients. Ninety percent of the patients were women, and I also saw many teenagers. The free time that had seemed to stretch out before me in July disappeared almost too rapidly.

In addition to my private practice, I was doing my control work with John Perry. I also became a member of the clinical faculty in the department of psychiatry at Stanford and the instructor for the only psychotherapy experience for the psychiatric residents that was available at the local state mental hospital, Agnews. I had met the residency director of Agnews, Dr. Elizabeth Jeffress, while I was still working at the NIMH, and that helped me get a position teaching the residents in that program. I did that for an hour and a half each week for six years. I could sense the residents' hunger for more psychotherapy experience, something they could not get in that setting. Meanwhile, my teaching duties in the department of psychiatry at Stanford were to supervise two residents an hour each per week. I was to continue to supervise residents for about twenty years.

In the fall of 1967, I was invited to participate in a large conference on suicide sponsored by San Francisco State University. Major speakers from around the world were asked to speak, and San Francisco State asked me to help with the planning of the conference, as I had reviewed Jim's book and also was on the National Institute of Mental Health Advisory Board for Suicide Prevention. I was interviewed on television by Caspar Weinberger, future secretary of defense in the Reagan administration, but at the time an interviewer for public television in the Bay Area. I arranged to bring Jim Hillman over from Zürich to be a keynote speaker at the conference. The conference on suicide was a success, and I enjoyed seeing Jim again, although the situation was complicated.

At the time of the conference, Jim's position as director of studies was under attack. A private correspondence with a woman patient had been intercepted by the woman's husband, and the husband wanted Jim out of his position as director of studies. (See my book, *The Jungians*, for a more complete description of this event.) Jim held out for some months, much to the consternation of the patrons and other influential Jungians, but eventually had to leave his position as director of studies at the Jung Institute in Zürich. Sadly, many of the patrons of the Jung Institute who wanted Jim to resign had been involved in significant boundary violations with patients themselves. One of those patrons was my father, who had been vociferous in wanting Jim to leave his position at the Institute. So when I saw Jim at this conference and we had a chance to talk, Jim questioned my position. At the time I did not know as much as I know now, but even then I was supportive of his being judged so harshly by first-generation analysts who had not been so pure themselves. Jim accepted my support, but I could also tell that he was not entirely convinced that I was behind him. It seemed to me that Jim had a difficult time separating me from my father.

Unfortunately, my inability to convince Jim of my support had long-term implications. Jim's suspicion of my motives precipitated a sort of emotional withdrawal that future events only amplified. However, he was still able to nominate me for second vice president of the IAAP in 1971, so there was still support for me. The fact that I had a strong clinical orientation, in contrast to Jim's more academic perspective, was a major theoretical difference.

All this manifested as a somewhat changeable attitude, a wind that blew hot and cold between us. At first I was somewhat bewildered by his unpredictable attitude. I continued to encounter Jim at Jungian congresses and at the Guggenbühls' house every couple of years. At times he was friendly, at other times dismissive. It was only later that I was able to trace the increasing rift between Jim and me back to this discussion about my father's hypocritical condemnation.

In 1968, I became an accredited Jungian analyst. Throughout this time I had continued to see Joe Henderson in analysis. Beginning in 1966, Joe had reduced his analytic practice to three weeks a month, leaving one week per month for vacation and writing, so after that point, I saw him three weeks a month. He was to continue this pattern for the next thirty-six years, although the pattern broke down during the last five or six years when he became increasingly frail.

By 1968, I was eligible to go to the international congress in Zürich and had thought of going with Jean and showing her my favorite places in Europe. However, my dreams warned me about the trip. In one dream I found myself on the crest of a high mountain as in the Swiss Alps, and I realized how dangerous it was for me to be so high. I had had many dreams like that where I was riding the crest of a wave or on the top of a mountain, and I knew that it meant that I was going too fast and that it was dangerous. I needed to slow down. Reluctantly, I gave up the idea of going to the 1968 congress.

By 1969, though, I thought I was ready to go back to Europe for the first time since the disastrous honeymoon of my first marriage. Jean, being a Midwesterner and having lived in Alaska, had never been to Europe. We visited my family in London and then went on to Zürich, where I introduced Jean to the Meiers, Liliane Frey, Aniela Jaffé, and the Hurwitz family, all close friends of my parents. Although Jean did not speak any European languages other than English, she seemed to like the ambience of Europe, and this was to be the first of many trips for us to different parts of the continent, usually including Switzerland, England, or both.

During this time in the Bay Area the hippie revolution and the psychedelic experience were at their peak. Jung became one of the gurus for those undergoing the experience of the collective unconscious via the psychedelic medium. Jung became popular and fashionable, and Jungian books began to gain popularity. In addition, the University of California extension programs, both in Berkeley and Santa Cruz, began to have a series of programs on various topics related to Jung. One of the first was on the subject of dreams, and I gave a revised version of the paper that I had given at the American Psychiatric Association meeting in Detroit in 1967. There were six hundred people in the audience, which was the largest audience that I had ever spoken in front of. I was never able to shake off my nervousness at being in front of so many people. The lecture went all right, but I knew that it was not really as good as it might have been. I participated in two or three other programs, "Jungian Analysis" and "Jung," at the University of California at Santa Cruz. These lectures were to smaller audiences and were less nerve-wracking and more satisfying.

I began to get involved in the San Francisco Jung institute committees, and already in 1969 I was made a member of the extended education committee serving along with Don Sandner and Tom Parker. At the time extended education was a small but emotionally explosive area of the institute. Since it was one of the few places where the institute made contact with the outer world, the members had strong, emotionally toned ideas of what we should present and who should represent us. We once had Edgar Casey, Jr., the son of the acknowledged psychic, scheduled to speak on our program, but Jo Wheelwright thought that would be bad for our image as a scientific institute. He exerted much pressure on our committee to disinvite him, which we reluctantly did.

I have continued on the extended education committee all these years, and I cannot seem to get off it. My connections with Jungians around the world make me a source of information when someone writes and wants to present in San Francisco. Because of the committee's interface with the collective, it has been a lightning rod for conflict. At times in the past a staff person has been in charge of organizing the program, but for the past twenty-five years, it has been run by analyst members, and this has worked out much better for everyone concerned. Although my wife wishes I would finish with the extended education committee, I always seem to hang on for another year.

The C.G. Jung Institute of San Francisco has had a long tradition of monthly dinner meetings. For many years we had Chinese dinners catered by Joe Jung's. For the first few years of my membership, business was handled at these monthly dinner meetings, and some of the meetings became emotionally intense, with Jo and Jane Wheelwright usually at the center of the storm. Two things changed. We decided to delegate most of the business to an executive committee, thereby taking the business out of the dinner meetings, and secondly, we changed from Chinese meals to the newly developing California cuisine. This meant that we could focus on either clinical or intellectual interests at the monthly meetings.

I was strongly interested in teaching Jung at the institute, and by 1970, I was teaching seminars on dreams and on the archetype of the *puer aeternus* to the candidates. In my seminar on dreams, I would present the dreams, and then ask the candidates to work backwards to the conscious situation of the dreamer. This was an unusual way to demonstrate the compensatory aspect of the unconscious, but it was also a chance for us to use our intuition about the dreamer. I continued these seminars until 1975, when Jean became a candidate and we both felt it would be better if I would withdraw from teaching her group. I did not realize at that time how long it would take me to get back into the regular teaching rotation at the institute. Besides Jean's candidacy, I was to become very involved with the International Association for Analytical Psychology, where I did much teaching and supervision, and I did not have time to teach internationally and at the local level at the same time.

In 1970, I realized that there were no courses for professional people who wanted to learn more about Jung but did not necessarily wish to become Jungian analysts. We began by offering one course each semester on a topic in analytical psychology. This program has grown and developed over the years and now is a staple of the larger extended education curriculum.

On December 22, 1970, our daughter Susannah was born. Jean, who by then had finished her internship and for the first time in her life was not working, took care of Susannah for the first two years. Then she started a psychiatric residency in San Francisco that required her to be away most of the day, and we hired a nanny who lovingly took care of Susannah. Since my office was in Menlo Park and was close by, I often came home during the day to check on things.

The period Jean was in her residency was stressful for our marriage, and we separated between October, 1973, and January, 1975, while we tried to work things out. The separation was painful, but it also resulted in profound psychological growth. Our marriage has steadily improved in the last thirty-four years, and other positive things came out of that dark period as well, among them a move from a rather poorly designed house in Atherton to a more conventional, two-story house in Palo Alto. Although the Atherton house had beautiful natural grounds, it was ill-suited for life with a young child. But the Palo Alto house was a good house in which to raise Susannah, and we still live there thirty-nine years later. However, the neighborhood has changed a great deal in the intervening years. When we first moved in, the area was middle class to upper middle class, but with the rapid growth of Silicon Valley, newcomers are inevitably corporate lawyers or upper-level executives from software companies. The neighborhood now is a mixture of old-timers and a new breed of recent arrivals. Some traditions have remained, however, including a tradition of putting up Christmas trees in the front yard, which has been observed each year since 1940. Around Christmas, people either drive or walk down our street to take in the decorations. It's a lovely tradition for young families, although it does cause some disturbance to my Jewish psyche.

After Jean finished her psychiatric residency, there was room in our new house for a psychotherapy office. Jean used it as an office for ten years before moving into our joint office building on Middlefield Road.

I remained focused on my analytic career. My early years at the institute, roughly from 1968 until 1976, were exciting ones. I rarely missed a dinner meeting, and I found the companionship and collegiality of the members very gratifying. It gave me a chance to see people like Elizabeth Osterman, Joe Henderson, Jo Wheelwright, Bill Alex, and others in a social setting, although I was definitely the youngest analyst during that first decade at the institute.

One other project came to me during the early days of my membership. Jo Wheelwright was asked to edit a series of essays on Jung that were about one hundred thousand words long and were to be included in a multi-volume work on psychology. He passed the project on to Tom Parker and me, and we shared the editing. All the classical Jungian terms, such as *anima, animus, archetype, psychological type*, etc., were covered in individual essays about two or three thousand words in length. Tom and I selected different members of the institute to write about the various topics. Unfortunately, when we were finished, the topics were spread around in a six-volume encyclopedia, the *International Encyclopedia of Psychiatry, Psychology, Psychoanalysis, and Neurology*, and the individual articles were difficult to locate. Also, the volumes had to be purchased as a set that was priced at six hundred dollars, an enormous amount at that time, so few encyclopedias were sold. Because of that, the material in the encyclopedia never had much of an impact on the Jungian community. When the encyclopedia was first published in 1977, the editor, Benjamin Wolman, would not allow us to publish the Jungian articles as a separate volume. He immediately threatened to sue us if we gathered the essays into a separate book, so the essays languished in obscurity.

In 1972, Jean and I decided to buy an office building in Palo Alto. This was the place we were going to settle down in, and I had seen from Jo Wheelwright how a home could easily be made into psychotherapeutic offices. I needed to find a building that was zoned properly for business uses, yet looked like a home. Darlene Hinton, the wife of my friend Ladson Hinton, had just become a real estate agent. She literally walked the streets of Palo Alto and found the house that Jean and I still both practice in. It was a residential house that could easily be converted into psychotherapeutic offices. I received commitments from Mary Jo Spencer and Ladson to stay there for five years, and we began to do the small amount of remodeling that was necessary to make the home into offices. At the time I felt uncomfortable doing real estate transactions because I thought that I should be an analyst exclusively, but in the long run it has really worked out well. The city of Palo Alto had very stringent building codes, dictating even the size of the plants that had to be planted. Fortunately, this was before Silicon Valley caused real estate prices to rapidly rise, and so, since we paid only $44,270 for the building, it was very affordable. Having such stability in terms of office space has allowed me to worry less about finances and even to take on projects which do not pay well, because I have been able to fall back on rents from the office building.

In 1972, the C.G. Jung Institute of San Francisco became the recipient of a grant from the Frances Wickes estate. Frances Wickes had been a Jungian analyst in New York who worked with many artistic people. She was initially trained as a schoolteacher and then later went to Zürich to see Jung. In 1927 she published a book, *The Inner World of Childhood*, which became a bestseller. She had been widowed early and had left all her business dealings to a New York stockbroker. She lived to be over ninety, and when she died in the early 1970s, she had amassed an estate worth two million dollars, a considerable amount in those days. Questions arose as to how this money would be distributed, and a committee was formed to address this question. The committee was made up of Mrs. Wickes's lawyer, Hazard Gillespie; Henry Murray, the eminent Harvard psychologist; Bill McGuire, executive editor of Jung's *Collected Works*; and George Hogle, a Bay Area analyst who had been in analysis with Mrs. Wickes in the 1940s and 1950s. George excused himself from any decisions involving the San Francisco institute, but the rest of the committee wanted to give the remaining one and a half million to the San Francisco institute. Before the Wickes committee could finalize that decision, they decided to have our institute evaluated by McKenzie Corporation, which was in the business of evaluating corporations. Our nonprofit was not their usual cup of tea, but they went about the business of interviewing a number of us, including me, and making their recommendation to the Wickes board. I was impressed by the depth of their questioning, and our institute received a clean bill of health as well as the final distribution from the Wickes Foundation. One hundred fifty thousand dollars was used to buy our present building on Gough Street, and the rest was put in an endowment which has sustained us over the years. When we first received the gift, our institute was able to live off the dividends from the endowment without touching the principal. We quickly found more and more projects to put the money into, though, and within a few years we were digging into the principal. In 1990, this produced a small crisis, and we have since become much stricter in how we allocate our resources.

In May, 1973, Jo Wheelwright had been asked to put together a Jungian panel for the annual American Psychiatric Association meeting being held in Honolulu, and I was selected for the panel. All the panel members were psychiatrists, and we spoke about different aspects of Jung's work. The presentation was at seven in the morning, and the room was filled to overflowing. It was the first formal Jungian presentation ever before an American Psychiatric Association audience, and it was highly successful.

Jo then talked to Leon Salzman, an influential member of the American Academy of Psychoanalysis, which at the time was the more liberal of the two national psychoanalytic associations. Jo persuaded Dr. Salzman to put those of us who had been on the American Psychiatric Association panel up for membership in the American Academy of Psychoanalysis. At the time Jo was the only Jungian member in the academy, but all of us were elected as members, which was very prestigious at the time. Later many members of the academy appeared to regret allowing us in, as at the time of admission they had not really checked how much supervision and analysis we had had. But I felt very proud of my membership and volunteered to be on panels at as many of the meetings as I could possibly attend. I would present the Jungian point of view, which was politely listened to. It was amazing to see how little they knew about analytical psychology and how distorted their views of Jung and analytical psychology were. I was on several panels, including dreams, transference, and history of psychoanalysis. Several members of the academy were interested in a presentation on "The Effect of the Gender of the Analyst." I presented the original Jungian model developed by Jung and Toni Wolff, where an analysand saw both a male and female analyst for appointments, either both on the same day or on consecutive days. At the time I had one patient who was seeing both me and a female analyst at different times, and it seemed to be working. The criticism of this method was that it dilutes the transference. Over time that criticism has won out, and I don't believe analysts still practice that way. However, I was asked to write up this technique, and it became the lead article in the *Journal of Contemporary Psychoanalysis*. Michael Fordham, who by then was a leading Jungian analyst from the UK, wrote a strong criticism of the technique. I was really pleased at the article's acceptance by a psychoanalytic journal. Michael appreciated that I had written up the method so clearly even though he disagreed with it. No one had written it up before.

In recent years the academy has become much friendlier to the Jungians, and they are encouraging us to present at all their conferences and become members of their Board of Trustees, etc. It is quite a shift from forty years ago.

The American Academy of Psychoanalysis has also become more conservative over the years. They restricted membership to physicians, and on two different occasions voted on the question of whether to allow psychologist members. As a result, the organization is still limited to psychiatrists, and, since few psychiatrists are pursuing psychoanalytic careers today, membership is declining. They changed their policy and accept any psychiatrist interested in dynamic psychiatric, changing their name to the American Academy of Psychoanalysis and Dynamic Psychiatry.

In those early years I was very involved in my clinical work and my focus was on seeing patients. In the beginning of my practice many patients did not know I had a Jungian orientation, and I liked that. I was always interested in the unconscious productions of my patients and I was tracking my own process by remaining in analysis with Joe Henderson. I published a number of papers on dreams and the therapeutic process and began to work on the history of analytical psychology.

In 1974 I published a paper which was probably the most clinically satisfying of my career. It was a case write-up entitled "A Case of Puer Identification." The patient had dreams which demonstrated what von Franz had written about in her monograph on the *puer aeternus* archetype, a popular subject within the Jungian community. It described a young man who was dominated by a mother complex and could not settle down, rather like the Peter Pan syndrome. He lived the provisional life and could not commit to a relationship or work situation.

While working on the paper, I had the good fortune to meet Fred Plaut, the editor of the *Journal of Analytical Psychology*, who was lecturing in San Francisco at the time. We spent several hours together, and with his additions, which came mainly from a more psychoanalytic approach, the paper was vastly improved. Working with Fred was the best editorial education I have ever had. The paper retained its classical Jungian approach, but with his help the developmental aspect was added, which grounded the paper in clinical language.

Another opportunity came my way in the fall of 1973. C.A. Meier, who had been my first analyst in Zürich in 1957, was retiring as professor at the ETH, which served as the MIT of Switzerland. Jung had held this professorship until his retirement in 1941, and Meier had been his successor. Now I was being asked whether I would be interested in moving to Switzerland and taking on the professorship. That certainly would have been a life-altering decision. My German was not perfect, but I felt I would have picked that up in a few months. However, we had just bought the office building and had begun to really put down roots in Palo Alto. As much as I loved to visit Zürich, I knew that living there would have been very different. At that time there was little social interaction with people when one lived there, although as visitors we were always more welcomed. I finally told Fredy Meier that I was very flattered to be asked, but moving to Zürich just would not fit in with my life. Interestingly enough, the professorship position remained unfilled for many years, and, when it was refilled, it was not filled by a Jungian. I saw it as a loss for the Jungian world to have lost its hold on the prestigious position Jung held for so many years.

Limiting my professional life to clinical matters came to an end in 1974, when I began to assume a leadership role in the Jungian world.

President of the Jung Institute

In 1974 I was approached out of the blue by the C.G. Jung Institute of San Francisco nominating committee and asked to become president-elect of the institute. I was flattered and immediately accepted the position, which meant that I would serve as president-elect for two years followed by two years as president. Serving as president-elect meant that I needed to attend executive committee meetings every Friday in San Francisco. In retrospect, that seemed rather easy to do.

When I became president-elect, the institute had just moved into its new quarters and was expanding rapidly. I had not appreciated the impact of an expanding role and had no idea what I was in for. Suddenly, every administrative decision seemed to come through the president. Unfortunately, I began my term with my lower back going out on me, and it really did not recover the entire two years.

It was a time of rapid change. First, Maury van Loben Sels, the original executive director of the institute, retired at the end of my first year. Up until this time, the institute had been run more or less as a family, and Maury fit into this structure very well since he knew many of the older members. We did not have a mechanism in place to search for a new executive director, but Joe Henderson knew someone he thought would be ideal for the position. Joe's suggested candidate, John Levy, had considerable experience working with nonprofit organizations in San Francisco and was well acquainted with Jungian psychology. So three analysts took John out for lunch, and we all liked him very much and were convinced that he was the person to replace Maury, which he did in the fall of 1977. During the interview we had explained to him that the institute was run by committees and that the committees had a great deal of autonomy. He said that he understood that, but over the following years, our committee structure gave him much difficulty.

Since I had already been president for a year at that time, I was the one who instructed him on his duties, and we started off well together, but twelve years later, at the end of John's tenure as executive director, I think he was very ready to leave. By the end, everything about the institute and the way it ran seemed to irritate him, and he was burned out after twelve years at the job. Today hiring a major employee of the institute would never be handled so informally. He or she would have to undergo a series of interviews with various institute committees, and it would be a long, drawn-out procedure.

During the early 1970s, US Jungian education was largely a coastal affair. There were four accredited Jungian institutes in the United States, situated in New York, San Francisco, Los Angeles, and Boston. In the fall of 1973, a fifth US institute was formed, a group which, unlike the existing institutes, had no clearly defined geographic center. The new group, the

Inter-Regional Society of Jungian Analysts, was to have a rotating meeting place somewhere in the United States. The idea was to provide an organizational framework for analysts returning from training in Zürich and analysts who were not part of the four existing institutes to meet and train, and the new group quickly established a national association and spread rapidly all over the United States.

In 1977, a group of Jungians met at Thayer Green's house in suburban New York City. As former president of the San Francisco institute, I was one of them. The older institutes were concerned about how the Inter-Regional Society was taking shape, so a meeting was called to discuss it. In truth, the Los Angeles and Boston representatives weren't particularly concerned with what the Inter-Regional Society was doing, but the institutes in New York and San Francisco cared a great deal. The Inter-Regional Society representative, James Hall, was usually a mild-mannered Texan, but he blew up at the meeting because he was getting a lot of heat. We were all trying to slow down the growth of the Inter-Regional, and we were questioning whether they were really offering adequate training.

This New York meeting became the first annual meeting of institute presidents of the United States, Canada, and Mexico. There are now many local Jung institutes spread around the country which also meet regularly. There have been many attempts to form a National Jung Society that would be more similar to the organizational structure in Europe, where all the Jungian groups are national. That has never worked in the US. Individual societies have not been willing to give up their autonomy to a national association, so the individual American societies are rather loosely attached to the IAAP.

For me, the first meeting of the United States Jungian societies was transitional. I attended as representative of the International Association for Analytical Psychology, but I was also immediate past president of the C.G. Jung Institute of San Francisco. However, from this point on in my professional career, my focus shifted to the international body. I did not turn my back on the local or American scene, but clearly my energy went to international issues.

8

EARLY RELATIONSHIP TO THE IAAP

In 1977, the IAAP meeting was held in Rome, and I was selected as one of the plenary speakers on dreams. My lecture was entitled "Dreams and Psychological Type," and it was well-received. After the lecture, I was interviewed by several Italian newspapers and journals. At that time, the delegates' meeting, during which the elections took place, occurred on the last day of the congress. That day Jean and I were invited to lunch by C.A. Meier, and the wine flowed plentifully. It was a social meal, no business.

Then we all went to the delegates' meeting. The only contested election was for the office of second vice president. I was nominated for the position by Jo Wheelwright. Nominations do not need a second according to Swiss law, but C.A. Meier stood up and seconded my nomination, which shocked me. Several other people were nominated as well. Some delegates seemed concerned that I was being nominated because my parents had both been analysts and I had a certain name recognition, and apparently they did not believe that I was qualified. Then Yechezkel Kluger stood up and made an impassioned speech in my favor, saying that he had known me since I was eight years old, that I had a sterling record wherever I had been, and that I definitely was qualified for the job. I won the election without a runoff.

The final banquet of the conference was held that evening, and Jim Hillman came up to me at the banquet. I knew that he and Meier had fallen out, and I was definitely sympathetic to Jim's position in their argument, although Fredy Meier and I remained on good terms. But Jim was obviously furious with me, and the intensity of his emotion left me utterly stunned.

He asked how I could still be friends with C.A. Meier and how I could let him nominate me for the vice presidency. He implied that at this point in our lives, I should have moved past my relationship with Meier. I don't quite know how I responded, although I too was surprised by Meier's nomination of me, especially since I'd had lunch with him just before the meeting and he had not discussed this with us over lunch. However, I had just been elected second vice president, and Jim and I had to work together for the next three years since he was the honorary secretary for the president, Adolf Guggenbühl-Craig. And we did manage to work together reasonably well, in spite of his discomfort with me. Then for Adolf's second term, Niel Micklem became the honorary secretary, and I no longer saw as much of Jim. But this episode did irreparable damage to Jim's and my relationship and created a lasting ambivalence.

That election began an eighteen-year stretch on the IAAP executive committee. I took each three-year term as it came up as I didn't want to commit myself to eighteen years up front. With each election I weighed whether I wanted to continue or whether it was time for me to do something else. Initially, I expected the election to bring monumental changes in my life, but in fact, almost nothing happened during the first year. I was the most junior member of the team and Adolf Guggenbühl-Craig and Jim Hillman did most of the work from Zürich, so nothing involved me. In addition, I was still president of the C.G. Jung Institute of San Francisco, where Jungian administration and politics took up most of my energy.

Getting to know Adolf and his wonderful family was a highlight of my entire experience in the IAAP. As soon as I was elected second vice-president, he and Anne invited me to stay with them whenever I came to Zürich, and I enjoyed their hospitality there for nearly thirty years. In the process I came to know the Guggenbühl children as well as the grandchildren as they arrived. When I first stayed with Adolf and Anne, not all their five children had married and they had no grandchildren at all. By the end of Adolf's life, they had eighteen grandchildren. For many years all the grandchildren went to grandma and grandpa's house on Wednesday. The household was sometimes chaotic, but it was so heartwarming to have them around, and I was fortunate to be there over the years on many Wednesdays. To have been even a small part of this family was one of the most meaningful experiences of my life.

On a professional level, Adolf became an immediate mentor to me. Although we were very different typologically, with Adolf being an introverted thinking type while I was an extraverted feeling type, we had many things in common. We were both psychiatrists, and we both had a strong international perspective on analytical psychology and world politics. Adolf had gained the wisdom of experience from his many years of administration in the Zürich and international Jungian communities, and he also held a position of respect in the general culture of Zürich. He came from a distinguished family with a long history in Switzerland; his father had been the editor of a well-known and influential weekly newspaper that had come out strongly against the Nazis in the late 1930s, which had not been a popular position at the time. In spite of Adolf's deep Jungian connections, he continued to function as a part-time general psychiatrist, and he liked to be called as an expert witness by the court of Zürich. He also kept his personal and family life separate from his professional life. When I attended the wedding of his son Alastair and his Turkish bride Yoncia in Istanbul, for example, most of the guests did not know that Adolf was a Jungian analyst. This contrasted with my experience growing up in a household where professional and social worlds intermingled. However, Adolf and Anne were most generous in inviting visiting Jungians to their home, so that was one area where the professional and personal overlapped.

What I quickly recognized was that the IAAP heard about the shadow side of analysts everywhere and that this was an important executive function of the IAAP. Adolf was extremely helpful to me in putting these shadow elements into perspective. He was far more lenient in his view of Jungian indiscretions than I was inclined to be, and I modified my attitudes under his tutelage.

Adolf and Jim Hillman were close friends, and their theoretical viewpoints were also close, especially in terms of the spiritual dimension of analytical psychology, perhaps because of Adolf's earlier studies in theology. However, as a psychiatrist Adolf was far more clinically oriented than Jim. My own theoretical views were somewhat different from either of their viewpoints, and I have been more focused on the interpersonal dialectic, an important attitude cultivated by the San Francisco analytic training program, than either Jim or Adolf. Over the years we had many discussions about all things Jungian, and we found common ground in many areas. Adolf and I were both pragmatic in our outlook and were not at all doctrinaire. Although we came from very different backgrounds, we found many areas of commonality. There was only one area of real conflict between us, which occurred some years later regarding a book I was writing.

In May, 1978, Adolf called a meeting of both the executive committee and the program committee of the IAAP. We met in a suburb of Zürich, in the garden of Adolf's house, where the business of both committees was conducted on the same day. "Money, Food, Drink, and Fashion, and Analytic Training" was the topic chosen for the next congress, to be held in San Francisco in September, 1980. We decided that no speaker who had ever before delivered a paper at an international congress would be invited to present in San Francisco. Holding a congress in the United States was a big risk since the dollar was still very strong, making America very expensive to citizens of other countries. It was questionable whether many Europeans would come, but Adolf and Jim were willing to risk that failure. The threat of an earthquake in a city famous for its great quake of 1906 was also seen as a strong deterrent to analysts traveling from all parts of the world.

The combined executive and program committees met for dinner at Adolf's house that Saturday evening, and Ann, Adolf's wife, prepared a beautiful dinner for all of us. Unfortunately, the German analyst Hannes Dieckmann had too much to drink, and later in the evening, when only a few of us lingered behind, he became very belligerent towards Jim Hillman, shouting obscenities and saying that Jim did not like him and was against the Germans.

It was a very uncomfortable situation for me. By the end of the evening, Hannes couldn't stand on his own and needed to be helped into a taxi. The shadow of that evening hung over the first term of Adolf's presidency.

Having the congress in San Francisco also meant that the presidents and honorary secretary needed to meet with the local San Francisco analysts and the society's executive committee. That visit took place in 1979, when Adolf, Hannes, and Jim came to San Francisco, and Adolf negotiated with the Palace Hotel in San Francisco to have the congress there. At the time the Palace was still a first-class hotel but badly in need of refurbishing. It has a famous history as it had survived the 1906 earthquake and many presidents had stayed there over the years. Its central garden court is a magnificent place to dine.

Since I was the only person from San Francisco on the IAAP executive committee, I became the unofficial congress liaison, meeting with local venues and reporting back to Zürich. Two months before the congress there was a hotel strike, and we feared the congress would be canceled, but fortunately the strike was resolved quickly and did not affect us. Contrary to our fears that people would not come, we had a large attendance, with many analysts from Europe using the occasion to see other parts of the United States en route to San Francisco. During the course of preparations for the congress, I met Ursula Egli, a Swiss woman who had moved to San Francisco and who spoke perfect English, German, French, and Italian. She was a superb organizer and became the point person for the congress, managing all registrations and scheduling.

We initiated something at this congress that has taken place at subsequent congresses in one form or another. On one evening, we arranged to invite everyone to dinner at a local analyst's home. The congress attendees were divided up into groups which were organized on a random basis so that analysts from different countries could meet one another. Small groups of analysts met at the homes of various local analysts and candidates. This meant organizing buses to carry people to all parts of the Bay Area, some at distances of up to forty miles from the city. Even then San Francisco had a large analyst membership, so we were able to organize dinner for 500 people, and, with very few hitches, we pulled it off. This was a highlight of the congress, and some form of private entertainment has been part of each succeeding congress.

Ursula made most of the arrangements, and since then she and I have worked together on many projects. As my involvement with the IAAP progressed, she became my secretary, and I know that she has worked for many other officers in the IAAP as well over the years. She is a most unusual person, and I cannot imagine how difficult my professional life would have been without Ursula's help. She was a marvelous editor as well for various books and articles, and most recently translated the correspondence between my father and Jung from German into English. I feel so lucky to have met her. She has become a dear friend over the many years since.

The 1980 congress itself was a huge success. Several analysts who have subsequently had a major influence on analytical psychology gave their maiden lectures at this congress, including John Beebe, Andrew Samuels, Russ Lockhart, and Sonja Marjasch. We also opened one evening lecture to the public with panelists John Perry, Jim Hillman, and Adolf Guggenbühl-Craig speaking about fashion, food, and money. Eleven hundred people attended. The congress had a positive outcome from every perspective, professional, financial, and social. No longer was there a fear of having an IAAP congress in the United States.

At the end of the congress some confusion arose regarding the site of the next congress. Berlin had graciously offered to host it, but at the very last moment the Israeli society put forth an invitation. The German members in attendance quickly deferred to the Israelis, so it was decided that the next congress would take place in Jerusalem. We decided against the typical late August date because Jerusalem was well-known for stifling heat in late summer, so we scheduled the congress to be held in March of 1983. The elections were pro forma, and we were all re-elected for another term. Jim Hillman resigned as honorary secretary, and Niel Micklem, an English doctor and analyst practicing in Zürich at the time, took over Jim's role as honorary secretary.

The presidents met with the Israeli organizing committee in Jerusalem in the spring of 1981 to prepare for the upcoming congress. As a Jew I had often been urged to visit Israel, but until that occasion I had never made the journey. I used the opportunity to bring my teenage son along with me and to spend some time touring the country. In 1981, Israel was still an idealistic nation, and the tension between Israelis and the neighboring Arab countries was not as openly polarized as it would become later on. Arriving a few days early in order to have time for sightseeing, my son and I stayed at the American Colony Hotel in the Palestinian section of Jerusalem. I happened to mention this to one of my family's oldest and dearest friends, Yechezkel Kluger, who had made aliyah with his wife Rivkah twelve years earlier. I was thoroughly chastised by Yechezkel for staying in the Arab quarter rather than a hotel in the Jewish quarter, although at the time it was a completely safe place to be and one could still walk freely throughout the city. Although during our meetings with the Israeli organizing committee we planned to stay at the Hilton Hotel in Jewish Jerusalem, many Jews stayed at the American Colony Hotel in the Arab quarter. In fact, while we were there I encountered Claude Frank, a wonderful Jewish classical pianist I had met previously in New York, who was on tour in Israel at the time.

Two of the main members of the organizing committee for the meeting in Israel were former members of the San Francisco Jung institute. The most senior person was William Alex, one of the first graduates of the Jung Institute in Zürich, who had practiced in Los Angeles and then San Francisco before moving to Jerusalem, where he thought he would stay forever. However, when his children moved back to the San Francisco area, he and his wife

Maria followed them. Bill never made the transition back to California as he could not regain his professional licenses to practice.

The other person on the organizing committee was Eli Weisstub, a Canadian psychiatrist who had trained at Stanford and then had gone through the San Francisco Jung institute analytic training program. After completing his training, Eli moved to Jerusalem, where he married Esti Galili, a child psychiatrist who later became a Jungian analyst. Eli later became vice president in the IAAP. He was interested in training issues as well as developing an ethics code for the IAAP.

Preparations for the congress went well. The topic chosen was "Symbolic and Clinical Approaches in Practice and Theory." By 1983 the developmental theory and practice that had been emerging in the United Kingdom had spread to many other Jungian centers, and, since there was much debate between the two schools, an entire congress was devoted to the subject.

By the time of the congress in March, 1983, many things had changed both for the IAAP and the world. In 1981, Adolf Guggenbühl-Craig had a serious heart attack and began a long convalescence. Hannes Dieckmann took over the reins as acting president of the IAAP, and he did a yeoman's job in carrying through Adolf's program. By January, 1983, Adolf was again having heart symptoms and went to the University Hospital in Zürich, where tests showed that he was on the verge of another major heart attack, requiring an emergency, seven-artery coronary bypass. I visited him in Zürich on my way to the Jerusalem congress. He did not look well, and I seriously doubted whether he would make it through his ordeal. But he did come through with flying colors and lived a fruitful life for another twenty-five years. However, there was no way that he could attend the congress in Israel, so Hannes Dieckmann stepped in and did an admirable job. However, I am sure it was a big disappointment for Adolf to have his IAAP presidency end on this note.

Despite Hannes Dieckmann's commendable efforts, the Jerusalem conference did not turn out as planned. In the fall of 1982, two Palestinian refugee camps in Lebanon were decimated by groups supported by the Israelis, and the mood of the country changed completely. Any idealism that had still existed in 1981 had disappeared by the time we returned to Jerusalem in March, 1983. Large settlements were being built on the West Bank, and these have continued to be a major point of contention between the Israelis and Arabs. Many European Jungian analysts refused to attend the 1983 congress in protest over Israeli actions in Lebanon, and it was a small and intimate congress.

At that time the major political issue on the Jungian front was the conflict in London between the symbolic and the developmental methods of analysis, and the conference was organized in an effort to resolve the split. Unfortunately, discussion between the two sides did not really occur, because adherents of either side only attended lectures promoting their preferred method. The AJA, the Association of Jungian Analysts, had been established in 1977 in Rome to allow Jungians with a more traditional Jungian background to form a group that would be more theoretically congenial for them than the developmentally oriented Society of Analytical Psychology (SAP). Mainly, those persons trained in Zürich, or other training centers where the traditional symbolic approach to analysis was taught, had wanted to find a Jungian home in the United Kingdom, where the only British group then in existence, the Society of Analytical Psychology, focused upon the developmental approach. The leaders of the newly formed Association of Jungian Analysts were Gerhard and Hella Adler, and most of the sympathies had gone with them in their struggle with Michael Fordham and the Society of Analytical Psychology. However, the Association of Jungian Analysts itself was divided, because analysts returning to the United Kingdom from their training in Zürich were now being told that additional control analysis or personal analysis with one or both of the Adlers was required before they could be accepted into the Association of Jungian Analysts. To those who had undergone full training in Zürich, this was an intolerable idea, and it was bringing about a reevaluation of the previous situation that had given rise to the split within the Society of Analytical Psychology. The spokesperson for the Association of Jungian Analysts was Martin Stone, who at the time was married to Miriam Adler, the daughter of Gerhard and Hella Adler. As a new analyst, he was put in an impossible situation.

The highly charged situation came to the attention of the IAAP executive committee, which had not yet developed a mechanism for handling this kind of problem. An informal committee of inquiry selected by Hannes Dieckmann was formed to meet with all the parties and make a recommendation back to the executive committee and the delegates at the next conference in Berlin. I was part of this committee, and over the course of the next three years I met with both sides of the Association of Jungian Analysts conflict, as well as with senior analysts of the Society of Analytical Psychology, usually individually. Emotions were high between the two factions of the Association of Jungian Analysts. Society of Analytical Psychology members had a stake in this conflict as well, because if the Association of Jungian Analysts split into two professional organizations, it would gain political clout within the IAAP, even though the Society of Analytical Psychology was already the larger and more established professional society. The committee of inquiry never met as a group, but each individual had met with members of every society. One month before the Berlin congress in 1986, I still had no idea how the situation would be resolved. Then, seemingly out of the blue, Hannes announced a solution. He never discussed the final resolution with me or the others on the committee beforehand, as I thought he would and believed he should have. His decision was that the Association of Jungian Analysts could split into two societies, to become the Association of Jungian Analysts and a new society called the Independent Group of Analytical Psychologists (IGAP). A fourth society also came into being at this time, a Jungian section within the preexisting British Association of Psychotherapists, BAP. I had never heard of this group before they were listed as a new society within the IAAP, although I was very well acquainted with one of its founders, Marianne Jacoby, an old friend of my parents. Since many members of the Society of Analytical Psychology were also members of the British Association of Psychotherapists, this evened out the political situation between the classical Jungians and the developmental Jungians in the United Kingdom.

Ultimately, the task assigned to the first committee of inquiry was decided by Hannes Dieckmann's negotiations with the United Kingdom groups but not with any members of the committee of inquiry, hardly a democratic process since the committee members never met as a group. In spite of the awkwardness of this situation, the committee of inquiry subsequently became a permanent committee within the IAAP structure, one which only functions when invited to do so and which does not intrude itself otherwise into the business of local societies.

The issue of Jung's relationship to Jews and to the Nazis also came up during the 1983 Jerusalem congress, but only indirectly and around the edges of the congress. The earlier Israeli society's invitation to host the congress, and the German society's instantaneous deference to them, had their history in World War II. Also, since the congress was in Jerusalem, home to Christianity, Judaism, and Islam, everyone was keenly aware of the religious and political issues staring us in the face. Many people wanted a discussion to occur between Israelis and Germans about the holocaust. However, the Israeli Jungians did not want it to be a part of the formal congress, so a group of Jews and Germans did meet informally, and the discussion continued through the next two congresses until it became a formal part of the congress in Paris in 1989.

New elections were held in the old pro forma way. Hannes Dieckmann became the president, I was elected first vice president, and the new second vice president was Bianca Garufi, an Italian analyst who was a member of Associazione Italiana per lo Studio della Psicologia Analitica (AIPA) and an enthusiastic supporter of Jim Hillman. Adolf had suggested that the officers of the IAAP be paid an honorarium. Up to this time all the officers had done their jobs on a volunteer basis with only travel expenses covered by the IAAP, but the work of the IAAP had increased markedly as the organization had grown. The payment of honoraria was approved by the delegates at the Jerusalem congress. The money had not been expected, but I was glad to have that small amount of money when I left my regular analytic practice to work for the IAAP.

First Vice Presidency, First Term

I left the congress in Jerusalem feeling that I was entering a new phase in my relationship to the IAAP. The Zürich influence of Guggenbühl-Craig, Hillman, and Micklem was fading, and Hannes Dieckmann and I were to become influential for the next three years. Hannes and I had an interesting relationship. As a young man he had served as a doctor on the Eastern Front during World War II, and after the war he had gone to Zürich for analysis and analytic training. Prior to World War II there had been a Jungian association in Berlin of which my father was a charter member. Hannes was quite aware of this fact. The organization had unraveled during the war years, but after the war Hannes became a founder and the president of the new German Jungian society, which was unique in that it shared the first two years of analytic training with the psychoanalytic society in Berlin. Hannes was the author of many books on analytical psychology and had become a prominent international Jungian speaker. After the war he had made a real study of the Holocaust, and I learned much about the Holocaust from Hannes. He was a strong supporter of Israel and of the Jews. His sister, Marianne Dieckmann, was the main assistant for Paul Berg, a professor of biochemistry at Stanford University Medical School who won a Nobel Prize for his work in developing the field of molecular biology. Hannes and his wife Ute were frequent visitors to Palo Alto, coming at least once a year to visit Marianne. We then developed a social relationship in addition to our professional relationship. I had the pleasure of several dinners with the Bergs and Dieckmanns at Marianne's home. The Dieckmanns had also bought a small farmhouse about a two-hour drive south of Paris, where they were spending more time. They invited me to visit them there.

Hannes chose a young psychiatrist and Jungian analyst in Berlin, Gustav Bovensiepen, as his honorary secretary. Gustav carried out many of the secretarial duties. Although he and I got along on a superficial basis, much tension existed beneath the surface. Also new to the executive committee of the IAAP were Luigi Zoja from Italy, Verena Kast from Switzerland, and Elie Humbert from France. Elie and I immediately made a positive connection with one another. He had a brilliant mind, and he was one of the most impressive people I have ever met in the Jungian world. I also met Murray Stein, who was on the program committee for this conference, for the first time. Both Elie and Murray were excellent additions to the intellectual mix growing in analytical psychology. I remained friends with Elie until his untimely death in 1991, and Murray and I have been friends until this day. I chose him as my honorary secretary when I became president in 1989.

Murray was also a Protestant minister who had a divinity degree from Yale and a PhD from the University of Chicago. He practiced in Chicago for many years until returning to semiretirement in Switzerland. He has been one of the more prolific writers and speakers in the Jungian field as well as being active in the administrative aspects of the IAAP. At present he is president of the International School of Analytical Psychology in Zürich. Both Luigi Zoja and Verena Kast were to play prominent roles in analytical psychology, both in terms of books and speeches and in terms of administrative policies. Both eventually became presidents of the IAAP and were very influential in European Jungian thought. Luigi, along with his wife Eva Pattis, a child psychologist and Jungian analyst, became active in South Africa, China, and South America. They truly became world Jungians and have helped many disadvantaged people in the process.

One of the most difficult issues confronting me was that many of the executive committee meetings for the next three years would take place in Berlin in preparation for the 1986 congress. Berlin was my mother's birthplace, and my father had grown up there and had had a thriving psychiatric practice until 1933, the year that Hitler came into power. I felt very ambivalent about travel to the city. Although I had made the trip twice prior to the 1986 congress, on both occasions I stayed in my hotel room as much as possible, not going out except for meetings and meals. I simply did not want to confront the feelings stirred by the city. Berlin was still divided, and one felt the effects of the war and the tensions between East and West everywhere. Although Hannes made it as comfortable as possible for all of us, no one could avoid the fact of the Berlin Wall. The title of the congress was appropriate, "The Archetype of Shadow in a Split World."

Fortunately, nothing eventful happened at the congress itself, and people seemed to enjoy themselves. As first vice president I gave the ten-minute opening address, welcoming the attendees and emphasizing how difficult it was for many Jews to attend this congress. This was greatly appreciated by many of the Jews who had come.

My father was eighty-five years old at the time of the congress, and he had written to Hannes mentioning that I was now going to become president of the IAAP. This upset Hannes immensely, and he rushed over to see if I really was going to run against him for the president's position. I assured him that my father was confused, for I had no such intention. Hannes was always apprehensive that I would run against him and try to get him out of office early. In this, he was not being completely paranoid. Some people held past indiscretions against Hannes. Just the fact that he was German stirred up old memories and wounds, and many analysts were uncomfortable having a German in charge of a European-based organization, as the IAAP was in those days. In fact, there had been an attempt to oust Hannes early, but I refused to go along with the plan, so it quickly vanished.

The composition of the IAAP executive committee was changed at the Berlin conference when the conference delegates voted to add a second position of second vice-president, which meant that delegates voting for the position of first vice president at the next congress would have a choice between two second vice presidents. Verena Kast was elected to the additional second vice-presidency, and at the time I welcomed her presence. Verena had charmed me with her engaging personality, and I knew that she commanded a lot of attention and respect from other women analysts. She was a well-known and popular author in the German-speaking countries. Verena, I believed, would be a valuable addition to the IAAP executive committee. Hannes and I were re-elected to our respective positions, and Murray Stein became the head of the program committee, which was becoming an increasingly important position as the organization grew.

Paris was chosen as the site of the next congress, to be held in 1989, and its chosen theme was "Personal and Archetypal Dynamics in the Analytical Relationship."

First Vice Presidency, Second Term

During my second term as first vice president, I found people increasingly turning to me. Hannes had stepped on people's toes over the years, while I tried to work with people, so I found that many Jungians preferred to deal with me.

Since the next congress was to be held in Paris, most of the organizing and program committee meetings were held there. Elie Humbert, the most influential French Jungian, was consulted on all important issues around the congress. Knowing that I would be giving the ten-minute introductory lecture at the Paris congress, I began to speak with a native French-speaking person for an hour and a half each week. It had been more than thirty years since I had made my first visit to Paris with my father, and I now could speak a passable French, and was still able to read French as well. It was quite a contrast with my first visit in 1953! My aim was to deliver that first ten-minute speech at the congress in French, and that is what I did. I know how much the French like to have foreigners speak French, even today where English, rather than French, has become the *lingua franca*.

Hannes and I divided the responsibilities. Hannes took care of most of the European issues, while I was more involved in the areas where English was the native language. We had a good working relationship, and there was much to do, for the world of analytical psychology was beginning to expand exponentially. A new group was forming in Cape Town, South Africa, another one in New Zealand and Australia, and all over the world we were hearing from people interested in learning more about Jung and analytical psychology. Travel began to increase. Hannes made a long journey to Cape Town, and I was given the responsibility of going to Australia and New Zealand. Both of these trips were costly in terms of both money and the energy of the IAAP, but they were absolutely necessary in terms of the development of new professional Jungian groups.

The trip to Australia and New Zealand was in August, 1988. My analyst wife Jean, my daughter Susannah, and her friend Shirin came along as well. Naturally, I paid for their passage out of personal funds and not from the IAAP. August was the middle of winter in the southern hemisphere, and we began the visit in Perth, Australia. Perth in 1988 felt a time warp back to the 1950s in Los Angeles. Even now it is a very remote location seventeen hundred miles from the nearest city. However, the most prominent Jungian in Australia was Rix Weaver, who lived in Perth. At the time Rix was in her mid-eighties, and she could not move around easily, but she had a number of analysands and students who took care of her.

The setting reminded me of Los Angeles in the 1940s in that the professional and personal relationships were completely intermingled. For instance, we might have dinner at a person's house, and then immediately switch from socializing and small talk to an interview about possible Jungian training at some future date. We brought in Stefan Neszpor, who was a psychiatrist but not a Jungian, to help with the interviews. We found it extremely helpful to have an outsider participating in the interview process.

While in Perth we stayed at the house of Muriel Stanley, the widow of a well-known virologist at the University of Western Australia. Muriel was a student of Jung as well as of yoga. When we arrived, she seated us at a round table, and to break the ice, said, "Let's have a picnic." We had a very good time staying at her house for a week while we did the interviews, and I gave a lecture to the Jungian group which was well attended. All of us loved the openness and freedom of Perth. Susannah and Shirin went out to see Margaret Thatcher, who was visiting at the time. They had a chance to shake hands with her, and she said, "It's good of you to come out."

After a most enjoyable five days in Perth, we flew back to Sydney, where there was a meeting of people who were interested in Jungian psychology. The meeting gathered all the people from Perth to the southern tip of New Zealand, a distance of six thousand miles, who were interested. We were baffled about how to form a professional group when there were such big distances involved. There were already a few analysts who had trained in either the United States or Europe who were practicing in Sydney, Melbourne, Wellington, and the South Island of New Zealand. The trainings were diverse, however, ranging from the more psychoanalytically oriented training of the Society of Analytical Psychology in London to the training of the classical Jung Institute in Zürich, and a wide range between. How were all these people going to coalesce into one group?

About fifty people attended this weekend meeting. Some had come from far-off places, and trying to satisfy the needs of such a diverse group was difficult. Personally, I was over-whelmed by the situation, and felt there was no way that the IAAP could begin to satisfy all the demands. The professional group in Australia and New Zealand was called ANZSJA, but not all the IAAP-accredited analysts were even members of this group. Some analysts, especially the ones who had trained in Zürich, were critical of training deficiencies of others, and they did not want to join. Those who had not trained in Zürich were more approachable and were interested in forming a professional group. There are also many younger students interested in learning more about Jung who wanted to know where they could receive further instruction. At the end of the weekend I was thoroughly exhausted, but I was satisfied that some new direction and focus was beginning to develop in a large region of the globe.

We took a week's vacation on Orpheus Island near the barrier reef before heading off to Wellington, New Zealand, and the final stage of our journey. Wellington is at the south end of the North Island, and it has a beautiful harbor that is sometimes compared to the harbor of San Francisco. However, the wind was strong enough to knock one over. As in Australia and in many other places, the New Zealand Jungian group had been founded by an older woman, Dorothea Norman Jones. She was a Kiwi who had trained in psychiatry in London and had her analytic training there as well before returning to New Zealand. By coincidence, she had been friends with the customs official in the London home office who had given permission to my parents to settle in the United Kingdom over fifty years earlier. She was an old woman at the time, and she seemed to be more interested in her horses than in developing Jungian psychology in New Zealand. That was fine with me, as she did not have the passion for Jung most other first-generation Jungians did.

The group in New Zealand was much smaller than in Australia. A couple of them had attended the meeting in Sydney, Australia, when we met with all the members of the ANZS-JA. As in Australia, the members had trained in different countries. At the time there were only four or five professional members, some in Wellington and others on the South Island. In the 1950s, my parents had strongly considered moving to New Zealand to escape all the atomic radiation in the northern hemisphere. That had captured my interest, and since then I had wanted to visit. I came to New Zealand with high expectations, but I found the Jungian group much less spirited than the Australian group, and, although the group was very welcoming, coming to New Zealand after Australia was a letdown. Everything seemed to be dominated by farmland and sheep. We did not go to the South Island, which is considered the more beautiful of the two islands and is the prime tourist destination. I was really glad to leave New Zealand and head for home.

This one-month trip to Australia and New Zealand was eye-opening. My childhood had been spent watching my parents establish a Jungian group in Los Angeles, and I myself had been a Jungian analyst for nearly twenty years before I made that trip. Yet here was a large area where analytical psychology was still in its infancy. Although there were also some very well-trained Jungians, and more to come in the near future, I felt in part like a missionary bringing Jung to the hinterlands. It was my first experience, aside from my childhood in

Los Angeles, where one could be on the ground floor of a developing professional society in analytical psychology.

Beginning a new professional society is not easy because there are so many conflicting demands, and in Australia and New Zealand, the wide geographical expanse that was occupied by only a few analysts made it especially challenging. To lessen the impact of incest, candidates would have to meet in a central location for most of the seminars, which would only be scheduled two or three times a year. Supervision at that time could be done by telephone, although it would not be easy. Still I came back from that trip quite satisfied with what we all had accomplished together. In the last twenty-five years Jungian analysis as a profession has grown tremendously, and there are active centers in many cities in Australia and New Zealand.

I made many such trips over my years as an officer of the IAAP. The last trip that I made as vice president was a three-stop European trip in the spring of 1989. My first stop was Barcelona, where Rosemary Douglas had begun to form a group of analysts. Rosemary was from an English family and had grown up in Patagonia. Her family sent her to England for her university studies. There she met and married a Spaniard, and they returned to Barcelona, where she endured the Spanish Civil War. She wanted a Jungian analysis, so during World War II she traveled through occupied France to go to Zürich, where she was in analysis with C.A. Meier. At the 1980 San Francisco congress she was accepted as an individual member of the IAAP. Few people knew of her, but Jim Hillman and Adolf Guggenbühl-Craig had recommended her, and she was voted in. By 1989, there were several psychologists associated with her who had had both analysis and supervision, and the numbers were sufficient to form a non-training group. It was necessary for someone from the IAAP to evaluate the quality of these candidates, and Hannes and I traveled to Barcelona to meet them. During my trip, Rosemary Douglas drove me back and forth from the Barcelona airport, and the fact that I survived her driving is a miracle.

Many of the candidates had made their analysis or supervision by going to France on weekends. While there, they would have several hours of analysis or supervision in a row so that they could obtain the requisite number of hours of supervision to become members of the IAAP. Basically, the people were qualified, but Rosemary was the only one who spoke good English, and my Spanish at the time was practically nonexistent. Both Hannes and I felt that they qualified to be a group member of the IAAP and should be recommended to the congress in August. I did not care for the process of getting supervision and analysis by having several hours in a single day, but clearly that was the only way that they could get the requisite number of hours, and we felt we had to accept this method.

Next, I headed to Vienna. For some time Hannes had been working with a group of candidates in Austria who wished to become Jungian analysts and members of the IAAP, and he went to Vienna on a regular basis to work with them. Nearly all of the candidates were approved at the 1983 Jerusalem congress, but one member of the group was not accepted, although I cannot recall the exact reason. In 1988, she asked to be reevaluated for membership in the IAAP. However, the situation was complicated by the fact that Hannes was staying with the rejected candidate whenever he went to Vienna, and the candidates all seemed aware that Hannes was having a relationship with her. Under the circumstances, Hannes asked me if I would interview her in Vienna, and I agreed.

This meeting turned out to be one of the most difficult tasks of my eighteen years on the executive committee of the IAAP. She was a medical doctor from Vienna but there was a problem with her credentials, although unfortunately I cannot recall the specific problem. I had the difficult task of letting her know that she would not be accepted at this later time, either. Hannes entrusted me to handle the situation diplomatically, and I believe I did so. The Austrian group was aware that I was in Vienna and knew why I had come, so I also met with them while I was there, and they were in accord with the way the situation with this woman candidate was handled.

The third object of the trip was to have an executive committee meeting in Paris to finalize everything for the congress that would take place at the end of August, 1989. The final mission of this trip was to make sure that both the program arrangements and the arrangements for the congress hotel and the venue at the UNESCO building were in order. I had a higher level of anxiety about this congress than I had had about previous ones, because I hoped to be elected president of the IAAP, although at that time the elections were still open for any other person to run for office. I faced the upcoming congress with a mixture of nervousness and anticipation.

9

IAAP PRESIDENCY, 1989 – 1992

By the time of the Paris congress, I felt that I was well prepared to be president. Boy, was I surprised! The congress did not unfold as I expected.

The meeting was held at the UNESCO building, and the congress hotel was the Westminster, which was a first-class hotel. We received summer rates, which made the hotel affordable, though barely so. The topic was "Personal and Archetypal Dynamics in the Analytical Relationship," and for a number of reasons—its location in Paris, the setting at the UNESCO building, and the topic—the congress attracted a large audience. My weeks of practicing French conversation with a local graduate student paid off, and I was able to deliver the ten-minute opening address in French, which I felt would be important to our French hosts. The French were gracious hosts, and we all worked with Jean Clausse, the husband of the president of the French society, Simone Clausse.

The founding and most influential member of the French analytic society was Elie Humbert. Elie had been a Catholic priest who had gone to Jung in the 1950s and was one of Jung's last patients. Elie later left the priesthood and married Myrtha Gruber, a young Swiss woman who later became a psychiatrist. I first met Elie in 1983 at the first executive meeting after the congress in Jerusalem. We immediately became friends and saw each other at every opportunity, which was at least twice a year because, since Hannes Dieckmann had a home just south of Paris, he scheduled meetings in Paris as well. Also, Elie's wife Myrtha came to San Francisco to work for several weeks with Mardi Horowitz, a prominent and creative psychoanalyst and psychotherapeutic researcher who was a professor of psychiatry at the University of California. Mardi and I had gone to high school together in Los Angeles and were both on the tennis team there, so we had known each other a long time.

Jean and I saw quite a bit of Myrtha that summer, and that strengthened the bond among the four of us. Elie had had a renal cell carcinoma removed before I met him, and he was supposedly cured. Unfortunately, it recurred, and by 1989, he was too sick to get out of bed, although his spirit was still completely there. We visited him at their wonderful fifteenth-century apartment on the Left Bank, and he lived on for another year. Elie was one of the most impressive persons that I have ever met, a towering giant in the Jungian world. All the French analysts looked up to him for a sense of direction in their personal and professional lives. Chiron Publications has published one of his books, entitled *Jung*, which is one of the most sophisticated and interesting introductions to Jung's work. For me, meeting Elie was one of the genuine benefits of having been associated with the IAAP. Our lives have aligned in another way as well, as I also fell ill with renal cell carcinoma. Fortunately new medications have been developed within the last ten years to treat this devastating cancer, but these were not available when Elie contracted his renal cell tumor. Both Elie and I, after surgery to remove our cancerous kidneys, were told that we were cured. But that was not the case for either of us, as is true for many cases of renal cell carcinoma, which can lie dormant for many years before cancer returns.

The Paris congress went along relatively smoothly, although some speakers went way beyond their time limits, and in doing so disrupted the schedule. One speaker, Carlos Byington, went over his allotted time by more than a half an hour and actually had to be almost physically removed from the platform.

The emotional highlight of the congress was the panel that discussed Jung and his alleged anti-Semitism. Jerome Bernstein, Adolf Guggenbühl-Craig, and Aryeh Maidenbaum were on the panel. Aryeh had uncovered a November, 1944, document from the Analytical Psychology Club in Zürich, signed by Toni Wolff and C.A. Meier, which stated that a quota on Jewish members should be limited to 10 percent. The audience was shocked by this fact, but I was not, as I had heard this already from Adolf Guggenbühl-Craig some years before. In 1944 many organizations and universities in the US had similar quota restrictions on Jews. Certainly when I applied to medical schools in the US in 1956, those quotas were still in effect at Harvard, Yale, and many other private medical schools throughout the United States. Other organizations also still had quotas, but the late 1950s were a time of transition. The quota system regarding Jews and other minorities would disappear over the next few years, and by the time I reached Yale Medical School in 1958, the percentage of Jews had risen to almost 40 percent. Having lived through these changes, the Analytical Psychology Club's quota system did not seem so shocking to me. What was surprising to me was the timing. November, 1944, was near the end of the war, and it was already apparent that the Allies would win. Why at that time? I do not know. I tried to talk to C.A. Meier about this, but he quickly became quite defensive, and I was never able to get an answer from him. What came out of the congress panel was that many people in the audience wanted a public apology from the Analytical Psychology Club, even though no one involved with the Analytical Psychology Club in 1989 had been a member in 1944, when the statute had been incorporated in their constitution. It did not make sense to me to write a letter of apology now, but Jerome was not very happy with my response, because he thought a letter should be written to Alfred Ribi, who was the president of the Analytical Psychology Club at the time. John Beebe was asked to compose a letter to be sent to the Analytical Psychology Club, and he, along with Jerome Bernstein, wrote the letter asking for an apology. I cannot remember the response of the Analytical Psychology Club, which is interesting in retrospect. However, the fact that the congress's letter was written satisfied the participants who attended that panel. That concluded the IAAP's official discussion on this sensitive subject, which had begun at the Jerusalem meeting in 1983. The topic is still hotly debated, and whenever I or others have spoken to a group of psychoanalysts, it is always among the first issues to be raised. Historians interested in Jung and analytical psychology have dug deeply into the archives in Zürich and elsewhere and have discovered many documents showing that, although Jung was not particularly positive towards Jews, he wrote letters in support of many European Jews who were able to escape the clutches of Nazism prior to World War II on the strength of Jung's recommendation. Still, this is a subject on which I have been attacked many times over my forty-five years as a Jungian analyst. The fact that my Jewish parents were in analysis with Jung during most of the 1930s without feeling a hint of anti-Semitism from him is something that doubters of Jung just cannot believe. Beyond that, they ask how I as a Jew can be a supporter of Jung. In largely Jewish audiences, this accusation is often voiced strongly. On the other hand, the fact that Jung helped my parents does not disprove that Jung was anti-Semitic.

In truth, the question of Jung's relationship to Judaism has plagued my entire professional career. It was the conscious reason why I undertook the publication of my father's correspondence with Jung, because at the time of the initial accusations against Jung in 1934, my father challenged Jung about his alleged anti-Semitism and being a member of the Nazi party. In those letters Jung most clearly outlines his views on Jews, Judaism, and Freud. I refer the reader to that correspondence. What troubles me is that few people have read the correspondence, while many people continue to make these accusations against Jung without bothering to read what Jung himself has said about Judaism.

At the congress, elections were held and I was elected president. I was not officially president-elect, but traditionally the first vice president became the president unless something highly unusual happened. Verena Kast's name had been placed in nomination as well, but she declined to run against me, I think in fear that it would be divisive for the organization. She seemed to feel that she needed to wait for her time, because she would almost certainly be elected president after my term.

The election that *was* contested was for the two second vice presidents. Luigi Zoja, Eli Weisstub, and Gustav Bovensiepen were the three candidates for the two positions. Gustav Bovensiepen had been the honorary secretary for Hannes Dieckmann, who was respected but not well liked in some quarters, and I think being associated with Hannes worked against Gustav. I knew Eli from San Francisco and Stanford because he had trained at Stanford and had been a graduate of the C.G. Jung Institute of San Francisco, so it was only natural that I would support his candidacy, especially to our own group. I did not campaign against Gustav or say anything especially positive about Eli except to our own delegates, but when Gustav lost the election to Luigi and Eli, he was very angry with me and accused me of going around and saying negative things about him. That was not true, but he would not believe my denials. Even today, almost twenty-five years later, I still believe that his association with Hannes and the lingering negative feelings towards Germany after World War II were the deciding factors against his being elected. The question of negative feelings toward Germany has hardly faded from the public eye. For example, in 2013, *The New York Times* reported on a Holocaust study which found that there were 42,500 concentration camps, slave labor camps, and prisons which contained Jews, gypsies, homosexuals, and ethnic minorities who were either pressed into forced labor or exterminated. No wonder there were and are lingering feelings against Germany.

I appointed Murray Stein to be my honorary secretary, a position that from the beginning had been more of an honorary position than anything else. The position was usually filled by a more junior person from the same Society the president belonged to, but Adolf changed that by first selecting Jim Hillman as his honorary secretary, followed by Niel Micklem, an English colleague who was then practicing in Zürich but who later went back to England. Niel died in December, 2013. He was a very fine English doctor and a very good Jungian analyst. At the time of the congress, he practiced in Zürich with Adolf, and the two had become good friends.

Over time, the position of honorary secretary had changed and, as the IAAP grew larger, was becoming a real working position. I wanted a colleague who was on equal terms with me rather than someone in a junior role. At first I thought of my dear friend Charles Klaif, and I had already asked him several years in advance if he would consider the position. He agreed to it, but then another good friend of both of ours sought me out and suggested that Charles was much too one-sided in his point of view, holding a stance that was too psychoanalytic. Our friend felt he would not be sympathetic to the archetypal point of view common in many of the other Jungian societies in the IAAP. I thought about it and realized that our mutual friend was probably right. Then Charles's wife developed breast cancer, and I used that as a good reason to suggest that he would probably be consumed with her care and would not have the time or energy to be the honorary secretary. He agreed on the surface, but obviously was deeply hurt by my not wanting him to be my honorary secretary, and it almost cost us our friendship. Unfortunately, his wife's breast cancer became a serious issue, and she died during my presidency.

Charles and I had made a trip to France in May, 1985. I had to be in Paris for an executive committee meeting, and Charles and I took the opportunity to visit Normandy and many other World War II sites. It was a very moving experience to visit the beaches and museums in that region. Charles's brother-in-law Ralph had asked Charles to travel with him earlier, but Charles's wife, Darlene, did not want her husband traveling with Ralph in France. They might have had too much fun in the wrong places! Darlene approved of his going with me, however, because she was confident that we would not get into any situations that he could not go home and tell his wife about. During the trip we also spent one night with Hannes and his wife at their farm south of Paris. It was a memorable trip for both of us. Charles died suddenly of a heart attack a few years after his wife's death, so, even though Charles did not become my honorary secretary, I look back on that trip with nostalgia. It was a great trip!

In reflection, I feel that what I had done with Charles was to make a decision too early, long before I should have. Planning too far ahead has been a lifelong pattern for me. One might say this is part of my extraverted intuitive character, but I also think it speaks to an underlying anxiety. I like to have things planned out far in advance. I had liked the way Adolf had handled the presidency of the IAAP, and the idea of an equal colleague as honorary secretary appealed to me. Charles Klaif would have been that. But then I wanted someone who had good relations to Zürich and had good connections with the European Jungian spirit. Murray Stein, who had organized the Ghost Ranch conferences in New Mexico, had proved to have a wide-reaching intelligence as well as exceptional organizational skills. For years these conferences had attracted a large Jungian audience, and I thought I could work with him. Murray was a good choice, and he and I worked well together for six years. Many of the forays into new areas both psychological and geographical were the result of suggestions from Murray.

Another shadow event associated with the 1989 congress was that Hannes had secretly promised the French Jungian society thirty thousand CHF from the IAAP to found a children's clinic in exchange for hosting the congress. This information shocked me, and I wondered what to do with it. Finally, I spoke with Adolf Guggenbühl-Craig, who also had not heard about this arrangement. He advised me to keep the issue quiet because the money had gone to a good cause, and I ended up not saying or doing anything. But when I look back now on how I handled that situation, I do not feel good about it. The payment should have come to the surface and to the attention of the executive committee, but I was just entering into my first term as president and I did not want to begin with a major confrontation. It was the result of my being too much of the nice guy and not putting my foot down. I did not

91

know if I was being self-righteous, but I found Hannes's sexual relationships, his drinking, and now this incident with the French society pretty hard to absorb. Later both Gustav and Hannes would attack me for spending too much money on travel for the IAAP, but by then I was in a position where I could not bring up all these events.

By the end of the Paris congress, East Germans had begun flooding into Hungary. No one knew what this meant at the time, but very quickly all of Eastern Europe was involved, and Communism collapsed in Poland, Czechoslovakia, Romania, the Balkans, and Bulgaria. In 1989 the IAAP began to receive communications from all the former Eastern Bloc countries saying that they were interested in Jung and asking how they might follow up on their interest. This was remarkable, because people had been secretly studying Jung when it was considered dangerous and they could have been imprisoned or killed for doing so.

After the congress, I headed back to Palo Alto to begin my term in the IAAP presidency, with Murray's assistance. The first of Murray's excellent suggestions was to have the new presidents meet in a retreat without any agenda. Murray suggested that we go to our house at Sea Ranch, a quiet introverted place on the northern coast of California. Murray had been there at another time with friends, and he knew it would be a quiet meditative place for us all to get to know each other a little better. We would be working together for the next six years, and we were all at least a generation younger than the previous several administrations of the IAAP. We represented new attitudes and brought a younger atmosphere into the organization. At first the retreat served the purpose of bringing us together, and in the beginning the working atmosphere among the presidents was very good. Things began to break down by the end of my second term, though. Unfortunately, I do not have a complete record of all that happened during my six years as president, and I am sure my memory overemphasizes some events and omits others.

My two terms preceded the coming of the internet. In 1989 the fax machine was still being developed, and Yvonne Trüeb, the executive secretary of the IAAP, was just beginning to use one. Initially I had to strongly encourage her to use a fax machine, because she did not open the box for several months after the congress. During those six years the fax and telephone were the main avenues of communication, along with normal mail. I cut down on my clinical work and devoted all day every Thursday to answering correspondence. A friend had suggested that I might contact Ursula Egli, who had helped with the organization of the IAAP congress in San Francisco in 1980, for some help with the voluminous correspondence. Ursula was Zürich-born and had come to San Francisco in the 1950s, when the United States seemed like a haven after World War II. She was fluent in English, German, French, and Italian, so that she was able to keep up with the extensive correspondence, which at the time was generally limited to those four languages. So I basically had two executive secretaries, one for the North American scene, and Yvonne, who handled European matters. This worked well in the beginning, but as time wore on Ursula took on more of the overall functions of the IAAP. Yvonne had a full-time job in Zürich with a foundation, so she gradually withdrew from the IAAP secretarial work. She did, however, continue working for the Jung Institute in Zürich. Both Ursula and Yvonne have continued to do specific tasks for future IAAP administrations at various times. At the time of this writing, Yvonne is still working part-time for the IAAP in Zürich and the Jung Institute, whereas Ursula has completely retired from all work, including the IAAP. I must give Ursula credit. She is an intelligent introverted person who managed the day-to-day business of the IAAP in an incredibly efficient and easy manner. She made me look very good, because she had all matters organized and under control. I owe a lot of whatever success I had as president to Ursula, and she continues to be a good friend to this day.

Yvonne and I have also remained in contact but in a different way. Her son, Hansruedi, and his family have twice spent a year either studying or on sabbatical in the Berkeley area. Before their first trip here, Ursula and I helped them find a house rental, and I was able to find a car for the family. Hansruedi and Liliane, a wonderful artist, and their children have had two wonderful years living in Northern California, and they have come back for vacations. Over the years we have developed a strong bond with the younger Trüebs and their four children. Hansruedi has become a successful lawyer in Zürich and works very hard, and it is always a pleasure to see them whenever we are there. So indirectly, Yvonne and I have communicated through Hansruedi all these years.

I had scarcely returned from the Paris congress before I began to receive requests to visit various Jungian societies. The first invitation came from Professor Harry Wilmer in Salado, Texas. He was hosting the fall meeting of the Inter-Regional Society in Salado, and he thought my presence there would be a calming one as the meetings were often contentious. He had also arranged a program where Montague Ullman and two other speakers presented an all-day conference for both the visiting analysts and candidates from the Inter-Regional Society and the local members of The Institute for the Humanities at Salado. Harry did not ask me to present but just to be there. Salado is a beautiful town among the rolling hills, and it is directly on the old Chisholm Trail, a famous trail of the old West. I had quite a positive transference on Harry, and I was eager to visit him in Salado.

When I first met Harry he was a professor at Stanford University in the department of psychiatry, and he had been my consultant on a therapeutic community inpatient unit at the county of San Mateo hospital. At that time he had almost completed his Freudian psychoanalytic training. He was also the best teacher I had during my residency. Harry had introduced the therapeutic community to psychiatric inpatient units in the United States, and he was a highly respected psychiatrist nationally. Since the time of my residency training, he had moved first to Langley Porter in San Francisco and then to the Temple White Clinic in Temple, Texas, before finally founding The Institute of the Humanities in Salado, Texas, where he invited prominent speakers in the humanities to lecture. Beginning in the late 1960s, he developed a profound interest in Jungian psychology, went into a Jungian analysis, and by 1974 had become an individual member of the IAAP.

Since Harry had already become a distinguished life fellow of the American Psychiatric Association, in May, 1973, he was able to get the Jungians a place on the American Psychiatric Association's annual conference in Honolulu. Jo Wheelwright, who was also a member of the American Psychiatric Association as well as the American Academy of Psychoanalysis, helped in making arrangements. I was part of the panel, which was the first formal Jungian presentation ever before an American Psychiatric Association audience, and it was very successful. But Harry really paved the way for the first Jungians to become members of the American Academy of Psychoanalysis. From that time until his death approximately ten years ago, he was a prolific writer and speaker at various Jungian congresses. Through the years I became acquainted with many members of his family, including his lovely wife Jane, as well as his five children. Harry had an incredible library, as well as numerous personal papers. Through the gracious help of Jane Wilmer and Stephanie Fariss, a former student of his and now a Jungian analyst in Chicago, much of the Jungian part of his library is now at a university in Taipei, Taiwan, where students can make use of his large collection.

A second request to visit came from Marie Abaque Klem in Mexico City, who wanted me to visit Mexico City and to meet with her several Jungian study groups. Marie Abaque Klem had trained in Zürich and was spending part of her time in Mexico City, where she was from, and part in Zürich. She had a number of people, mainly women, who were in analysis with her, and at the same time she was running several Jungian study groups. I did not want to go to Mexico City, chiefly because of health concerns about the unsafe water there. I suggested that she come to San Francisco, where we could talk about the situation in Mexico City.

Marie was not the first to try to introduce Jung in Mexico City. There had been a couple of other attempts where people from the US had gone to Mexico City and tried to organize Jungian training. Up until that point nothing had materialized, and in time I realized, reluctantly, that I would have to go there and take my chances about getting sick. So I arranged to go for a long weekend in October, 1989. I was met at the airport and taken care of from that moment until I left on Sunday.

Not only were the groups mainly women, but they were also mainly Jewish women. It was even more specific than that in that the Jewish women were divided into Middle Eastern Jewish women and those of Eastern European Russian extraction. These two groups had strong cultural differences, and it took me a while to grasp the situation. I was quite familiar with the Eastern European Jewish culture, because that was the background of most of the kids I knew growing up in Los Angeles. Many of these Eastern European Jews in Mexico had wanted to come to the United States but had not been admitted because of the quota system, so they had ended up in Mexico instead. On the other hand, the Middle Eastern Jews had a very different cultural heritage, and their customs and foods were remarkably different. They had their own Middle Eastern synagogues which were separate from the Eastern European ones. The two groups knew each other and socialized, and they were respectful of each other, but the cultural mores were different. Yet here they were together in these Jungian study groups. I must say they were generally attractive women, married with children and servants, and wealthy. I was quite taken by them, and it put me in touch with the early trip to Guatemala that I had taken with my father in 1946 to see his mother and relatives there. So in the end the 1989 trip that I approached with so much apprehension turned into a very pleasant trip, and I was treated royally by these attractive Mexican women therapists.

When I came back I organized some of my San Francisco colleagues who I thought might enjoy teaching in Mexico City. I cannot remember exactly how many people contributed to the program, but several lecturers did go there and were paid by the Mexican Jungian study group. I also suggested that members of the study groups attend the next national meeting in the United States, which was to be in Los Angeles, as I thought that would be a good introduction for them into a larger Jungian professional group. Several of them did attend the national meeting in Los Angeles in the fall of 1990.

For the next decade I traveled two times a year to organize, teach, and participate in organized psychological conferences in Mexico. However, I never saw Marie Abaque Klem again. She withdrew from the Jungian study groups, and Patrizia Michan, Julie Rubinstein, and Jacqueline Gerson became the people that I worked with the most. I met Jackie and Julie on my first trip to Mexico City but didn't meet Patrizia until 1992. The three of them were part of a small group of people who wanted to become Jungian analysts and were eager for training experiences. Most of the people were wealthy enough to make regular trips to the US for analysis and supervision.

Patrizia was from the Middle Eastern Jewish community, and she owned a three-story building which she used as both a teaching and clinical facility. It had a large seminar room and facilities for simultaneous translation. It was a wonderful setting in which to give seminars and see people in supervision.

A major event for this growing Jungian community occurred in October, 1992. A program on "Archetypes and Mexican Culture" was put on by one of the major universities in Mexico City. Sonja Marjasch, Theo Abt, and I were invited as guest speakers to this large conference. Prior to the conference, I was interviewed by several prominent Mexico City newspapers.

Sonja and I already knew each other pretty well from Zürich, where we spoke often. She was very active and traveled widely until old age in spite of a congenital deformity which made walking difficult. Sonja was a very popular analyst in Zürich and was an extremely gifted, perceptive, and wise woman. On one occasion she made a comment to me at a dinner party in Zürich that I've never forgotten. At the time I was vice president of the IAAP and would soon be president, and I was very much a public figure in the Jungian world. She noted, however, how ambivalent I was about being in the spotlight, and she got me to reflect on this tension. One part of me has always gravitated toward the limelight while an equally strong part has preferred to stay in the background. I can still feel how much my mother wanted me to obtain a position of prominence, while at the same time I realize that I have never been sure whether such a role was natural to me or not. Today I am a more private person than I once was, and I choose my public speaking engagements according to what they mean to me personally, rather than simply proceeding with talks simply because it is expected. I tend to gravitate toward audiences and cities I like and subjects that are important to me, which is all the more important since travel has become much more difficult with passing years and my energy for speaking has waned.

In 1992, however, Sonja and I participated in the Mexican conference, but Theo Abt from Zürich could not attend. Instead, Sven Dorner, a Jungian candidate from the New England society, did the lecture on alchemy. Sven was from a cross-cultural background since one of his parents had been from the US and the other from Mexico, so he was comfortable in both worlds. He was quickly drawn to the emerging Jungian groups in Mexico, and he organized separate Jungian study and training groups in both Mexico City and Oaxaca. However, he never really entered into the Jungian mainstream in Mexico City, and he also never completed his training in the United States and has never been recognized as an accredited Jungian analyst. However, he still unofficially practices and trains in Mexico City. For a time he was in jail in Mexico City for tax irregularities and brought his young son to stay with him in his cell, which I found hard to imagine. I saw him recently at an International Association of Jungian Studies conference in Braga, Portugal. Our conversation was cordial, but to me he is a carrier of what I see as the shadow of some Jungian developing groups.

The developments in Mexico represented an important introduction to my first term as IAAP president. After going there several times, I realized that I shouldn't be trying to coordinate the group alone but that others should be brought into the situation. At first I suggested to Murray Stein that he visit Mexico City, which he did, and he also was caught up in the intriguing situation developing there. He and Patrizia developed a strong working relationship through her *centro*. Then Murray invited Beverley Zabriskie to come down, and she too was drawn to the favorable situation for teaching, supervising, and seeing individual clients. Both Murray and Beverley became much more involved with Mexico, and I slowly began to withdraw from the group. With the rest of the IAAP to think about, I could not spend so much time and energy on the Mexican situation.

However, the group of Mexican therapists who wanted to become Jungian analysts grew over time, and those who were interested traveled to the United States for their analysis and supervision. Jackie Gerson gravitated toward San Francisco, Julie Rubinstein toward Chicago, and Patrizia toward New York, with some of her work done in San Diego. By the end of my second term as IAAP president, Patrizia had become an individual member from Mexico, and several others were on their way toward individual membership. At the same time, I saw tensions and rivalries developing within the group, although they really did not flare up until after the end of my second term. I taught at the Mexican group about twice a year until 2000. In the end I think they got a bit tired of me, and with everything that was going on down there, I wanted to withdraw as well.

I've reflected often on my experience with this group of women from Mexico who entered training. They were mainly Jewish women, and I felt that I understood more of my father's psychology through having met them. After spending more time in Mexico, I saw that his Guatemalan birth was a deeper influence than I had realized. My mother's German Jewish family background had been the dominant influence in my own childhood, but my experience with these Jewish women in Mexico made me more conscious of the deep impact my father's Guatemalan background had on him, and thereby on me.

The IAAP presidency, of course, brought up many other demands, often from outside North America. In January, 1990, I made my first trip overseas as president of the IAAP. The UK Society of Analytical Psychology, which owned the *Journal of Analytical Psychology*, was prepared to make it a joint UK and US journal, with joint editorship, and a meeting was called to explore this question. Rosemary Gordon, Judith Hubback, and Andrew Samuels were the British representatives, and John Beebe, Murray Stein, and I were the American representatives. It was cold and windy when we arrived in London. We spent two days in a Holiday Inn working out how the joint arrangement would work. It was not easy to resolve, because it meant that the Society of Analytical Psychology was giving up control of the *Journal*, which they had begun in 1955 under the direction of Michael Fordham. Over time, the *Journal* had become the voice of the developmental school of analytical psychology, and now it was going to have to open itself up to the Americans, who represented a much more diverse spectrum of viewpoints toward analytical psychology. Over the next few years, the *Journal* would have some rocky moments as the publishers wrestled with questions of what to publish and what not to publish based upon the various perspectives represented by the American and British points of view. Who had the final authority to either say *yes* or *no* to publication? I was outside of almost all of these discussions, but I do recall that it was difficult for the Brits to let go of the questions about what was published in the *Journal of Analytical Psychology*. Of course, since they had been the sole publishers for the first thirty-five years of the *Journal's* existence, that is very understandable. The adjustment to equal authority on the editorial board for both the US and the UK representatives took many years. Throughout this time, the Society of Analytical Psychology in the UK was the owner of the *Journal* and was financially responsible for publication. Although at the time of the London meeting I had been on the *Journal* advisory board for many years, and I have continued in that role ever since, I have never been asked for my opinion about individual articles or specific policies, although from time to time I have been asked to write on a specific topic.

After the meeting about the *Journal of Analytical Psychology*, I had made plans to meet the first Russian who had expressed an interest in Jung. Valery Zelensky, a psychologist who wanted to publish Jung and Jungian books in Russian, was visiting London for several weeks, and Andrew Samuels had arranged a meeting with him. I was both excited and apprehensive, but Andrew and I met him for breakfast one morning, the first of many meetings I would have with Zelensky over the next few years. It was a cordial meeting, but I was mystified. Initially he seemed to be coming from a foreign planet, and I did not get much of a sense of him as a person at that first meeting.

The first executive committee meeting over which I presided was in May, 1990. By then several members of the executive committee had received inquiries from individuals in the Eastern Bloc, and we realized that people all over the Soviet Union and the Eastern Bloc were studying Jung in secret. We all wondered about the appropriate method to reach out to all these searching individuals, and we finally hit upon a multipronged approach.

I was delegated to go to Moscow and Leningrad and discuss the translation and publication of the *Collected Works* of Jung into Russian. I had contacted Olivier Bernier, the executive director of the Van Waveren Foundation, who had promised four thousand US dollars for each volume of the *Collected Works* that was translated into Russian. By the spring of 1990 the Soviet Union was already beginning to unravel, and dollars and other Western "hard currencies" were preferred over the erratic Soviet ruble. Dangling four thousand US dollars for each volume of the *Collected Works* was an attractive offer.

One of the people that I contacted in May, 1990, was Gerda Niedieck, the agent for the Jung estate who handled all the translations of the *Collected Works* of Jung. In her prime she had been an excellent literary agent and had some of the most famous authors of the twentieth century as her clients. However, by the time that I had met her, she had developed organic brain disease and would perseverate for several hours, which made for painful and extremely long meetings. I spent many hours with her while I was in Zürich for the executive committee meeting, but I found out very little. However, I did learn that the Soviet Union did not abide by international copyright laws. Anyone in the Soviet Union could translate Jung into Russian, and there would be no recourse if the translation were found to be inaccurate. I also learned of a three-volume Russian translation of Jung that had been compiled by Emilii Medtner, a Russian émigré who had studied in Zürich during and after World War I. Medtner had come from a family interested in music and mysticism and had been in analysis with Jung shortly after his break with Freud. His three-volume translation mainly contained

Jung's early papers, but Jung had authorized Medtner's Russian translation, and it had been published in Zürich. I found out in later visits to the Soviet Union and Russia that many people had this three-volume set on their bookshelves, hidden behind another layer of books.

Through Renos Papadopoulos I had also been introduced to a young group of Russian psychotherapists who were beginning to do individual psychotherapy in their apartments. They were not specifically Jungian, but they were very interested in depth psychology. Many different people with different orientations were clamoring to present their theories to this young group of psychotherapists.

Every detail of the planning, as well as the trip itself, was unusual. The first order of business was to obtain visas for the Soviet Union. In San Francisco there was a travel agency specializing in this, and I made contact with them well in advance. I was assured that the visa process would be a simple matter, but at the time of departure for Switzerland and then the trip to Moscow and Leningrad, we still did not have our visas. We spent several days in Zürich, holding the executive committee meeting and meeting with various people about the upcoming trip, and still the visas had not arrived. On May 16, we headed to the airport for the Swissair flight to Moscow, and we were assured that the visas would arrive by personal carrier from Basel. I have no idea why they were coming from Basel, but we sat in the airport lounge and waited. Finally, we were dramatically handed our visas by courier. It was a very unsettling way to begin a trip to a country still under communist rule. By spring of 1990, most of the former Soviet republics had overthrown communism, but the Soviet Union was resisting change.

We arrived at the airport in Moscow and were met by a young Russian couple who spoke excellent English—Julia Aloshina and Pavel Schnevneski—and were taken to the flat of Seriozha and Marina Agrechov. These four young people were central to the psychotherapy group developing in Moscow. Other members of their group were there as well, and we were served a beautiful Russian spread, which was described as a "leetle snack." It was the warmest of welcomes to begin our visit.

We were put up at the Intourist Hotel near the Kremlin. It was the quintessential Soviet experience, from the creepy certainty that our room was bugged to the dour-faced blonde matron sitting in the hall overseeing each coming and going. We had been warned that we should bring gifts of cigarettes and chocolate for these watchdogs guarding each floor. Our room looked down onto the Kremlin and Red Square, both hazy through the dirty grey window glass. The hotel had an antiquated telephone system, and we never discovered the actual telephone number for our room. However, people who wanted to get in touch with us somehow knew how to reach us. They would call at all hours, day and night, and, since there was no message service, people would just call repeatedly until we were back in the room and answered. Several prostitutes adorned the small, cramped hotel lobby, and I was approached several times when I was alone there.

I had been given two or three names of potential publishers for the Russian edition of the *Collected Works*, and I called them from our room and set up some appointments. They seemed eager to publish the volumes given the rate, and we chose one publisher who was eager to do the whole series. He wanted to begin with volume fifteen of the *Collected Works*, which contains articles on Picasso, James Joyce, Freud, and other cultural figures. They were not interested in beginning with the more clinically relevant volumes, such as "Two Essays On Analytical Psychology." We mentioned that we were going to Leningrad as well and arranged for a further meeting there.

The overnight train to Leningrad was filled with drunken passengers, and it was not a comfortable trip. We arrived in Leningrad and met our assigned driver and escort, a young man named Sasha who spoke not a word of English. We learned that a Russian airliner had just crashed at the Leningrad airport, and many passengers had been killed. His sister, her husband, and their infant had been on the flight, and other passengers had changed seats with them so they could be together. Because of that, they had survived the crash. When we left Leningrad a few days later, we saw the carcass of the airplane lying next to the runway. We were there again a year later, by which time the prerevolutionary name "St. Petersburg" had been restored, but the skeleton of the plane was still there.

In Leningrad we stayed at the Pribaltiyskaya Hotel, the Soviet equivalent of the Intourist Hotel in Moscow, with all the same amenities and distractions, but located far out of town on the Baltic Sea. Jean and I both gave seminars at the Institute of Psychoanalysis in St. Petersburg. Michael Reshetnikov, a young psychiatrist who was eagerly searching to learn more about Western depth psychology, was our host. His office had pictures of Lenin and Gorbachev, and the atmosphere was quite Soviet in nature. We also renewed our contact with Valery Zelensky, who was becoming more active in publishing Jungian books in Russian. I got into the habit of drinking quite a bit of vodka as well as a wonderful Georgian cognac that was comparable to French cognac. Russians enjoy their vodka, and there were numerous toasts at all these lunches and dinners. Sometimes there was very little time between two events, so I had to be extremely careful with the amount of alcohol that I drank. We also visited the Bechterev Institute, a world-famous neuropsychological institute where Pavlov did his research more than one hundred years ago. Of all the places that we visited, they seemed the most guarded in their responses to us, and it was not exactly a warm welcome. Jean, who had been a student nurse at a large state mental hospital in the mid-fifties, found the conditions and the layout similar to what she had seen then.

The publisher and I agreed on the terms of a contract for Russian publication of the *Collected Works*, beginning with volume fifteen. I agreed to sign on behalf of the IAAP as well as to return to Moscow for the Moscow International Book Fair, the largest book fair in the Eastern Bloc countries and the Soviet Union, which would be held three months later.

Upon my return to California, I had a dream in which I was hanging onto the tail of a 747 airliner in flight. I interpreted the dream as compensatory and assumed that it must be telling me that I had begun to view travel to the Soviet Union as just another commuter trip. I realized that this kind of travel was quite dangerous for me because of the psychological inflation it produced and that I needed to think seriously whether these sorts of trips were really necessary.

Suddenly, in that three-month interval between our departure from the Soviet Union and the agreed-upon date of our return, Boris Yeltsin came into power! The old guard communist leaders, including Gorbachev, were out. It appeared that communism was on its last legs. Then, in August, 1991, the old guard staged a successful coup and regained control of the Soviet Union for two or three days, before popular acclaim for Yeltsin brought him back into power. However, in the short period that the old guard was in charge, they canceled the Moscow book fair, and I was in a quandary about whether I should cancel my trip as well. While in Leningrad I had learned of a Russian man, Sasha Etkind, a psychologist and historian, who was then on sabbatical in Palo Alto. We met and were seeing each other regularly, and of course what was happening in the Soviet Union was affecting him deeply. I asked my close friend Bob Hinshaw, a Jungian analyst and publisher of Daimon Verlag press in Switzerland, to accompany me on the return trip to Russia and sign the contract with the Russian publishers, then follow up on the process with them. We debated whether to make the trip then or put it off, and we finally decided to go and sign the contract. We really were not sure what we were signing and what it meant, but we proceeded in spite of that. Some months later we had the first copy of what we thought were to be many volumes of the *Collected Works*. I still have several copies of the book, which includes a short introduction by Joe Henderson. Unfortunately, that translation of volume fifteen was the only book which came out. In spite of numerous attempts, Bob Hinshaw was never able to contact the publishers again.

I had put a good deal of effort into this project, and its failure was one of the most frustrating events of my presidency. I was just too removed geographically to be able to be effective, especially in those pre-internet days given that the phone system in Russia was antiquated. I still have four copies of the book, but we never received news of its production, distribution, or sales. The project was gone with the wind.

Certainly the breakdown of communism and the "Iron Curtain" was one of the most important events of the twentieth century. Since the end of World War II, the world had been divided into the Communist countries and the free world, and this divide had existed for so long that it seemed permanent. Then, seemingly overnight, communism collapsed, and we Westerners moved in with our various wares hoping to influence a whole continent of people who had been cut off from the rest of the world for a very long time. So much was lost in the gap between the Slavic perspective and our Western one. For instance, the Russians were really not familiar with all the past conflict between psychoanalysis and analytical psychology, and the Russian psychotherapists had no concept of maintaining a boundary between office and home. Their tiny apartments were a combination of everything, living room, dining room, bedroom, and office. I realized quickly that these young psychotherapists were not necessarily going to become Jungian analysts, and I abandoned any ideas of a zealous Jungian mission early on. What I did realize that some of the many burgeoning therapists would gravitate toward Jung eventually, and my goal was to introduce Jung's ideas to them and see where those ideas landed and caught hold.

Regardless of that, we were very impressed by the intelligence and sophisticated thought of the young people we met. We became very fond of Julia, Pavel, and their young daughter, who was then only three years old. Seriozha, his wife Marina, and their two young daughters were a most hospitable family, and the couple was a gravitational center for the Russian psychological group. Seriozha's untimely death by heart failure in his mid-forties was a tragedy for the nascent organization, and we were deeply saddened by his loss.

I think the most touching experience for me occurred on my third visit, when Jean and our college-age daughter accompanied me. We were invited to visit the parents of a young psychologist, Igor Kadyrov, one of those who preferred the study of object relations over Jung. Jean and I took a real liking to him and he to us. He wanted us to meet his parents, who were settled in Moscow after living in Kiev for many years. His father had been a pilot in Murmansk during the Cold War, tasked with searching out American planes that might violate Soviet space. To him the American was still an enemy, and he had never met anyone from the US. Communication was difficult as neither of Igor's parents spoke English. Igor's mother was gracious and welcoming, eager to make us feel at home, but his father did not know what to make of us and sat in grim silence with his arms crossed over his chest. I am not sure how Igor's father came around, but he finally did acknowledge us. Perhaps it was the presence of our daughter, who has a knack for reaching out to people in a friendly way. He finally saw that we were another family much like his own family, not their enemies. To me making this connection, watching our family go from enemies to persons in his eyes, was one of the most meaningful exchanges of my three visits to Russia and the Soviet Union.

Prior to my making this trip, my old friend Sonja Marjasch had contacted me. Sonja's family had originally come from Russia, and in 1992 she had a cousin there who was experiencing health issues. She asked me to meet with her cousin as he needed heart surgery, and it was not available in Russia at the time. It was a secret meeting because he was not allowed into the hotel. We did meet in the lobby and communicated briefly. Unfortunately, I could not really help him.

The next year Seriozha and Igor came to visit us in California, and we took them down the coast to Monterey, Carmel, and Big Sur, which was a wonderful immersion in a new landscape and a new culture. Heading south through the Salinas River Valley, Seriozha exclaimed, "Steinbeck country!" He had read John Steinbeck's novels in his high school classes in English literature.

I do not believe that any of that original group of Russian psychotherapists became interested in Jung. Igor Kadyrov trained as a psychoanalyst in Germany, and we hear about him through a mutual friend. Julia and Pavel entered psychoanalytic training in the US. Although I have met Russian Jungian analysts and candidates in subsequent years, none of them were part of that original group.

Perhaps it would have turned out differently if Seriozha had lived. He had attended an international psychoanalytic congress in Barcelona, and while there he developed chest pain. Instead of going to see a doctor, he drank some vodka and cognac to ease the pain, but he died soon after, a very Russian ending to his life.

South Africa

Another major undertaking during my first term was evaluating the group in Cape Town, South Africa. The group had begun with a South African child psychologist, Vera Bührmann, who had trained as a Jungian analyst in London shortly after World War II, then returned to South Africa. In addition, the novelist Laurens van der Post, a friend of the British Royal family and an ardent supporter of Jung, was born and grew up in South Africa, and he wanted to establish a Jungian community in Cape Town. Van der Post agreed to support an analyst from the United Kingdom for five years if he or she would live and work in Cape Town. The analyst Julian David accepted this offer and agreed to analyze the many qualified psychologists and psychiatrists who sought out his services. The Cape Town group developed around these two early analysts, with Julian David doing analysis and Vera Bührmann doing the supervision. This was a unique situation, but the distance between Cape Town and any other Jungian center made this the only viable alternative. However, it was stressful for everyone involved, and Julian David had a heart attack early on in his stay. Patrick Tummon, an Irishman who had trained at the Jung Institute in Zürich, moved to Cape Town some time during the five-year period that Julian David was there. Lee Roloff from Chicago had also begun traveling to Cape Town to teach, and he had developed a strong commitment to the group there. Lee and I had met in Chicago, and he gave me his impressions of all the individuals in the group.

Because Cape Town was so far from California, and in order to save the IAAP money, I traveled there alone. In retrospect, I realize that was a mistake, because it placed a tremendous burden on me. When I arrived in Cape Town, Vera picked me up from the airport. She was already in her mid-80s, and driving with her was literally putting one's life at risk. We had never spoken at length, but she told me right away that I had a reputation for going into new situations like this and ferreting out what was happening very quickly. She told me the students knew that as well, and as a result, they were very wary of my visit. She immediately brought me to meet the Cape Town group, and you could have cut the tension in the room with a knife. My task was to interview each of the sixteen potential Jungian analysts individually for two hours, and I did so over the next week and a half. We also had several group meetings, and I gave two public lectures. I did uncover a boundary violation which disqualified one of the candidates. Making a decision in this case was not easy, and I consulted with Murray Stein about the situation because I did not want the sole responsibility on my shoulders. On the whole, though, it was a fine group of therapists, and it was truly satisfying to interview them. In May, 1992, eight of the candidates were presented to the executive committee of the IAAP, which approved of all of them. In addition, many of these candidates came to the IAAP international meeting in Chicago in August, 1992, where they were officially approved by the delegates to individually become analysts and to form a professional society. The remaining eight therapists, who had not had sufficient analysis and supervision to be eligible, continued with the new group.

All this was taking place at a time of great social and political change in South Africa. Mandela had been released from prison early in 1990, and I arrived about two years later, in March, 1992. I think that all the Jungian candidates supported abolishing apartheid, and I know that some of them had been politically active in the whole process. A crucial vote in South African politics, a referendum to abolish apartheid, took place the last two days I was there. It took a full two days to tally the vote, but it abolished apartheid forever. I was in Pretoria at the time, and there was a great celebration. That evening, in the midst of the celebration, I left Johannesburg to return to Zürich, feeling truly blessed to be able to witness such monumental social change. I write this paragraph three days after the death of Nelson Mandela, as the entire world joins to remember his amazing ability to transcend hatred. He was a force of character so strong that, under his leadership, South Africa was able to emerge as a fledgling democracy without descending into violent revolution, which would have been profoundly destructive for both the black and white populations.

All these changes in the world at large, the breakdown of communism and the abolition of apartheid, took place between 1989 and 1992. It made for an incredibly busy first term of my presidency, and the travel needed to offer a Jungian presence in these situations was immense.

This was a huge change from previous IAAP administrations, which had not been called to respond to social changes of this magnitude.

Of course, the ongoing administrative work of the IAAP needed to be tended to at the same time. The next congress, which was to be in Chicago in August of 1992, had to be organized. That meant we had to have a congress theme, a program committee, and a local organizing committee. The theme chosen was the "The Transcendent Function: Individual and Collective Aspects," a concept that did not have a parallel in psychoanalysis. The Chicago Jungians were in the process of buying a rather large building which would house both the institute and some of the individual analysts who were in private practice. Perhaps they were eager to have the international Jungian community see how well the Chicago Jungians were doing, but the acquisition turned out to be too costly a venture for the institute in the long run, and many years later this building was sold. A single individual had lent the money to the Chicago institute, but eventually he wanted the loan to be repaid. At that point the Chicago Jungian professional society underwent major changes in its structure as well as its location. The continuing education part of the institute was downsized considerably, and certain individual analysts essentially left to go off on their own.

Preparations began to house the 1992 international congress in Chicago at the Hilton Hotel, the flagship hotel of the Hilton chain. Peter Mudd, who had been the executive director of the Chicago Jung institute and who had not been in favor of buying the large building in Evanston, became the point man in Chicago to coordinate the congress. Peter had extensive experience in planning conferences, but I felt that he was also upset with me for having chosen Murray as my honorary secretary as that effectively barred Peter from a position on the international executive committee at that time. The president can choose the secretary from his own group, and in that way one can have two members from the same group, but otherwise it has not been possible to elect two individuals from the same society. There are so many groups that need and want to be represented that it would be unfair for any group to have more than one voting member on this select committee.

Peter was a wonderful organizer, and the preparations for the congress went smoothly. One innovation that we introduced at this congress was for the IAAP to pay for five individuals from former Eastern Bloc countries to attend the congress. In 1992 these individuals were from Bulgaria, Lithuania, Hungary, and the Soviet Union. From such meager beginnings, we now have probably close to a third of the attendees coming from former Eastern Bloc countries and Asia. This represents quite a shift and indicates the direction that analytical psychology is heading in the future.

Otherwise, there was little out of the ordinary about the congress in Chicago. All the officers were reelected without opposition. The delegates' meeting was the least controversial delegates' meeting I can remember. There were some stirrings among the delegates to adopt a statement concerning human rights, but the time had not yet arrived for that to be a major issue.

The Kirsch family (from left: James Kirsch, Tom Kirsch, Hilde Kirsch) walking on Hampstead Heath or in the Big Wood, London, 1937.

Swiss Jungian analyst and psychiatrist C.A. Meier, successor to Jung as the ETH professor of psychology and first president of the Jung Institute in Zürich, and Mary Crile, a family friend, Los Angeles, 1958.

Right: Passenger liner Samaria, which carried the Kirsch family across the Atlantic during the Battle of Britain. Image by Kenneth D. Shoesmith.

Below: Excerpt from the ship's manifest from the Samaria, listing the Kirsch family among the passengers traveling from Liverpool to New York, September 23, 1940, through October 3, 1940. Library of Congress image.

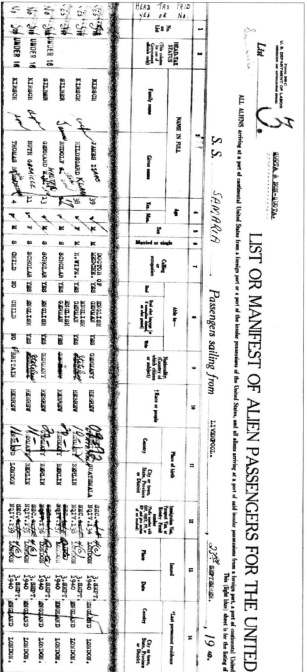

North-South meeting of Jungian analysts in Carmel, California, 1959.
From left: Jungian analysts John Perry, Jane Wheelwright, Melvin Kettner,
William Alex, and Max Zeller. Max was also a family friend.

Lower left: Psychiatrist and Jungian analyst Joe Henderson, Los Angeles,
1959. Joe was co-founder of the San Francisco Jung Institute and was
generally considered to be the dean of Jungian analysts in the United States.

Lower right: Liliane Frey-Rohn, a close associate of Jung and a senior analyst
at the Jung Institute in Zürich, about 1960.

Rivkah Schaerf Kluger (left) and Hilde Kirsch,
Los Angeles, about 1960. Rivkah was a Biblical
scholar and a Jungian analyst who practiced in
Zürich, Los Angeles, and Haifa.

James Kirsch and Sigi Hurwitz, Zürich, mid-1960s. From left, James Kirsch, father
of Thomas Kirsch, and Sigi Hurwitz, Jewish Kabbalah scholar, teacher at the Jung
Institute in Zürich, Jung's dentist, and close family friend.

Jungian analysts James Hillman and Hilde Kirsch, Los Angeles, 1966.

Zürich dinner party, 1970s. From left: Dora Kalff, founder of sandplay therapy; James Kirsch; Hilde Kirsch; Sam Francis, contemporary painter; and Jungian analyst Liliane Frey-Rohn.

Above left: James Rudolf Silber, referred to as Jimmy in the family and Jim by friends and colleagues, early 1950s. Jim was a psychiatrist and in midlife became a Jungian analyst.

Above right: Gerhard Walter Silber, who changed his name to Gerald Silver when he became a naturalized US citizen in 1946, playing with his son Paul Silver, 1959. He was referred to as Jerry by family and friends.

Jim and Jerry were the sons of Hermann Silber and Hilde Kirschstein Silber (later Hilde Kirsch).

Ruth Gabriele Kirsch, daughter of James and
Eva Kirsch, Los Angeles, 1950.

Tom Kirsch's father and son, Los Angeles, early 1980s.
From left, David Kirsch and James Kirsch.

Lower left: Psychiatrist and Jungian analyst Charles Klaif, friend and colleague, Kirsch home in Palo Alto, about 1978.

Lower right: Swiss Jungian analyst, publisher, friend, and colleague Bob Hinshaw, mid-1980s.

Jungian analyst Elie Humbert, leader of the French
Jungian group for many years, Paris, 1985.

Picnic near Giverny, France, 1985. From left, Myrtha Gruber-Humbert, Tom
Kirsch (with back to camera), Jungian analyst Elie Humbert, and Jan Stein.

Jo Wheelwright, psychiatrist and Jungian analyst, former president of the IAAP, and international figure in Jungian psychology, at the Hollister ranch outside Santa Barbara, mid-1980s.

Jungian analysts Ute Dieckmann (left) and Hannes Dieckmann, former president of the IAAP, at the San Francisco Jung Institute, mid-1980s.

Adolf Guggenbühl-Craig was a highly respected Jungian analyst in Zürich, having been the president of the Jung Institute and later on president of the IAAP. Picture taken at the dinner table in his home around 1990.

Jungian analyst Joe Henderson in his San Francisco office around 1990.

London meeting to merge the British Journal of Analytical Psychology with the US edition, 1990. From left: British Jungian analyst Judith Hubback; San Francisco Jungian analyst John Beebe, colleague and friend; and British Jungian analyst Rosemary Gordon.

Andrew Samuels, British Jungian analyst, friend, and colleague, in London, 1992, during a visit with Joe Henderson to deliver a lecture to the four London Jungian groups.

The grounds of the Russian White House about two weeks after Boris Yeltsin's August, 1991, confrontation with Soviet tanks, leading to the end of the Communist regime. Rubble from blockades still littered the grounds. The sign affixed to the fence post reads, "Do Not Forget."

Therapist group in the apartment of Michael Reshetnikov, Leningrad (now St. Petersburg), 1991, during an IAAP trip to Leningrad to arrange for the translation of Jung into Russian. From left: Julia Rybutina, translator; Misha Yarish, psychologist; Jean Kirsch; Michael Reshetnikov's two children; Michael Reshetnikov, psychiatrist and head of the Psychoanalytic Institute, Leningrad; Valery Zelensky, Jungian publisher in Leningrad.

Seriosha Agrichev, the leader of the Russian psychotherapist association in Moscow during the early 1990s, on the California coast in 1995. He was a brilliant man who died young.

Russian student Igor Kadyrov on a visit to the California coast, 1995. Although he studied Jung following the breakup of the former Soviet Union, Igor eventually became a psychoanalyst with a strong interest in object relations theory.

David Tresan, San Francisco Jungian analyst, friend, and colleague, in the Kirsch home in Palo Alto, 1992.

C. A. Meier, celebrating his ninetieth birthday in Zürich in May, 1995.

IAAP congress dinner, Zürich, 1995. From left: Swiss Jungian analyst Hans-Jürg
Brunner and Italian Jungian analyst Luigi Zoja, former president of the IAAP.

The late Mario Jacoby, Swiss Jungian analyst, friend, and colleague,
and Jungian analyst Jean Kirsch, Zürich, July, 2006.

Group of San Francisco Jungians in the office of Joe Henderson, 1996. From left: Tom Singer, Richard Stein, Joe Henderson, Tom Kirsch, David Tresan, David Richman, Nancy Haugen. All are Jungian analysts in San Francisco except Nancy Haugen, who is a Jungian psychotherapist.

Joe Henderson and Senator Bill Bradley at the Bolinas Rod and Gun Club at a conference in 1996. This was their first meeting, and they developed a close relationship over the next few years. Bradley is a well-known politician, writer, and former basketball star.

Psychiatrist Harry Wilmer, Jungian analyst, professor, and head of The Institute for the Humanities at Salado, Texas, at Joe Henderson's one hundredth birthday celebration in Marin, California, 2003.

Jungian analysts Linda Carter, American editor of the *Journal of Analytical Psychology*, and Joe Cambray, former president of the IAAP, in Tanglewood, Massachusetts, personal visit, 2005.

Henry, constant companion for ten years
and sorely missed, Thanksgiving, 2006.

Family photo, London, about 2010. From left: Claire Kirstein, daughter of Peter
Kirstein; professor Peter Kirstein, Tom Kirsch's cousin; Tom Kirsch.

Swiss Jungian analyst, publisher, friend, and colleague Bob Hinshaw and Susannah Kirsch, daughter of Tom and Jean Kirsch, at Tom Kirsch's seventieth birthday celebration in the Zürich backyard of Jan and Murray Stein, 2006.

Andreas Jung, grandson of C. G. Jung, and Jan Stein, Zürich, 2014.

Ladson Hinton, III, and his three sons, panel discussion at the 2010 IAAP congress in Montreal (from left: Laban Hinton, Ph.D., professor of anthropology and global affairs, UNESCO Chair in Genocide Prevention, Rutgers University; Ladson Hinton, III, M.D., Seattle Jungian analyst, colleague, and friend as well as member of the San Francisco Jung Institute for forty-five years; Ladson Hinton, IV, M.D., professor of psychiatry, University of California, Davis; and Devon Hinton, M.D., associate professor of psychiatry at Mass General Hospital, Harvard University.

Psychiatrist and Jungian analyst Joerg Rasche, who made arrangements for the plaque marking the site of James Kirsch's 1933 Berlin office, and his wife, physician Beate Kortendieck-Rasche, at the 2010 IAAP congress in Montreal.

Richard Wilhelm conference speakers with a bust of Richard Wilhelm in Qingdao, China, where Wilhelm worked for twenty years as a missionary and translated the *I Ching* into German, October, 2013. From left: Murray Stein, Jean Kirsch, Bettina Wilhelm (Richard Wilhelm's granddaughter), John Beebe, Heyong Shen (*I Ching* conference organizer), Tom Kirsch.

Speakers at the First International Conference of Analytical Psychology, Taipei, Taiwan, October, 2013. From left: Jungian analyst and Korean professor Bou-Yong Rhi, psychiatrist and founder of the Jungian professional group in Korea; and Professor Heyong Shen, first Jungian analyst in China.

Tom Singer, San Francisco Jungian analyst,
friend, and colleague, on vacation in 2013.

Murray Stein, Jungian analyst, friend, colleague, and
former president of the IAAP, in Zürich, June, 2014.

10

IAAP PRESIDENCY,
SECOND TERM, 1992 – 1995

The second term of my presidency continued in much the same vein as the first term. Although world events at that time were not as dramatic as the breakdown of the Berlin wall, it was still an eventful time.

Brazil

At the congress in Chicago I had spoken with Ana Lia Aufranc, president of the Brazilian Jung society, the first professional Jungian organization established in South America. A new group had recently formed in Brazil which included former members of the original society plus other members who had trained in Zürich. There was a great deal of conflict between the two groups, although the exact nature of the conflict was unclear. It seemed to be more of a personality conflict than anything else, but the executive committee was concerned. The original Brazilian group was not anxious to have anyone from the IAAP come to Brazil, but everyone on the international executive committee thought it was imperative that someone from the IAAP make the trip to Brazil and assess the situation.

However, a year before I made the trip to Brazil in August, 1993, Andrew Samuels had been a guest speaker of the original Brazilian Jungian group, and I had asked him to have a meeting with the other group while he was in Brazil. At the time the older, more established group had no problem with Andrew meeting with members of the new group. But after the meeting occurred, the established group was furious with Andrew and me for suggesting that Andrew meet with the new group. After all, the older group had paid a large sum to bring Andrew from England to Brazil, and the other group had paid nothing at all. The group footing the bill felt that the non-contributing group had no right to have Andrew speak with them.

This has been an issue generally among different Jungian communities. It happens frequently on the West Coast of the United States when someone from Europe is invited to speak at a particular Jungian society. Once the arrangements are made, one or two other Jungian organizations may invite the same person to speak at their society, and those groups only pay the person's airfare domestically, which is much less than the transatlantic fare. Sometimes the transatlantic fare is shared by two or three societies, but that does not happen very often. In the case of the Brazilians, there was a lot of anger directed at both Andrew and me for having suggested that Andrew meet with the newer group. I am sure that added fuel to the fire, and by the time my daughter and I traveled to Brazil, I encountered a lot of hostility, while my college-age daughter was treated very well.

Hence, I was not really welcomed there. I felt the hostility from the moment that I landed in São Paulo. But, since this was an official IAAP visit and my expenses were paid by the IAAP, I had the freedom to meet with anyone I liked. There was a welcoming gathering that included members from both groups, and one could feel the tension in the air. I met with members of the established and newer group, assessing the situation. Although the second group was not yet formally recognized by the IAAP, the solution seemed to require having two professional societies in Brazil.

One person who was not a member of either group was Roberto Gambini. I found meeting with him a breath of fresh air. Roberto had trained in Zürich and was very much of that ilk. He also had a master's in anthropology from the University of Chicago, so he had a particular interest in the tribes of the Amazon. We made an immediate connection, something I failed to achieve with members of either of the two conflicting groups.

Economically, Brazil was in a state of hyperinflation. Whenever one used a credit card, one percent per day was added to the bill until the due date of the payment. Such a financial situation made me extremely uncomfortable, and I can only imagine how the Brazilians felt about the situation. Security was tight in São Paulo, and Rio de Janeiro was even worse.

After our visit to São Paulo, my daughter Susannah and I traveled on to Rio to meet with members of the newer group. Rio was considered a much more dangerous city than São Paulo, and we were never left alone. Carjacking was rampant, and, since we were not used to living in the sort of hypervigilance that was the norm for the Brazilians, all of them were concerned about our safety. For instance, we were taken on a brief tour of Rio and stopped at a vista point in a large park in the middle of the city. There was one other car parked there, and the two women who were our hosts became very anxious about the people in that car. Nothing happened, but their apprehension showed the anxiety people lived under. My daughter wanted to drive in a favela and see firsthand how the poor lived, so the Brazilians took us through part of one, and the windows of our car were closed the whole time.

While in Rio we met with Walter and Paula Boechat, who had trained in Zürich. They were leaders of the new group but were members of both the new and older groups. The Boechats and Roberto Gambini were the only people with whom I was able to make a real personal connection. They invited us to dinner at their house one evening. Again, as in so many places in Central and South America, the house was surrounded by a large, protective wall. I was told that so many people had been carjacked that this had become a common occurrence.

Early Sunday morning, the last day of our trip, we were picked up by a taxi driver to head to the airport. The airport road passed through several tunnels, and after one of them, the taxi driver pulled over to the side of the road. He told us he had to change a flat tire, but I was certain that it was a setup to steal our bags. The driver stopped a spot between two tunnels where there were no people, only cars whizzing past on their way to the airport. Fortunately, the taxi really did have a flat tire and the rest of the drive was uneventful, but Susannah and I were greatly relieved when the taxi pulled into the airport without further incident.

On the flight back to the United States I began to feel ill with what turned out to be a bad viral upper respiratory infection. The trip had been filled with tension and hostility from what were obviously warring factions, but it had been successful in the sense that I abandoned any idea of reconciling the groups and realized that there needed to be two professional Jungian societies in Brazil. Nonetheless, it was one of the more difficult trips of my presidency. Other Jungian groups not affiliated with the IAAP have invited me down since then and have been willing to pay generously, but I chose not to repeat the trip. Although I met many lovely people there, and Rio is an absolutely beautiful city physically with its large hills, grand vistas, and spectacular beaches, the economic situation and the threat of crime marred the experience for me. Brazil emerged from that economic downturn, but I read that those planning for soccer's FIFA World Cup there in 2014 encountered many of the same problems.

Small European Countries

During the early 1990s I made visits to several small European countries that were developing professional Jungian groups. By this time the large European Jungian organizations, Switzerland, Germany, France, Italy, and the UK, had all settled into functioning professional societies, but that left countries like Denmark, Austria, Spain, the Netherlands, and Belgium, which were all in various stages of development with issues unique to their culture and circumstances.

Austria

During Adolf Guggenbühl-Craig's presidency, Hannes Dieckmann, the first vice president of the IAAP, went to Vienna on a regular basis to work with a group of eight candidates who wished to become Jungian analysts. Two of them were from Salzburg, and the remaining six were from Vienna. As mentioned earlier, one of these candidates was involved with Hannes and had a problem with her credentials, and she was not accepted as an analyst. All the others were, and they formed the professional Austrian society of Jungian analysts. Unfortunately, there was a great deal of tension between the Viennese and Salzburg analysts, and the Salzburg people, especially Frau Bock, kept writing to the IAAP expressing displeasure at how the IAAP had handled the Austrian group. She had reason to be upset about the process, but her repeated complaints to the IAAP became very irritating to the executive committee. At the same time the rejected candidate wanted to be reconsidered for IAAP membership, and I made a trip to Vienna in 1989 to talk to both the rejected woman and the other members of the Austrian group. The meeting did not change the situation for the rejected candidate, who was again denied on professional grounds, and the discussion with the aggrieved members of the Austrian group never really deepened. The tensions remained, and Frau Bock continued to protest what was going on in Austria long after my term was over. Many of the analysts left Austria for other areas, and by the time of the Copenhagen congress in 2013, the roster of Austrian analysts was completely comprised of new names, which was a relief to me.

Belgium

Belgium was another conflict hot spot. There had been a professional society in Belgium for many years. In fact, Jef Dehing, a Belgian member, had been the editor of the IAAP newsletter for many years and had attended many executive committee meetings. As president, I was invited to attend a meeting of the professional group in Brussels, and I did that as part of one of my European trips to Switzerland. The group was extremely cordial, and at first I did not pick up any degree of tension in the air. However, very shortly after that trip, the IAAP executive committee was informed that the group was breaking up into two separate professional societies. At first the split seemed to be based on language as there were some Flemish-speaking analysts and some French-speaking analysts. I asked Luigi Zoja to visit Belgium and report back about what was happening. From him I learned that the split was not only over language, but that one group was interested in British object relations theory and the other group was more classically Jungian-oriented. The split was clear, and both societies had reconstituted into separate professional societies.

I did not have any further interaction with the Belgians after this, except that I spent one day with André de Koning, who had trained with the Belgians although he was from the Netherlands. In the course of our discussion, I mentioned how much I had loved Perth, Australia, and that the group there was open to having new members. He and his wife were interested in leaving Europe and finding a new adventure to follow. They took me up on my suggestion about Perth, and the next time that I saw them, they had bought a house outside of Perth, and André had become an integral member of the Perth group as well as ANZSJA, the combined Australian and New Zealand group of Jungian analysts.

Denmark

The Danish Jungian situation was another complicated one. One Danish individual, Eigil Nyborg, had gone to Zürich in 1951 and had received his diploma from the Jung Institute in 1956. After graduation he returned to Copenhagen and brought Jungian psychology to Denmark. He was a gifted therapist, but he did not keep good boundaries and became overinvolved with his patients. This meant that training to become a Jungian analyst became almost impossible. Two individuals, including a dentist, Ole Vedfelt, and Pia Skogemann, had become individual members through the IAAP, and another woman, Kirsten Rasmussen, had graduated from the Zürich Institute. There were many others who wanted training, and since the Danes did not have a training program, a plan was developed for the Danish candidates to travel to London several times a year for training seminars, supervision, and analysis with the four Jungian groups there. This way they would receive seminars from the various viewpoints prevalent in the field of analytical psychology. Andrew Samuels arranged the program in London, and it was an extremely successful one. It began in the late 1980s and went on through the early 1990s. At the conclusion of this program, all its students needed to be evaluated by the IAAP, and so Verena Kast and I traveled to Copenhagen in 1993. We spent two very long days interviewing the candidates who had gone through the Danish segment of the London training program, and we also interviewed the founder, Eigil Nyborg.

All the candidates were very good and passed. At the 2013 IAAP congress in Copenhagen, I had the opportunity to speak with Misser Berg about that experience. She said that it made them feel that they belonged to the international Jungian community, which was a very good feeling. I liked hearing that some twenty years after the fact. Also, returning twenty years later to an international congress in Copenhagen showed me how much the Danish Jung society had grown and matured, which was also very satisfying.

The one fly in the ointment was the 1993 interview with Eigil Nyborg himself. I found myself extremely angry with him for his indiscrete behavior with woman patients, and I let him know what a mess he had made of the situation. I know he triggered my father complex since my father had exhibited much of the same behavior and had made things difficult in Los Angeles. What was refreshing to learn was that Mr. Nyborg had married one of his patients, Vibeke Vedel, and that she described their marriage until his death as a very satisfying one. In fact, Vibeke had become the president of the Danish society and was instrumental in helping to organize the most recent congress in Copenhagen. Verena Kast and I had interviewed her for individual membership in the IAAP separately from all the other candidates, and we found that she had an excellent grasp of analytical psychology.

The Netherlands

I was asked to visit Amsterdam to see if we could put together a professional group there. Members had trained in different institutes, such as Zürich, London, and the Belgian society. There was very little cohesiveness among the members, and I was not sure how to proceed. Patricia de Hoogh-Rowntree from the UK had moved to Amsterdam and had married a Dutchman named de Hoogh, but he died of a heart attack very soon after the marriage, and she returned to practice in the UK. She showed more interest in organizing a professional society than the others, but after her departure there was not enough energy to proceed further. I liked all the people individually, but I could not organize a group from California. What I enjoyed most in Amsterdam was the classical music at the Concertgebouw, and each evening after my meetings with the Dutch I would wait patiently in line to purchase returned tickets to the concerts. I heard some of the most wonderful music there, and the sound was extraordinary. I did go back to Amsterdam after my presidency and gave a weekend workshop to a lay Jungian group. Another Dutch man, Robbie Bosnak, was peripherally involved with the Dutch Jungians. He still visited Holland from time to time and was interested in how the Netherlands group was functioning. Robbie traveled all over the world, but now he has settled in Santa Barbara, California.

Spain

Spain made a slow entry into analytical psychology. The influence of Franco was a considerable drag on the development of analytical psychology, but Rosemary Douglas had gotten it off the ground. In 1989, when I was IAAP vice president, I made a trip to visit the group, and by the time of the Paris congress later that year, the candidates had managed to get enough hours of analysis and supervision to become a non-training professional group. I enjoyed Barcelona and the individual candidates, but I did not think that the Spanish group was a strong one, and I have not followed up with any of the individuals. Later I went to Barcelona for a history of psychoanalysis meeting, and in 2004 the IAAP had its international congress there. Barcelona is a great city and all the trips were most enjoyable, except for the very late dinners, which are not good for those who, like me, suffer from GERD (Gastro-Esophageal Reflux Disease), where one is not supposed to eat much before going to bed because of the danger of reflux.

Three European Countries with an Interest in Jung

Hungary

Prior to the breakdown of Communism in the Eastern Bloc countries in 1989 and 1990, Hungary had the greatest amount of freedom of thought. For example, one could buy the *International Herald Tribune* in Budapest when we were visiting in 1986. That visit was purely personal and did not involve any work with Jungians. However, we were shown around by a Jewish Communist who took us to all the Soviet places. At the time of our visit, there was a large international medical congress in progress in Budapest, and we were not able to find hotel rooms, so our group of ten stayed in a bed and breakfast. The rooms were antiquated and in a terrible state of repair, and Budapest seemed like a pretty grim place.

By 1992 Hungary had been freed of Communism, as had the other Eastern Bloc countries, and there was a group of about fifty people who were studying Jung. The leader Ferenc Sülé, a psychiatrist, wanted me to visit the group, so while in Zürich I flew to Budapest for three days and met with the Jungian group there. I consulted with Judith Luif, a Hungarian

Jew who had left during the 1956 Hungarian revolution, settled in Zürich, and trained to become a Jungian analyst. She had returned periodically to meet with the Hungarian Jungians but had not offered any regular analysis. She had a friend in Budapest who showed me around to many of the numerous Jewish sites in the city. What I had not realized was that in 1944 the Swiss vice-consul, Carl Lutz, had saved the lives of sixty-two thousand Jews by handing out identity cards, arranging visas for many of them to go to Palestine, and finding "safe houses" in Budapest for others. He was able to negotiate with the Nazis and the Arrow Cross, the Nazi organization in Hungary. After the war he was honored by being named one of the "Righteous Among the Nations" at the Yad Vashem Memorial in Israel.

I also learned that a Hungarian Catholic priest who was familiar with Jung had visited Switzerland prior to World War II and arranged for some of Jung's writings to be translated into Hungarian. In addition, the 1975 exhibition in honor of Jung's one hundredth birthday traveled all around Hungary. During my second term as president, I met with the Jungian group in Budapest, which was the first Jungian group in Eastern Europe. Like so many other informal groups studying Jung, the Budapest group needed an analyst, but as of the time of my visit, they had not been able to attract one. However, Hungary's relative freedom allowed the Hungarian Psychoanalytic Association to survive both the Nazis and Communism, and recently, the San Francisco Jung institute has had an international student from Hungary, Zsolt Deak, who is in the process of training to become a Jungian analyst in Hungary. Training is not easy, because there are no recognized Jungian analysts in Hungary, which means that he has to travel to obtain analysis. At present, he is going to Vienna regularly for analysis.

Ireland

Many people are captivated by Jung's writings, and Jungian groups have arisen all over the world. I have generally been supportive of these reading groups as they have oriented people to their dreams and inner life and helped them find meaning in their lives. At times, though, individuals with some knowledge and experience of the unconscious can become inflated and want to become missionaries for Jung. I have seen that on several occasions, and even experienced some of it myself when I began my Jungian analysis in San Francisco. Later, when I was president of the IAAP, a couple of individuals sought me out and wanted to "receive accreditation" as a Jungian.

The situation in Ireland was complex. Several Irish people who were interested in analytical psychology had gone to the UK and trained with one of the recognized Jungian training centers there. In some cases they had remained in the UK, and now some of the UK Irish analysts wanted to form an Irish Society of Analytical Psychology in England. I made it clear that this was impossible and that if they wanted to form an Irish society, they would have to return to Ireland and form it there.

Other Irish therapists had trained in London and had returned to Ireland to practice, but at the time of my presidency, there were not enough of those to form a professional society. Instead, there was a group interested in Jung that included both analysts and lay members. I had mail contact with a Mrs. O'Mally, who was president at the time. She had invited me to speak to their group when I was president, but I never could quite arrange a time that fit my schedule. Many UK analysts did speak to the Irish group and provided support and supervision, and at present there is a small Irish professional society.

All this was well and good, but then an Indian woman who had read Jung and wanted to spread the word was able to attract a large number of people in Ireland and form a group to study Jung's psychology. She obtained the approval of Laurens van der Post, who had been a close friend of Jung, and he wrote her expressing support for her group and what she was doing with her students. She also arranged to write a column in the *Irish Times*, the largest newspaper in Dublin at the time, where she analyzed people's dreams. People would send in dreams, and she would publish an analysis. Needless to say, I was extremely upset to read all this, since the woman had had no formal training as an analyst at all. This was purely a case of "wild analysis."

Around this time she contacted me, and we arranged to meet in London on one of my trips. She was a very soft-spoken and approachable woman, and I liked her personally. I could see how she could attract a large following because she was charismatic. With as much diplomacy as I could muster, I explained to her that I could not support what she was doing. I told her she needed to go into analysis and complete some training in Jungian psychology, and I added that she was running quite a risk analyzing dreams of people in the newspaper. She left the meeting on a cordial note, and I never did find out what happened to her. I cannot imagine that she stopped doing what she was doing, but I have heard nothing further about her.

Sweden

During my second term, I was contacted by a group of three young people from wealthy families in Sweden. The three of them had read a good bit of Jung, but they had never been in analysis. However, they hoped to start a master's program in analytical psychology in Stockholm, and to facilitate that, they wanted to be recognized as Jungian analysts. They sought me out, and I met them in Amsterdam on one of my European trips. Again I listened as they presented a case for making them Jungian analysts, explaining how good their recognition would be for Sweden and the field of analytical psychology. At that time there were only a couple of very introverted analysts practicing in Sweden, and they had no interest in forming a professional organization. The Swedish advocates didn't get much satisfaction from me, so they went on to Zürich with the idea of obtaining recognition from the Jung Institute. Although the Jung Institute was skeptical about what they were doing, there was also interest in negotiating some sort of arrangement with them. Many of the students attending the Jung Institute at that time were from Sweden, but none had returned to Sweden to practice. Almost all of them remained in Switzerland after they finished their training.

Suggestions such as these were some of the more surprising requests of my presidency. I learned that the IAAP, as the only recognized international professional body of Jungian analysts, received many such unexpected offers, and the president was called upon to decide how to respond in each case. These two proposals from Ireland and Sweden had the most impact since both groups had the potential to form an altogether new type of Jungian body made up of Jungian-oriented therapists who had not had any analysis. The groups would have had only a reading knowledge of Jung, and it is unclear what kind of basic psychotherapeutic training they would have had, if any. These two requests were the most serious offers of this sort I received during my presidency, but overall there were many such irregular requests for recognition.

China

During my second term as president, I traveled to China, which was probably the most significant trip of the term. Murray Stein, who was still living in Chicago, had met Heyong Shen, a visiting professor from South China Normal University in Guangzhou who had received a Fulbright scholarship to a university in central Illinois. Heyong went to Chicago to meet with Murray and told him about his interest in Jungian psychology. This request sparked Murray's curiosity, and he soon decided that we should go to China and see what was developing there in terms of analytical psychology. At first I was extremely skeptical, because I didn't expect to find a major interest in analytical psychology, and the IAAP had not really received any requests to visit. I was also very concerned about the cost of such a trip, because, since none of us could speak Mandarin, we would require a full-time guide and translator with us at all times. None of this dissuaded Murray, who continued to suggest we visit.

Around the same time I had attended an American Academy of Psychoanalysis meeting in San Francisco and had met an important Korean psychiatrist named Dongshick Rhee, who was a member of the Korean Academy of Psychotherapists. There was to be an international meeting of the International General Medical Society of Psychotherapy in Seoul, Korea, in August, 1994. This was the organization that Jung had been president of in the 1930s, and this would be its first meeting outside of Europe. Dongshick Rhee enthusiastically invited me to give a major talk at this international conference in Seoul. I considered this and decided that a combined visit to Korea and China would make sense. The IAAP had its strongest Asian Jungian presence in Korea under the able direction of a professor, Bou-Yong Rhi, who had studied in Zürich and who was at the time the preeminent psychiatrist in Korea. He headed the department of psychiatry at Seoul National University, which was considered the "Harvard" of Korea, and was both a classical Jungian analyst and a modern-day biochemist with many publications in the field. Until that time, the only Jungian to have visited Bou-Yong Rhi was Adolf Guggenbühl-Craig, who visited when he was president of the IAAP. Adolf had told me a lot about that visit, which had impressed him greatly. Bou-Yong Rhi had developed a fairly large group of people interested in Jungian psychology, and Adolf encouraged me to pay him a visit. In addition, Rhi had known and liked my father very much, and through that connection had referred patients to me. Some of these patients had gone on to fellowships in the Sleep Research Center at Stanford under William Dement, a physician and professor who was one of the cofounders of REM research. I had also been introduced to Professor Bou-Yong Rhi at several IAAP congresses, and I felt there was good rapport between us. So, between being a major speaker at the conference and meeting with Professor Rhi and his students, there was much to do in Korea.

Around the same time, I learned that a Chinese man working in the department of water for the city of Los Angeles had translated several of Jung's books into Mandarin. He was friends with Yehua Zhu-Levine, who had immigrated to the United States during the Cultural Revolution. She had influential contacts in China and was interested in Jung's psychology, and some of her friends in China were even more interested than she was. Her husband was an American Jewish man who worked as a cameraman in the movie industry. (This would later turn out to be beneficial since he filmed some of the lectures that Murray and I gave in Beijing. Those videos were later transferred to DVD, and we were able to give a copy to Heyong Shen and bring a copy back to China in 2013.) Murray and I worked out an arrangement with Yehua to serve as our guide and translator while we were in China. The cost of the trip was mounting, but by this time the commitments both in Korea and China had been made, and we were going.

Murray brought his wife and granddaughter on the trip, and I took Jean. We met in Hong Kong, which in 1994 was still under British rule. After getting over the worst of the jetlag, we took the two-hour train ride to Guangzhou, where we were met by Heyong Shen. In comparison to Hong Kong, Guangzhou seemed bleak. At that time there were very few cars and almost no traffic lights, but the streets were crowded with carts, bicycles, and people on foot. We stayed at a luxury hotel, the White Swan, where we saw a number of American families who were in the process of adopting baby girls belonging to families who wanted sons but were constrained by China's one-child policy. Both Murray and I gave lectures at the South China Normal University that were well-received. I was especially pleased that the Chinese had accepted my lecture on "Jung and Tao," because I was very unsure how it would be regarded. Later we visited a mental hospital which reminded me of some of the back wards of American state mental hospitals.

From Guangzhou we traveled to Beijing, where we again toured hospitals and Murray and I lectured at several of them. Murray had a travel agent's card, so we were able to stay at the Peninsula Hotel, a first-class hotel that was quite luxurious, for an extremely reasonable price. It was an interesting experience in that, although the hotel chain is American and the manager was an American, only the first six or eight floors were for public guests, while the upper floors were for the Chinese military. On one occasion I met two women on the elevator who had just come down from one of the military floors, and they were giggling to themselves about whether they should try to induce me to go with them, but they left without trying to persuade me.

Heyong Shen had taken the train from Guangzhou to Beijing and joined us for our experiences in Beijing. He recognized that this initial visit of Jungians into China was significant. We were able to visit many major sites, such as the Great Wall and Tiananmen Square, and Yehua introduced us to some Chinese book publishers and an amazing Qigong practitioner. I had never seen Qigong practiced, but I found the results amazing. Many muscle groups and areas of tension could be released without touching the person at all.

Although I had doubted the value of the trip because it was extremely expensive in terms of IAAP funds, in retrospect, that single trip opened up China to analytical psychology. The interest in analytical psychology that has blossomed in China and other parts of Asia over the past twenty years has more than justified the cost of that initial trip.

China has remained a lifelong interest for me. Since that first Asian trip, I have returned seven times, and both Jean and I later became involved in Taiwan and their developing group. I have realized that Jung was strongly connected to the Chinese psyche through his contact with *The Secret of the Golden Flower*, the *I Ching*, and Richard Wilhelm and his lifelong study of Taoism and Buddhism. The Chinese have also recognized that, more than any other Western psychologist, Jung both had a deep understanding of the ancient Chinese ways and lived his life in accord with those principles.

After Beijing, Murray's family went home and Jean and I went on to Korea. Our China experience had been a most memorable one.

Korea

In 1994 one could not travel directly from China to Korea, so we spent the whole day getting from Beijing to Seoul, Korea. We had to go to Tokyo, and from there we could travel on to Seoul. In Seoul we were part of the Sixteenth International Congress of Psychotherapy, which was organized mainly by the Swiss members who were primarily practitioners of existential analysis. Medard Boss had been the founding and leading member of this group, which had been heavily influenced by Martin Heidegger. Although I am not aware of any association between Jung and Heidegger, Boss had been in a supervisory group with Jung in Zürich for many years, and relations between the existentialists and the Jungians at the conference were congenial. I gave my talk on "Jung and Tao," which I had written for this conference and which went over well. In the question-and-answer period, a Korean psychiatrist inquired about Jung's anti-Semitism and whether he was a Nazi. I found myself thinking that one could not get away from that question at any non-Jungian professional meeting! I answered by asking why no one questions Heidegger's being a Nazi party member from 1933 until the end of the Third Reich and his firing of his Jewish mentor Edmund Husserl, a founder of phenomenology? This does not stop people from studying Heidegger, but questions about Nazism seem to stop people from reading Jung. As a Swiss citizen, Jung could not have been a member of the Nazi party, but he did interact with the Nazis because he was president of the very organization which was sponsoring the conference at which I was then speaking. It upset me at the time that this issue came up in Korea, especially from a Korean psychiatrist, but I finally found my peace with this issue in Versailles some years later.

Dongshick Rhee was glad that I was there, and I felt I was receiving VIP treatment. The Korean Jungians attended the conference and gave some of the lectures, but they were not prominent at the meeting. I believe that Dongshick Rhee and Professor Rhi were colleagues but not really friends.

While at the conference I met a researcher and professor from the University of Chicago, David Orlinsky, who has since become a lifelong friend. David is a leading psychotherapy researcher who over the last twenty-five years has developed a self-evaluating questionnaire for therapists that asks them to express what they believe makes psychotherapy work. He has had the questionnaire translated into several languages, including Korean. I took the test while in Korea and found that answering it actually made me very anxious, and I found the questions both penetrating and thought-provoking. David is an extraverted feeling type, and our personalities have many similarities. Only the distance between Chicago and San Francisco keeps us from seeing each other more.

The conference ran for four days, and after that we were in the hands of Professor Rhi, who had his own program for us, some of which was very subtle. For the first weekend we were invited to the heart of South Korea into areas that contained old burial mounds, a hidden Buddha figure in a secluded area in the mountains, and much that was at the root of Korean culture. Then we returned to Seoul and were put up in the most beautiful hotel, the Hotel Shilla. Professor Rhi thought that, as president of the IAAP, I should stay at the same hotel in which Presidents Bush and Clinton had stayed when they came to Korea. It was a wonderful place and one of the nicest hotels that I have ever stayed in. Jean and I were enormously appreciative of the Koreans' hospitality.

During this time I gave a lecture on Jungian psychology at one of the major hospitals, and then Jean and I had a case seminar with some psychiatrists and psychologists from the hospital, during which Donghyuk Suh presented a case to us and we commented on it. The students were not very familiar with some of the developments in contemporary psychoanalysis, such as object relations theory and Kohut's self-psychology. We could tell that Donghyuk Suh was very interested in our remarks regarding modern psychoanalytic clinical theory and practice.

Professor Rhi also asked Donghyuk Suh to take us out of town to the Korean Folk Village, a recreation of a typical Korean village from the late 1700s. It was a fascinating trip, and it gave us a good opportunity to speak with Donghyuk. After we came back to Seoul, the three of us had dinner together, and Donghyuk asked about the possibility of spending a year or two in San Francisco at our institute.

The San Francisco International Student Program developed from this conversation. Jean immediately picked up on the idea and started imagining ways that it might work. Over the next year she held numerous meetings with members of the institute and also connected with other universities, because a student would have to be matriculating at a university in order to obtain permission to see patients in our clinic. These meetings took up an inordinate amount of time, but Jean and the rest of us stuck with the process, and we were able to get approval both from the San Francisco Jungian community and from the CIIS, the California Institute of Integral Studies. Donghyuk had saved up enough money to be able to bring his wife and family to the Bay Area. The young girls went to a public school, and, as part of a pilot project, Donghyuk became our first international student. Since then having an international student has become a permanent part of the institute program, and funds have been put aside to support the student. So far Donghyuk has been the only student who has had sufficient resources to make the trip on his own. Every other student has received help from our institute, either in terms of donations from members or as part of the overall budget of the institute.

I was extremely sad to leave Korea, and it was the most painful leave-taking of any of the IAAP trips. The hospitality had been so wonderful and so well-conceived. We were well taken care of, and at the same time it was all done quietly and without fanfare, so that one almost did not realize that the process was going on. I am sure that Professor Rhi wanted us to spend lots of time with Donghyuk Suh in the hope that we would find a way to bring him to San Francisco for further training. Later on Donghyuk did become an individual member of the IAAP, and he eventually joined the Korean Association of Jungian Analysts.

Last Year of the Presidency

The last year of my presidency felt different from all the others. At this point I had been a part of the executive committee of the IAAP for seventeen years. The culture of the organization was changing rapidly, and some people thought that I had become a fixture in my role within it. As my time with the executive committee came to an end, I felt the reality of being a "lame duck president," and Verena Kast challenged me more and more. I believe she saw me as part of the "old guard patriarchy," and she seemed to use every opportunity to paint me as unsympathetic to the woman's movement and to the feminine. Executive committee meetings became increasingly unpleasant, yet I realized that it was not really appropriate to try to defend myself, that I had to let this dynamic play itself out. It reached its zenith at the delegates' meeting at the Zürich congress in August, 1995, when Verena could barely be civil to me as I handed the presidency over to her. Her brusqueness had one positive effect, however, and that was for me to be glad to leave the IAAP executive committee. I think that, had everything been harmonious at the end, it would have been more difficult to say goodbye.

Nonetheless, the year leading up to that delegates' meeting was an eventful one. The first Pan-European Jungian meeting took place at the end of January, 1995, in Paris. The conference itself has been eclipsed in my memory by recollection of dinner in the basement of the Louvre seated between Coline Covington and Angela Connolly. The setting was stunning, and it was my first encounter with these two women.

The *Eurostar* train under the English Channel had just opened, and Murray Stein and I traveled to London, where we had arranged to interview sixteen individual candidates from different countries. Verena Kast had been critical of me for devoting so much time and energy to these individual candidates, but I sensed that each of these individual candidates, who were from countries where there was no professional society, would immediately become the focus of the professional Jungian society in that country. I felt it was terribly important that these candidates be examined thoroughly, so we had arranged that members from the four UK societies would be examiners, along with the president, honorary secretary, and vice presidents of the IAAP. This process took the better part of a week in London.

Each of the candidates had written up a case of up to fifty pages, so there was lots of reading and discussion in addition to doing the interviews. It was a highly successful undertaking with almost everyone passing. This initial experiment in bringing candidates together was the beginning of the router program and the developing group concept, which have become such a large part of the work of the IAAP. Routers are individuals who are in Jungian training but are from countries where there is no professional Jungian society, so they are supervised directly by the IAAP. A developing group is made up of individuals who are interested in analytical psychology but who are not necessarily interested in becoming Jungian analysts. Developing groups have a mixture of people, both routers and people who are just interested in learning more about Jungian psychology.

The next event was a correspondence with Alain and Sophie de Mijolla. They were French psychoanalysts who were preparing a comprehensive psychoanalytic dictionary in three volumes. They did not have any Jungian items on their list, but they were open to incorporating twenty Jungian items, including biographies of Jung and Toni Wolff. In July, 1995, the International Psychoanalytic Association had its meeting in San Francisco, and the de Mijollas met with all the editors, including me. They viewed the dictionary as a long-term project, and this was the organizing meeting for the different sections. A project of this magnitude has many logistical problems and requires uniformity in how each item is written. I chose several people to write on the different Jungian items, and I wrote separate biographical sketches on Jung and Toni Wolff. Fortunately, Ursula Egli easily figured out the instructions, and we produced the write-ups on time and in the correct format, which astonished the de Mijollas. I imagine that they expected us to be airheads and not really connected to the real world of publishing.

During that last year of my presidency I was asked to interview a number of candidates in Venezuela. Having had the experience of going to South Africa alone, I was not going to make the same mistake a second time. I asked Betty Meador, a trusted friend and colleague, to join me in interviewing a number of candidates who wanted to become analysts. There were several individual members in Venezuela, Rafael López-Pedraza, Fernando Risquez, and Rita and Axel Capriles. The Capriles and Rafael had trained in Zürich and were classically oriented. Risquez was an Army psychiatrist who was identified with the military establishment and was more of a clinician than a Jungian. There was no professional society in Venezuela at the time, and we were examining candidates who would follow the leadership of either Risquez or the Zürich-oriented analysts.

Like Rio, Caracas was a dangerous city, so they did not leave us alone for a minute except for the times when we were in the hotel. We interviewed the candidates, who for the most part were well qualified. No special issues came up during the interviews, and we recommended that several should take the exam to become individual members, though that happened after I left the presidency.

The Zürich congress in August, 1995, was to be my last formal meeting as president. Prior to the meeting Jean and I had stayed with Tom and Jane Singer on the island of Ios. It was a beautiful site, and while there I was completely relaxed, but as soon as I checked into the hotel in Zürich, I felt my whole body tense up. It was a remarkable change!

The first bit of bad news was that the French group had changed their position on a statement that was to be approved by the delegates on the "Rights of Man." At the previous congress in Chicago, the delegates had recommended inserting a non-discrimination clause into the constitution, and the language was to be voted upon at this congress. Six weeks before the congress in Zürich, the French had reacted to the wording and changed their vote to reflect that they were now against the statement as presented. To untangle the confusion that this created was daunting. We felt we would have to postpone the vote on that clause and remove it from the agenda of the delegates' meeting. This change should have been sufficient warning that the delegates' meeting was going to be tough. It was!

This was the first IAAP congress in Zürich since 1968, and it attracted many people. Over seven hundred were in attendance, and there had been more papers submitted than at any previous congress. The theme of the congress was "Open Questions in Analytical Psychology," which allowed for a wide range of papers. We continued to invite people from the Eastern Bloc countries as well as Heyong Shen from China, whom we had met there the previous year. The conference was well organized, with many tours and excursions in Zürich and a trip by boat on the lake past Jung's house. The congress should have been the culmination of my eighteen years on the executive committee, but instead, it was a nightmare! There were so many conflicts, some of which I can no longer remember except that every meal involved meeting with someone about some issue. I definitely was not a free man.

The worst time for me at the congress was the delegates' meeting itself. Initially, the delegates' meeting was going well, until Hannes Dieckmann and Gustav Bovensiepen brought up the issue of presidential travel, expressing criticism of the amount of travel I had done as president. My impression is that members view travel as a perk of being president. Travel then becomes a sensitive item in the budget, because members become somewhat envious of it and wonder if all of it is really necessary. Dieckmann and Bovensiepen received a lot of support from other delegates, who were also critical of the amount of travel I had done, but I was absolutely shocked that this criticism had come from the two of them. I just stood up at the podium, wondering how I could respond. For the moment I was paralyzed. Immediately I thought of the trip that I had made to Vienna for Hannes, but I could not bring that up in a public meeting. It was an expensive trip to meet with this woman doctor who wanted to become an individual member, a woman Hannes had lived with while doing the training in Vienna many years before. I had made that trip to protect Hannes from shame and humiliation, although I realized that Hannes's behavior in this incident had, unfortunately, not been that out of character. The Austrian candidates had accepted the arrangement, but it would have been difficult for them to object because they wanted to be accepted as analysts. With all these thoughts going on in my mind, it stirred up my father complex, so I became silent so that my father complex would not express itself. I had known too many older male analysts who had been involved with their patients, and witnessing this behavior had had a wounding effect on my psyche. It was one of the major issues that originally had brought me into analysis. So I was not going to expose this major complex to all the delegates and really ruin my image as the last act of my presidency.

Actually this exchange affected me for the rest of the delegates' meeting. Since that time I have given the issue of travel a lot of attention. What I have realized is that my presidency was transitional for the IAAP. Prior to my presidency, the central focus of the IAAP had been European, with its center in Zürich. There were many American members, of course, but the center was in continental Europe and the UK, and travel to new groups was minimal. During my two terms as president, all that had changed. South Africa, Mexico, South America, and Russia and Eastern Europe had all requested visits from the president of the IAAP, and I had responded to these requests. The one place where the IAAP had taken the initiative in reaching out was in China, and I had had grave doubts about making that trip, in large part because of the expense. However, it turned out to be a most fruitful encounter, and the connections to Asia that the experience opened up have been far-reaching. There are now developing groups in Macao, Shanghai, Beijing, Hong Kong, Taiwan, and Guangzhou, and there have been numerous conferences in different cities of Asia. It is the most dynamic area of the world for analytical psychology.

It is only in retrospect that I have realized how much the focus of the IAAP changed during my presidency. I knew at the time that the opening to Eastern Europe and the Soviet Union was immensely important, but all the other presidential trips just seemed to arise on their own. I think that my presidency set a pattern which only has become more pronounced with each succeeding administration. Developing groups, routers, and individual membership have all become important functions of the IAAP, although they have not always been embraced by the membership. There is still criticism of the amount of money and energy that goes into the aid and development of new Jungian professional groups in various parts of the world.

When I think back to that delegates' meeting in Zürich in 1995, and as I am writing it up now, I wish that I could have handled the moment better and not let it get under my skin. What was also clear to me was that I was not acting as a missionary. I had had that missionary zeal as a young analysand and had realized that it was part of my parental complexes. My parents had been missionaries in several different settings and countries, and I had identified with their missionary spirit as a young man contained by the parental psyches. Also, when I began analysis in San Francisco, it was so freeing for me personally that I wanted all my friends to do likewise, though of course not with my analyst. I wanted him for myself. As I got deeper into my analysis, though, I realized the limits of any analysis, Jungian or Freudian, and at the same time valued my own Jungian analysis. Thus, during my presidency I felt quite secure in my Jungian identity and did not feel the need to "convert" anyone to becoming a Jungian. What helped enormously was that I went back to seeing Joe Henderson, not so much for analysis but more as someone who knew the international world of the Jungians with whom I could share my experiences. He was very interested in what was developing in the Jungian world, and at the same time he provided a sense of stability when I got off center. I was extremely fortunate that he was still around and mentally present while I was going through the various stages from second vice president all the way through to finishing the presidency in 1995.

The second incident of the delegates' meeting which distressed me was the way Verena Kast dealt with me at the conclusion of my second term as president. I had just given my final paper speaking about all that had happened in the IAAP while I was president and what it had meant to me personally. I had worked extremely hard and felt I had accomplished a great deal, and I was sad in letting go of the office. It had been a great ride. Verena was not able to thank me for my service to the IAAP, and she could not get me off the podium fast enough, a rather tactless dismissal that was noticed by many of the delegates in attendance. She acted without any feeling for me, though her attitude made it much easier for me to move on from the presidency and get on with the rest of my life. Still, it was a very disappointing ending to a long and creative aspect of my professional life.

11

POST-IAAP PRESIDENCY, 1995 – 2003

The transition from eighteen years of service on the international executive committee to being off the committee altogether was not an easy one. Past presidents have dealt with this issue in different ways. Some have continued to have some other affiliation with the international executive committee, such as being on the international ethics committee. Some have continued lecturing and traveling as before, and others have withdrawn from the international scene completely. After my term ended, I still had two unfinished projects which it seemed to me were appropriate to continue, at least for the next few months.

The first project was the international psychoanalytic dictionary which was to be published in French by Alain and Sophie de Mijolla. The congress in Zürich was in August, 1995, and the dictionary project was finished by October, 1995. The IAAP continued to support this important project to its conclusion.

The second project was a return visit to the Australian and New Zealand Society of Jungian Analysts, ANZSJA, for their meeting in Freemantle, Australia, in March, 1996. The geographical distances in Australia and New Zealand are so great that it is a tremendous effort to bring the members together for a meeting. Since Jean and I had been at their first organizational meeting in 1988 in Sydney, the members very much wanted us to attend this meeting in Freemantle, which is just off the western coast on the Indian Ocean near Perth. Both Jean and I helped them with their organizational issues, and they made us honorary members of their society. The professional training of the various members was diverse and included the entire spectrum from developmental to the most classical. This meant that the training program created by ANZSJA also had to be acceptable to the full range of thought regarding analytical psychology, which was not an easy task. However, a compromise was settled upon at this meeting, so that analytic training in Australia and New Zealand could begin without candidates having to go to the UK, Switzerland, or some other geographical area. Unfortunately, some of the analysts at either end of the analytic spectrum did not join ANZSJA initially, and as far as I know never did.

After the weeklong meeting in Freemantle, Jean and I joined Craig San Roque in Alice Springs, where Craig and Leon Petchkovsky lived at the time. They both had been very active with the aboriginal population, which had a serious problem with substance abuse in the form of glue sniffing. Craig very gently introduced us to some of the leaders, and we were taken out into the bush for a ceremonial feast that included barbecued kangaroo tail. After this wonderful primitive experience, Jean and I headed to the Great Barrier Reef for a few days of vacation, then flew home.

I had accepted speaking engagements for the next year or two in Melbourne and in Cape Town, South Africa, although I had declined other invitations to far-off lands. I found myself having frequent minor illnesses after my presidential term ended. After the last of these had passed, I realized that my body was reacting to all these time changes and I needed to reduce international travel. So, with much reluctance, I informed the sponsors in Melbourne and Cape Town that I could not fulfill my obligations to them. I knew by doing so I would never receive another invitation to either of these places, but both my body and psyche needed to slow down. It was the right thing for me to do.

I was not finished with the IAAP, though, and I began to consider the idea of publishing a history of the Jungian movement. Having grown up in a Jungian household as the son of two first-generation Jungian analysts, and now having been on the international executive committee for eighteen years, I had a fairly unique perspective over a forty-year period of Jungian life. At the conclusion of my presidency, there were over twenty-five hundred members of the IAAP distributed around the globe. I felt it was time to do a Jungian history. So I contacted Routledge Publishing Company in the UK, and I was encouraged by Andrew Samuels to submit a proposal for such a book. This proposal was accepted, and in the summer of 1996, I began the project of writing a history of the Jungian movement, which was to be entitled *The Jungians*. The contract included some travel money so that I could interview individuals at some of the professional societies that I did not know well.

I happened to receive notice that this proposal had been accepted while attending a *Journal of Analytical Psychology* conference in Maine. One of the speakers at this congress was James Grotstein, and I mentioned the history project and contract to him. His reaction was unexpected. He was extremely suspicious of biographies and biographers in general, and, because of his prior experiences in this realm, it was obvious he did not place much value on what I was doing. Grotstein had been a student of Wilfred Bion in Los Angeles, and, as one of the better-known Bion students, he had often been asked to speak about him. His interactions with those biographers had not always turned out well, and he had become increasingly suspicious of both biographers and biographies. He was warning me about what I was getting myself into, and I came to see the wisdom in his warning over the next few years as I worked on the book.

Shortly after the end of my second term as IAAP president in 1995, I had learned more about using computers, and I got on a listserv run by then-professor John Hollwitz of Creighton University in Omaha, Nebraska. Richard Noll was on the listserv as well, and his comments were rife with all sorts of half-truths about Jung, including claims that Jung had founded a cult and that various secret rites related to the Mithraic religion had been conducted at the time of his death. I found myself reacting strongly to these assertions and coming to Jung's defense, much as I had with previous allegations about Jung's purported Nazism.

In retrospect, what happened next is quite humorous. Noll's second book on Jung, called *The Aryan Christ: The Secret Life of Carl Jung*, had just been published, and Noll was making a book tour that included Palo Alto. I decided to attend. In the course of the reading, Noll made his assertion about Jung forming a cult, and I asked about Jung's funeral and memorial service. I knew that the service had been held in Küsnacht, that it was a very ordinary Protestant burial service not connected with any cult, and that Jung had been interred in the family plot, and I said as much. Noll became very agitated and wanted to know how I knew this. I said that there were photos of Jung's gravesite on the internet and I happened to have a copy of the program for the service, which was a conventional Protestant one. Suddenly, Noll recognized who I was, and he was flustered for the rest of the book reading.

The next morning Noll appeared on the program *Forum* on public radio, which was hosted by Michael Krasny. Krasny had initially wanted me to be on the program with Richard Noll, but Noll had said that if I was on the program, he would not appear. Still, Michael Krasny was concerned about how the local Jungian community would react to having Richard Noll on the show, and so he arranged for me to ask a question when the program was opened to the listening audience. I again brought up the issue of Jung's conventional funeral, and Noll recognized my voice and stated loudly that, "Tom Kirsch is a stalker." Since the program *Forum* had a wide audience in the Bay Area and was also available nationally, many people I knew heard his comment. My friends were amused by the label, and, looking back on this event, I have to agree. Noll dropped his attacks on Jung and the Jungian community shortly after that. Every tradition has someone who has been disillusioned, becomes an irritant for a while, and then is forgotten. Richard Noll was that person for the Jungian community. Still, his defamatory chronicle reinforced my desire for a genuine history of Jung and the Jungian movement.

Biographers of Jung

One might include Richard Noll as an ostensible Jung biographer, but I also had significant contact with two other Jung biographers in the early 1990s. Initially I had been approached by Gerda Niedieck, the literary agent who was responsible for all of Jung's work, who arranged for me to have a meeting with representatives of the Jung family to discuss the possibility of my writing a definitive biography of Jung. I met with the family in Zürich for several hours, and, by the end of the time, I realized that this was not something I wanted to do. First of all, it would have been so time-consuming that I would have had to give up my clinical practice of Jungian analysis; secondly, I would have needed to spend many months over the course of several years in Zürich and other archival places, such as the Library of Congress in Washington; and finally, my German was not good enough to read and understand all the material that was only in that language. So, although I felt honored to be asked, I declined the offer.

The person who accepted the challenge of undertaking Jung's biography was Deirdre Bair. Deirdre was a well-known biographer who had won a National Book Award for her biography of Beckett. She had also written award-winning biographies of Simone de Beauvoir and Anaïs Nin, and so in many ways she was an appropriate choice to write Jung's life story. She did not consider herself a Jungian per se, but she came into the project with a positive view of Jungian theory, and Paul Roazen, a noted psychoanalytic historian, had encouraged her to take on the project of writing a biography of Jung. We arranged to meet each other in the spring of 1995 when I was in New York for a conference entitled "Jung: Yesterday, Today, and Tomorrow" that had been arranged by the C.G. Jung Foundation of New York and sponsored by the Van Waveren Foundation. She seemed to be exploring what kind of support she would receive from the Jungian community if she were to accept the contract. She also spoke with Andrew Samuels and Beverley Zabriskie, two other important and influential figures in the Jungian world who were also part of the conference. I supported Deirdre, and we began a friendship that continues to this day. She has gone on to other projects, but she is still involved in Jungian psychology and is asked to speak at various Jungian conferences. However, I don't believe that she initially realized the enormity of the task that she had undertaken. Jung himself had said that it would take more than one biographer to detail his life, because there were so many facets to it. It took her much longer than she had anticipated, and she had to contend with some major health issues during the course of the project. Still, she took on her subject with a great deal of energy and found herself immersed in archival material at the ETH (The Swiss Polytechnical Institute) in Zürich, where there was so much material on Jung. She also received assistance with the important German language material.

Deirdre had also been an investigative journalist, and she uncovered much new material. For instance, she met with the nephews of Toni Wolff, who were very cooperative, and obtained first-hand material about Aunt Toni from them. As she had not been familiar with the Jungian community, she had to familiarize herself with all the different currents in the Jungian world. This was not easy, and she ran into the conflicts between different individuals. She had a good relationship with the Jung family at the beginning of the project, and the family provided her the material that she wanted. However, over the course of writing the biography, for reasons that are not clear to me, she ended up alienating the family.

Deirdre was fluent in French, and her biographies on de Beauvoir and Nin had been widely read in France, where Deirdre had quite a following. Élisabeth Roudinesco, a prominent French psychoanalytic historian, was friends with Deirdre and could not abide the fact that she was writing a biography of Jung. Roudinesco was a Jewish holocaust survivor who had been born in Romania near the end of the war, and in her view Jung was a Nazi and an anti-Semite, and she could find nothing redeeming to say about him. Deirdre uncovered material indicating that Jung had been contacted by the Allies in 1944 and had, at their request, submitted psychological profiles of major Nazi figures, including Hitler, prior to the Allied invasion. However, this evidence of Jung's cooperation with the Allied cause did not change Roudinesco's opinion or, sadly, the opinion of many other psychoanalysts who had concluded that Jung was a Nazi and an anti-Semite.

Deirdre and I had lively discussions about many aspects of Jung's life and his biography, and I made some introductions to help her gather background information. She sent me an early draft of her manuscript, which I read with great interest. It was a large manuscript, and I remember having several comments about the early draft. I did not see another draft until the book was in galley proofs, and it was really too late to change very much.

At the same time, Sonu Shamdasani was working on his biography of Jung. Sonu had become interested in Jung as an adolescent and had been studying everything connected to Jung for many years. I had met him in the late 1980s while he was still working for the Freud Museum in London, and we had some very interesting lunches talking about Jung and some of his early followers. Sonu was also good friends with the pianist and Jungian analyst Joel Ryce-Menuhin and his wife Yaltah. He knew of my interest in classical music, and we spent several "artistic evenings" together listening to classical music.

When Joe Henderson and I came to London in 1992 for him to deliver a lecture to the four London Jungian groups, I arranged to have lunch with Sonu and Joe. Joe was fairly quiet during the lunch, but I think that they both enjoyed meeting one another. At the time Sonu wanted me to organize a historical Jungian conference. He had made that suggestion during my IAAP presidency, and at that time I did not have the energy to put on any extra conferences, but I knew that at some later point I would be interested in putting on a history conference. By the mid-1990s, Sonu had left the Freud Museum and was working at the Wellcome Institute.

I knew Sonu as a Jung scholar, and he had more information about Jung than anyone else I knew. However, he had come to see Jung's biography as his territory since he had been working on *Jung and the Making of Modern Psychology* for some time. As he saw it, Deirdre was coming in as an outsider and was going to publish her biography before his. In 2005 the Jungian groups in London invited both Deirdre and Sonu to present their material on Jung in successive months. Deirdre presented her material a month before Sonu, and, when Sonu came to present, he did not speak about his own work at all but instead spent the entire lecture citing all the mistakes in Deirdre's book. Although some people in the audience loved the fact that he took on Deirdre, many of them were shocked that he had devoted his entire lecture to attacking her book. I had to agree, although I was on friendly terms with Sonu at the time and did not want to alienate either him or Deirdre. I realized that there would be errors in any book of the magnitude of Deirdre's *Jung*. In fact, Sonu had similar criticisms when my book *The Jungians* came out.

Deirdre's biography of Jung has much to recommend it. It is a valuable source of information about many different aspects of Jung's life, and it brought up much new information about Jung's life as well. However, there are some errors in the manuscript, which disappointed many Jungians. In my opinion the strengths in the manuscript far outweigh the errors, but if one is particularly interested in one of the areas that Deirdre does not get quite right, one can become pretty irritated. I value the biography for what is positive and can make my own judgments about the rest.

An important issue came up with the German edition that I followed, although I was not involved in it directly. In the European publishing world there is a concept called the *Persönlichkeitschutze*, which means that in a biography one cannot make damaging remarks about any person in the book. It literally means that anyone in any book is protected. The Jung estate felt that the law of *Persönlichkeitschutze* had not been adhered to in Deirdre's biography, and this delayed the publication of her biography for almost a year and necessitated certain changes.

12

THE JUNGIANS

I embarked on research for my book, *The Jungians*, soon after signing the contract with Routledge in June, 1996, as I felt it would be a wonderful way to come to terms with my experiences in the IAAP. Martin Stone and Moira Duckworth recommended that I make a quick trip to London to interview Baroness Vera von der Heydt, who had had a significant number of hours of analysis with Jung and who was already ninety-seven years old. Her life had been most dramatic as she had married a baron at a young age, with the Kaiser in attendance at her wedding. She had participated in numerous seminars at the School of Wisdom in Darmstadt when Jung was in attendance, and then, when the Nazis came to power, had immigrated to the UK. In 1996 she was living in a Catholic rest home in London, and the message was that she would not survive much longer. My contract included some travel money for interviews, so I traveled to London to see her in December, 1996, and she related some of the remarkable experiences of her life over the course of a two-hour interview. Unfortunately, it has never been published. One week after I interviewed her, she died.

On that same trip I also interviewed David Howell, Marianne Jacoby, and Molly Tuby, all old-timers in the Jungian world in London. David had been one of the early psychiatrists of the Society of Analytical Psychology, the major Jungian professional society for many years, and Molly Tuby had been one of the early members of the Analytical Psychology Club in London that had formed in 1922. Marianne Jacoby had been a founding member of the British Association of Psychotherapy, Jungian section, and had been friends with my parents from their days in Germany. She was also an astrologer and did a reading of me in 1936 shortly after I was born. In 1974 I had a chance to get an update to my chart from her, and she was like family to me. It was a satisfying trip, the first of many I was to undertake in the course of writing of the book.

Since in the course of the trip I was passing through Zürich, I interviewed Adolf Guggenbühl-Craig and Mario Jacoby, who were the real doyens there, as well as three people from the Research- and Training Centre for Depth Psychology According to the Ideas of C.G. Jung and Marie-Louise von Franz. They were Gotthilf Isler, Theo Abt, and another Greek analyst, Emmanuel (Manolis) Kennedy, who had been brought up in Zürich. Talking to them rekindled the attitudes I remembered so vividly from my own early days in Zürich. They were all very interested in the unconscious, had little interest in the collective, and did not care at all about their professional persona. They claimed little interest in being part of the IAAP, which seemed too collective for them. All the teaching at the Centre was from the texts of Jung and von Franz, and the faculty felt this was sufficient to make their students good Jungian analysts. Since then, however, I have heard that some of the students have sought out more professional recognition so that it would be easier to work in their home countries.

I had first met Dora Kalff beginning in 1953 when I was still a teenager. Her house, built before Columbus discovered America, was stunning and made a lasting impression on me. She was a good friend of my parents, especially my mother, and I was well acquainted with the importance of sand tray. I knew that I needed a chapter on the history of sandplay in my book, because it was too important a part of Jungian theory to be left out. Personally, I found Dora quite the prima donna, but she was also an extremely gifted healer. I never was a part of her inner circle, but we always had a pleasant relationship, and because of the friendship between her and my mother, Dora often invited me to her home in Zürich.

One other aspect of the Jungian experience in Zürich was the Klinik am Zürichberg. This was a psychiatric hospital where patients who needed long-term inpatient care were seen in a Jungian setting. C.A. Meier was the titular head, but Toni Frey was the effective leader of the hospital. By the time that I was writing up the history of the Klinik, it had lost almost all of its Jungian foundation due to an enormous conflict between Toni Frey and C.A. Meier which had ended up in the courts in Zürich. The conflict had focused on the medical director of the Klinik. Meier wanted a non-Jungian medical doctor, and Toni Frey objected strongly to this. When I wrote this up for my book, *The Jungians*, I unconsciously took the side of Meier, most likely out of my old transference to him. This got me into great difficulty with Toni Frey, who up until then had been a good friend who had visited us in California and had been someone who I visited regularly in Zürich. Before publishing the chapter on the Klinik I had showed it to Adolf Guggenbühl-Craig, who had vetted it for me, but had made no comment about how I had written this part of Zürich story. I thought it was balanced, but I had underplayed the important role that Toni had played in making the Klinik run and overemphasized the importance of Meier. Sadly, this basically cost me my friendship with Toni, although I visited him when he was recovering from a gastrointestinal disorder at a *kurort*. I was always sorry that I had not gotten the story about the Klinik am Zürichberg right, and I was upset with Adolf as well for not catching my error.

I felt I needed to make a trip to Italy and Israel, places which had strong Jungian professional societies and which I did not know that well. In 1998 I interviewed Luigi Zoja in Milan and then went to Rome and interviewed Paolo Aite, Aldo Carotenuto, and Mario Realfonzo from Naples. Realfonzo had worked with Ernst Bernhard and provided a beautiful picture of Bernhard for the book. None of the Italian Jungians really spoke more than conversational English, so Roberto Gambini, who had been in Milan for an executive committee meeting, came down to Rome and acted as my translator. This had been arranged on the spur of the moment in Milan, and I don't know what would have happened if Roberto had not been there. Thanks to him, the Italian part of the trip was very rewarding.

From Italy I flew on to Israel, where I stayed with Esti and Eli Weisstub. I had known the Weisstubs for a long time, and we had renewed our friendship both from Stanford, California, and during the time I spent on the executive committee of the IAAP. The Weisstubs had a beautiful old house built along the old Ottoman Empire railroad line, and from there I interviewed a number of people. At that time there was just one Israeli society, and so it was not difficult to navigate the field.

I was particularly interested in interviewing people who had known Erich Neumann. Neumann had died of a rare cancer in 1960, but most of the analysts in Israel had been deeply influenced by his work. I interviewed Gusty Dreifuss, a Swiss Jew, who had graduated from the Zürich Institute and then had made aliyah to Israel. He practiced in Haifa, and I stayed with him for a couple of days. He took me to a kibbutz overlooking the Golan Heights where Geula Gat, a long-time student of Neumann, lived and worked. She was originally from Germany and a Christian who had come to Palestine in the late 1920s with a Jewish girlfriend and had never left. When she first started working with the children in that area, she was the only one doing therapy working with dreams and drawings according to the theories of Erich Neumann. Since then she had received numerous awards for the work she had done with children in the area. When I saw her she was advanced in years and had lost her husband to gunfire from the nearby Golan Heights, but she still had lots of energy and was amazing old woman.

From the kibbutz I went on to Tel Aviv to visit Dvorah Kutzinski. This was the first time I had ever been in Tel Aviv, and I got completely lost trying to find her apartment. I arrived very late and in a sweat. She immediately suggested that I take a shower, which I gladly did, because I was drenched from running around and trying to find her place. Dvorah had come to Tel Aviv from Prague, and every other member of her family had been killed in the holocaust. She had become an analysand of Neumann's and became completely devoted to him and to spreading his writings. I probably learned more about Neumann from her than anywhere else. She told me about a seminar on dreams that he held weekly as well as other seminars on subjects that he later developed into books. Neumann lived with his wife and two children in a small apartment in which he had groups for training. The Neumanns' son, Micha, became a Freudian psychoanalyst, and their daughter, Rali, became a sandplay therapist in Jerusalem. I had known Rali in Zürich in the late 1950s when she studied there and I was in Zürich for analysis. We became quite friendly at the time, but we had lost contact when she returned to Israel and I to the United States. However, she was open to being interviewed about her parents and their work in Israel, so I went to see her. This time spent in Israel was a very pleasant interlude. It was peaceful there at that period, and the whole stay was without incident.

I made one more trip before writing up a draft of the book. I needed to go to Berlin and interview Hannes Dieckmann, Hans-Joachim Wilke, and Eberhard Jung. In the years after World War II, they had been a group of youthful Jungians who were instrumental in once again beginning a Jungian organization in Berlin. I spent a smoked-filled evening listening as they discussed the beginnings of the Jung group after the war. It was not a particularly comfortable evening, but I did obtain the history. Dieckmann, especially, was aware of the fact that my father had been a charter member of the earlier C.G. Jung Gesellschaft that had been founded in 1931 and knew how he had fled Germany as Hitler came to power.

I did a great deal of research on Jung and his relationship to the Nazis, and I could not find any evidence that he had had any connection with The Göring Institute, which was the main psychotherapy training institute during the Third Reich. Geoffrey Cox, who had written extensively about therapy in the Third Reich, offered a great deal of assistance. Some time previously I had interviewed Theo Seifert, an analyst in Stuttgart, when he had visited San Francisco on a vacation, and we talked at great length about the German Jungian situation at that time. He wrote me after the book was published, saying that the way that I had described Jung's position during the Nazi period was very evenhanded. He added that he thought it was the most objective description at that time, which pleased me greatly. However, I tried on numerous occasions to interview Jim Hillman, but he never acknowledged my requests for an interview. He only responded after the book came out—with very strong criticism.

After the trip to Berlin, I was ready to put the book together, and by June, 1999, I had my manuscript written. I had my uber-secretary, Ursula Egli, read it, and instead of saying that it was great, she said that it needed lots of editing and that we should go over the whole text one more time. She felt there were too many repetitious words that I needed to change. So for the next month, at every free moment, we went over more and more of the text until finally we had finished a complete editing. Initially I was extremely disappointed that I had to undertake this, but in the end I was greatly relieved that we had done it. It made for a much better book, and many people have said what a good writer I was! Little did they know how much editing help I had had.

Publication of *The Jungians*

In May of 2000, *The Jungians* was published in the UK. It came out as a hardcover, with a paperback edition to follow the next year. At the end of June, the first launch was scheduled in New York. Beverley Zabriskie kindly offered her house to have a launch of the book and planned for wine and cheese for all the attendees. Analysts from the Jung institute in New York and other psychoanalytic colleagues turned out for the occasion, and all the books that Routledge had brought were sold. It was quite an effort for Beverley and Philip as they had just returned from a trip to South America earlier that day, and I was extremely grateful to them both for having gone to so much effort to bring this about. It seemed like an auspicious beginning.

In July, 2000, Jean and I went to Europe, where there was to be another gathering in the UK. Before that event I presented a small paper on Jung as Freud's first critic at the Association Internationale d'Histoire de la Psychanalyse in Versailles. What should have been a rather innocuous presentation instead turned into a real fiasco, one I have since written up in a book edited by Tom Singer and Sam Kimbles. I had just finished speaking when a female analyst from New York stood up and announced that there was an elephant in the room, that Jung was a Nazi and anti-Semite and was involved in perpetrating the holocaust.

At that moment I completely lost my cool and became as emotional as I have ever been at any meeting. I knew that this woman wasn't alone in her assessment, that for all her emotionality, she was just repeating what many psychoanalysts believed, so I defended Jung to the hilt. There were several prominent psychoanalysts at the meeting, and that probably made it even worse for me. Some people praised me for my outburst, while others, including my wife, were upset with me for losing it.

From Versailles we went on to London, where my dear friend Andrew Samuels had organized a UK launch at his house. Many of the important analysts of the four London groups were in attendance. It was satisfying to realize that they wanted to attend this gathering.

In London I had a long breakfast with Sonu Shamdasani. Sonu had wanted the IAAP to have a greater interest in the history of analytical psychology, and especially Jung. As president of the IAAP, I listened to his request, but I did not have the energy to organize another conference in addition to the international congresses. We had met regularly whenever I was in London, and we had discussed my book project. However, I did not have him read the manuscript before it was published. I knew that if I had done that, it would have delayed the project by a year or two. Sonu was very particular about details, and I wanted this book to be completely my own, mistakes and all.

We had breakfast at the Durrants Hotel in London. He began by saying that, as a friend, he would have to spend eight hours a day for a week to correct all the mistakes he'd found in the book. I was extremely upset by this comment, but I felt that I should listen to him. He was coming to San Francisco a couple of months later, and I suggested that we get together for an afternoon and go over the list of errors he had found. I knew that in a historical book like this, it was easy to make mistakes in the details, so I said that I would bring a pad of yellow paper and we would go over them all.

We did get together in San Francisco and he did find some errors in the details, but not too many considering the number of facts that there were in the book. He had two main criticisms. First, he disagreed with my statement that the transference between Toni Wolff and Jung had not been fully resolved when they developed their personal relationship. As an analyst, I know that transferences and counter-transferences can linger for many years. Second, I referred to the split between London and Zürich as part of the split between the UK and continental Europe that had been going on for centuries. I traced the conflict back to David Hume and the British empiricists on the one hand and Immanuel Kant and continental philosophy on the other. Sonu did not like this comparison. After going through all Sonu's criticisms, although there were places in the books where I had typed the wrong year or made similar small errors that I would like to correct, I still stand by my overall statements about Jung and Toni Wolff and the split between Britain and continental Europe.

After the European promotional trip for *The Jungians*, I arranged some additional domestic trips on my own nickel to speak about the book, visiting other major Jungian centers like Boston, Los Angeles, Portland, and Seattle. Reviews of the book in the Jungian journals were extremely positive, except for one review by James Astor in the *Journal of Analytical Psychology*. He did not like that I had dedicated the book to Joe Henderson, my analyst, and he revealed some personal information about me that I still do not know how he obtained. The book was also reviewed by several psychoanalytic journals, and overall their reviews were very positive. All in all, I was pleased about the reception that the book received. It had definitely been worth the effort.

13

HISTORY CONFERENCES

After my book, *The Jungians*, came out, the extended education committee of the C.G. Jung Institute of San Francisco decided to have a weekend conference around its general theme of a history of analytical psychology. *The Journal of Analytical Psychology*, under the editorship of Joe Cambray, cosponsored the event, which was scheduled to occur just before Thanksgiving, 2000, with the conference papers to be published in a special issue of the *Journal*. Sonu Shamdasani, Joe Cambray, and I decided upon the speakers, selecting them from among the notable and influential people of the Jungian world, each of whom carried a piece of our history. The list included Luigi Zoja, Murray Stein, Beverley Zabriskie, Ernst Falzeder, Jay Sherry, Dyane Sherwood, Michael Horne, and Andrew Samuels. We drew a large crowd, nearly three hundred people, most of whom participated for the entire weekend.

Sonu spoke three times as scheduled, and criticized several different analysts over the course of his lectures. Although each analyst he mentioned had extensive clinical experience, he seemed not to see their differences in terms of an individual's varied emphasis on particular Jungian concepts. He failed to recognize the exigencies of the analytical relationship, the scientific expectation that a founder's hypotheses and theories should be extended or modified on the basis of clinical experience and subsequent knowledge, or arguments that necessarily arise in that process of growth. Instead he threw in comments about conflicts between Jungian analysts that seemed to highlight their general ignorance and failure to correctly interpret Jung. The implication was that their differences and conflicts made them look foolish.

When Andrew Samuels finally had the podium on the final day of the conference, he responded to these implications. He questioned why Sonu always presented Jungian analysts in a negative light, as if disagreements over approaches to understanding a subject indicated ignorance. Did not historians also disagree, sometimes heatedly, about their subject? Was it not also possible that he, Sonu Shamdasani, might someday disagree so strongly with Ernst Falzeder on some topic that they might not be on friendly terms thereafter? This so upset Sonu that he left the auditorium, walking directly in front of the podium on his way out. He threatened to return to London immediately. He was persuaded to join a group of speakers at a planned dinner, where the gentle persuasion of San Francisco analyst Sam Naifeh kept Sonu from leaving on the spot. People talked about this dramatic moment for years to come.

Since both Sonu and Andrew, along with Luigi Zoja, were our houseguests, the hour-long ride back to Palo Alto was very uncomfortable. Sonu and Andrew had been friends for many years, but this blow-up essentially ended their friendship. I have always been grateful to Andrew for taking on Sonu for his sweeping contempt for Jungian analysts. He consistently implied in all his criticisms that he was the only one who really understood the true way to read Jung, and that analysts are nothing but impostors, exploiting Jung's ideas, simply to make money without having a true understanding of what he wrote. During that time Sonu gave me a pass because I actually had had contact with Jung and because my parents, especially my father, really did understand Jung. Actually, my father had often expressed similar beliefs about Jungian analysts, and I was accustomed to hearing such statements, which I did not know what to do with.

However, in spite of these complications, the history conference was well-received. The enthusiasm of the audience for learning more about the history of the Jungian movement encouraged the extended education committee of the C.G. Jung Institute of San Francisco and the editors of the *Journal of Analytical Psychology*. Our second conference was held in Tiburon on the north shore of San Francisco Bay in 2002. With the exception of André Haynal, a prominent psychoanalyst from Switzerland who was scheduled to be in Los Angeles for another meeting around the same time, our presenters were North American. The program included a panel of Jungians and psychoanalysts who compared the work of Ferenczi and Jung, since there is some overlap in many of their ideas, such as the dialectical relationship in therapy and an interest in the occult. Other prominent speakers included Peter Homans, distinguished professor in the humanities at the University of Chicago, who had written *Jung in Context*, and Bill McGuire, who had been editor-in-chief of Princeton University Press during the preparation of Jung's *Collected Works* in English. I gave a paper on the correspondence between Toni Wolff and my father, which I found to be a difficult task because the letters discussed my father's personal complexes in detail, and I had had enough of those already. This history conference was less dramatically contentious than the first one, but its intellectual content was of high quality. Baruch Gould had recently become our director of extended education, and organizing this conference together was the beginning of our mutually deep relationship.

The third history conference came a year later, just after the release of Deirdre Bair's biography of Jung. Deirdre spoke about her new biography, and David Tresan lectured on Jung's concept of psychic energy. Angela Graf Nold informed us about the scientific culture and international reputation of the Burghölzli Sanatorium in Zürich during Jung's time, and David Lee spoke about Oskar Pfister, a Swiss Protestant minister and one of the original members of the Swiss Psychoanalytic Society who later became a follower of Freud. Additionally, a new movie on the relationship between Jung and Sabina Spielrein, *The Soul Keeper* by Roberto Faenza, had been extremely popular in Italy. Simultaneously, a quiet documentary by Elisabeth Márton, *My Name Was Sabina Spielrein*, was in circulation. Based on the actual letters between Spielrein, Jung, Freud, and Bleuler, Márton recreated the remarkable life of Sabina Spielrein. She also had access to Russian sources, so the film was rich in historical documentation. It became popular among Freudian psychoanalysts and Jewish groups. I saw the film again at an International Psychoanalytic meeting in New Orleans, where the Freudian analysts were enthusiastic in their response, which made me curious. Spielrein had obviously been an important early figure in psychoanalysis, yet she had been almost totally disregarded because she had ended up in the Soviet Union, and for many years no one knew her fate. Only with the breakdown of Communism did we begin to get a fuller picture of her catastrophic end. Her life followed the trajectory of many of the tragedies of the twentieth century, and she fell victim to many of them—the Russian revolution, Stalin's ultimate suppression of psychoanalysis in Russia, and, most tragically, the juggernaut of Nazi anti-Semitism, which she could not believe credible given her idealization of German culture, art, and science. All this was carefully documented and cinematically presented by Elisabeth Márton.

Our fourth and last history conference had an interesting beginning. The focus was to be on religion and Jung's psychology. However, we also wanted to bring Andreas Jung, one of Jung's grandsons, to the conference. Murray Stein, with whom I was in steady contact, came up with the idea that Andreas, an architect whose professional position was to assess the preservation of architecturally important and historical buildings in Zürich, might speak about Jung's house in Küsnacht. I thought this was a fine idea, so we plotted ahead.

Some years prior I had been introduced to Franz Jung, Jung's only son, by Frances Slocumb, who knew him well. Franz was an old man at the time, but we developed an immediate connection, and from then on when I was in Zürich, I would go over to the house at 228 Seestrasse in Küsnacht, and we would have long discussions, during which he expressed himself on a number of subjects. During the course of those visits I also met Franz's sons, Andreas and Peter.

Murray and I both had been invited to speak at a *Journal of Analytical Psychology* conference in Oxford in the spring of 2005. After the conference, Murray returned to his home in Goldiwil, above the Lake of Thun, and Jean and I made the short hop to Zürich, specifically to meet the Jungs. We had arranged a luncheon meeting with Andreas and his wife Vreni at the Veltliner Café, a venerable old restaurant in the Old Town of Zürich. Within minutes we realized our affinity, and lunch was great fun! Vreni Jung had voluntarily organized Jung's correspondence in the ETH archives and she told us it contained a correspondence between Joe Henderson and Jung, which neither Joe nor anyone else in San Francisco had known. As a consequence of this meeting, I was able to arrange for Joe to swiftly receive copies of these letters—at the time he was already 102 years old. Joe was really astonished and pleased.

During lunch we tried our best to persuade Andreas and Vreni to make the trip to San Francisco and for Andreas to present his architectural studies of Jung's venerable house on the shores of the Lake of Zürich, in which he—as a son of Jung's only son, Franz—and his wife Vreni had raised their family and still resided. That was not so easily done. They were strongly rooted in Swiss culture and did not readily assent to international travel, but we had previously been aided in our persuasive efforts by their children, who had insisted they make a trip to Peru and Machu Picchu, which they had done and thoroughly enjoyed. Eventually they agreed to come to San Francisco and planned to vacation afterwards in the Indian country of the American Southwest, much as Jung himself had. Jung had written about his trip to the Southwest in his autobiography, *Memories, Dreams, Reflections.*

In addition to inviting Andreas Jung to the conference, we invited Ann Lammers, who had just finished editing the correspondence between Jung and Victor White; John Dourley, a Catholic priest and Jungian analyst; Steven Joseph, who spoke about Jung and the Kabbalah; David Tresan, speaking about Jung's relationship to transcendence; and Murray Stein, who presented a paper on "Jung and Christianity." It was an exciting weekend on the shores of San Francisco Bay with glorious views of the headlands and the Golden Gate Bridge.

The conference was full to overflowing with enthusiastic attendees. The night before the conference opened we hosted a convivial dinner at our house in Palo Alto, which set the tone for the whole event. The lectures were uniformly excellent, and Andreas absolutely charmed the entire audience with his presentation on Jung's house. The conference was a success in every way.

We did not know it at the time, but this was the last of the formal history conferences. Since then, Jean and I have stayed in touch with Andreas and Vreni, always making arrangements to see them whenever we are in Zürich. Sometimes we host a dinner in Zürich and sometimes we are invited to swim and have dinner at their house in Küsnacht, and our friendship has deepened over the years.

I was surprised at the interest in these history conferences. Members of the local Jungian community came in large numbers, and the first conference attracted an international audience, with attendees from Hong Kong, Canada, and Mexico. Our community was very interested in hearing about our origins and roots, and the fact that we could attract international speakers of great renown to present made for very lively conferences.

14

NEW DIRECTIONS

By 2003 I had finished my book, *The Jungians*, completed presentations about it in Europe and the US, and helped organize some of the history conferences that arose out of the book's publication. I was ready for a new project or two, though I was not conscious of the fact that I was looking for a new project, because many opportunities were coming my way without my searching them out. I rarely sought out new projects or speaking engagements, but I seemed to receive them anyway. If they did not materialize, I found I was increasingly happy to stay close to home. I had spent years promoting Jung and analytical psychology around the world, and as I approached the age of seventy, I thought it time to slow down a bit. My health was reasonably good except for a chronic low back problem that I had had since my late twenties. I had become a regular swimmer, which had helped the back problem, and I had tried various non-traditional medical therapies, which also helped. My back was actually doing better as I neared age 70 than it had been at age 28. I thought my back problems were probably related to having played so much tennis in my youth, and that at that time there were virtually no treatments for back problems besides surgery, and even surgery was not a particularly safe option.

Adventures into Asia

In July, 2006, a project arose which was completely unexpected. One evening a couple days before Jean and I were scheduled to fly to Europe, I received a phone call from a Taiwanese couple, Steve and Jenny Chang, who were in San Francisco with Heyong Shen. Heyong Shen had been our host in China in 1994 and became the first accredited Jungian analyst in China several years after our visit. He also had been an international student at our institute for two years, and during that time I'd grown to know him well. The Changs were business people, and they wanted to come down to Palo Alto the next day for lunch and meet with me. My schedule that day was full because we were leaving the next day for Europe, but, as luck would have it, my patient who had been scheduled around the noon hour cancelled due to illness, and so I had the time to see them.

The next day the Changs arrived at my office in Palo Alto and announced that they were the founders of a large Taiwan computer anti-virus company, Trend Micro. We formed an immediate connection because I had their software on all three of my computers and had researched it extensively before buying it. So here were a couple of synchronicities that had allowed this propitious meeting to take place. During lunch they asked me what I was doing professionally right now. I had been gathering up my father's correspondence with Jung with an eye toward publication, and I explained the project to them and said that I had an editor who was working on them. We already had a contract with Routledge, but we were raising money to fund the project. Correspondences are expensive to publish because they require much archival work to get permissions from the people mentioned in the letters.

They asked me if I needed more money to complete the project, and I said enthusiastically, "Yes!" They offered a very generous amount, which we thought would be enough to finish it. However, more letters were found, and the project ended up being larger and more expensive than originally budgeted, but the funding from the Changs was substantial and allowed the project to move along nicely. However, their generosity had a hitch. They wanted Jean and me to come to Taiwan and teach their students about Jung and analytical psychology. Inwardly I groaned, because I had no desire to travel to Taiwan, and I knew that Jean would balk at going to this new place. My orientation had always been toward Europe, and I had had little interest in Asia, although I had made a trip to China and Korea in 1994. That trip didn't arise out of personal desire but because I was asked to visit as president of the IAAP. But in 2006, I accepted the proposal knowing full well that it was worth their generous donation to commit to this teaching assignment. When I presented the proposal to Jean later, she did balk, but eventually she agreed to make the trip as her contribution to having my father's correspondence with Jung published. I delayed our departure till fall, 2007, as far into the future as I could reasonably extend it. We planned to spend two weeks in Taiwan, then we were also invited to China for a week, and after that Jenny was going to take us to Kyoto for four days. We had plenty of time between the July, 2006, luncheon and our final departure, giving us a long stretch to prepare our workshops, but we would leave only six weeks after coming back from an IAAP meeting in South Africa. Having two major trips scheduled so close to one another did not please Jean at all, and I was not too happy about that, either.

In the beginning of October, 2007, we flew nonstop to Taipei from San Francisco, arriving at 6 a.m. two days later. We had one day of relative relaxation before the first of two weekend seminars would begin. What neither of us had realized was that we were the first Western Jungians to be in Taipei. Kazuhiko Higuchi from Japan had come to teach and Martin Kalff to provide training in sandplay, but no Jungian analyst from the West had ever gone to Taiwan before.

On the day of the first seminar, there was a large typhoon which completely closed down the city of Taipei. Given the weather, we thought no one would come to the seminar, but 40 out of the 50 people who had signed up made it in spite of the storm. What we had not realized was that most of the psychologists and therapists in Taiwan had had some connection in the West, either in the US or the UK, and so were familiar with Western thinking. Many of them spoke English, although not everyone spoke or understood English well enough to follow the lecture completely without translation, so it was still necessary to have simultaneous translation into Mandarin. The Taiwanese were very respectful to both of us. To them Jean and I represented elders, and there was also the projection that we were "true authorities." Neither of us were comfortable with that particular projection, and I had a strong negative reaction to it. I had a dream after the first day in which I was going up very high on a bridge that seemed to stop in midair, and I realized that I needed to come down from that height. What I took away from that dream was that I needed to be more grounded and less concerned about whether or not I was an "authority." The second day of that first weekend seminar went much better, and I was much more relaxed as I talked about dreams and other Jungian themes. The students were very interested in sandplay, and so Jean's presentations were equally well-received. What Jean and I quickly realized was that this was a situation where we were treated equally because the students did not know much about either of our backgrounds. In the rest of the world my connection to Jung through my parents always puts me in the limelight, but here we were equal and were treated that way, which was very good for our relationship.

In addition to our workshops, we also did individual supervision, and of course some people asked for hours of analysis. I ended up Skyping with a couple of people for many years, and so did Jean. Both Jean and I fell in love with Taiwan and its people. Jean said later that she knew immediately that this would be a life-changing experience, and that was why she protested so much about making the trip. We have ended up going back each year for the past six years to teach and supervise, and it has been a life-altering experience for both of us. The Taiwanese students have treated us with such special warmth, and their enthusiasm has been unbounded. Jung and analytical psychology really excite many of the students and therapists, a different response from European audiences, who have heard all this material forever and sometimes seem bored with presentations.

On that first trip we also spent a week in mainland China as well as an unexpected stop-over in Hong Kong. We had not gotten visas to go into China, so we had to get express visas in Hong Kong. The Hong Kong Jungians were most helpful, and since then we have gone back to teach there as well. In mainland China we were taken care of by Heyong Shen and his wife, Gao Lan. We visited Guangzhou, which we had not seen for thirteen years, and it had grown so much that it was completely unrecognizable. Heyong had many students at the university, and I cannot ever remember having my picture taken so many times with so many different people. We were definitely not used to that kind of attention!

From Guangzhou we flew to Shanghai to meet with students interested in analytical psychology. I also spoke at Fudan University, one of the oldest and most prestigious of Chinese universities. The students did not speak English, so the lecture was simultaneously translated, but it seemed that I was not getting through to the students. I have never figured out why the simultaneous translation did not really reached them. Shanghai was impressive with its canyons filled with high rises, like New York on steroids. Mainland China was overwhelming, and both Jean and I realized that we could not do such a long trip in Asia again. We only went back to China one other time in the fall of 2013.

But we were hooked on going back to Taiwan from then on. I have made yearly trips, and Jean has made all the trips except one. On that first trip I had a serious talk with Heyong Shen in China, and he said that if we got involved in Taiwan, they would have a rapid development of analytical psychology there. I listened politely to the flattering statement and quietly wondered to myself what would happen and how Jungian psychology would develop there. In fact analytical psychology has developed rapidly in Taiwan, but not necessarily because of Jean and me.

The next year's trip was to Taipei and Hong Kong. I felt that we needed to reciprocate for their helping us out with the visa to China the year before. I honestly cannot remember the sequence of the topics that we discussed in 2008, but they included dreams, transference, synchronicity, individuation, the approach to the unconscious, and an introduction to the pictures from the *Rosarium Philosophorum*. We also did case conferences for the therapists and saw the patients we had been Skyping with.

After that first trip, Jean and I had written a long report detailing all the significant events that we could remember. The report had been circulated among the international executive committee members. A conference on psychotherapy was scheduled for spring, 2009, in Shanghai, and members of the international executive committee were going to attend. As part of the Shanghai trip, they made a site visit to Taipei and approved the Taiwan group as a developing group, as the group was definitely ready for this next step. Angela Connolly and a couple of other analysts gave seminars to the students. Joe Cambray, who was president of the IAAP at that time, and the other executive committee members thought that I would be a good liaison person to serve as intermediary between the Taiwanese developing group and the IAAP, and I felt honored to be given that position. Under IAAP rules, the liaison person cannot provide analysis but can offer seminars and supervision, while others provide personal analysis. The IAAP contributes some money for travel each year to facilitate this arrangement. The developing group in Taiwan has received four thousand Swiss francs in IAAP funds each year to continue the liaison contact, while Jenny and Steve Chang, working through the Taiwan Institute of Psychotherapy, have generously helped to pay for hotel and food expenses as well as extra flight costs.

After the Shanghai conference, the IAAP approved Taiwan as a developing group. The number of people showing an interest in analytical psychology was growing, and the number of people attending open seminars was increasing as well since more analysts who were going to Asia were contracting to speak in Taiwan.

In 2010 Liza Ravitz and I went to Taiwan and Hong Kong to teach, and Liza loved the experience. In fact, she loved it so much that she and her husband Sam decided that they would like to spend a year in Taipei. Sam had a business that he could run from anywhere in the world that had an internet connection, and Liza planned to analyze and teach. They ended up staying two years, departing Taiwan in May, 2014. It was a rich experience for both of them as well as a real opportunity for the Taiwanese, who have been fortunate in having Liza there full time since usually those in a developing group generally have to bear the expense of going to another city, often a fair distance away, in order to receive concentrated hours of personal analysis. For her part Liza has enjoyed having these very talented people as her analysands. In addition to analysis, Liza had a position at a university, where she taught sandplay and Jungian theory. Her presence in Taiwan greatly accelerated Jean's and my dream about the development of analytical psychology in Taiwan, and the Taiwanese have been extremely welcoming to visiting Jungian analysts from all over the world, so many have wanted to return to teach again.

By 2013, the Taiwanese were feeling more ambitious and decided to have an international conference in Taipei in the fall. It was coordinated with another conference arranged by Heyong Shen in Qingdao to honor Richard Wilhelm and the *I Ching*. The two conferences came on back-to-back weekends so that many of the presenters could be there for both conferences. I was able to speak to both groups, and the experiences were very different but both exceptional.

The conference in Taiwan brought in speakers from Japan, Korea, China, Italy, Switzerland, and the US. It was truly a dialogue between East and West, and discussion was encouraged. I was privileged, along with Murray Stein, to be honorary co-president of the conference. The Taiwanese also published a book of fifteen of my papers that had been translated into Mandarin. The papers ranged from early clinical papers on analysis and dreams to later papers on the history of Jung and analytical psychology. Translating and publishing this group of papers had been an enormous outlay of time and effort that I felt keenly. Wen-Yu Cheng, a psychologist who I had first met in Taipei, oversaw the project of translating the different chapters. He recently completed two years as our international student at the San Francisco Jung institute. He is now going on to obtain his doctorate degree at a local psychological graduate school, and at the same time he continues to be a part of the candidates' group at the C.G. Jung Institute of San Francisco. International students do not often have this relationship with the candidates, but Wen-Yu is a special person and has had a strong impact on the San Francisco Jung institute. In many ways the combination of the international conference and the publication of my papers into Mandarin seemed to fulfill the task that I had felt called to do in Taiwan. The group there now had ten or more routers who were on their way to becoming Jungian analysts, and analytical psychology had a solid grounding there.

The conference on the *I Ching* was conducted with a depth and reverence for the ancient Chinese text, which is probably the most sacred text that I have experienced in my life. Over the years it has had a profound effect on my life and the direction that it has taken, and to now have an entire four-day conference focused on different aspects of the *I Ching* was a rare privilege. Over the years Jean had become very interested in the *I Ching*, while I perhaps had shied away a bit, but the conference reawakened my earlier interest.

At the conference I met Christa Robinson, who had been head of the Eranos Foundation at the time it had been studying the *I Ching*, and I felt a deep affinity with her. I did an *I Ching* reading with her, and realized how stuck I had been in writing this memoir. Even when speaking privately, it was difficult to speak about the shadow of people in the Jungian world, and I realized it would be even more difficult when the memoir was published. She helped me see that I could not be gratuitously angry, but that the anger had to be objectively expressed. That freed me to begin writing again after having been blocked for some time, and I have been able to express negative feelings about people, but I have worked hard not to allow a nastiness to intrude. I have continued to speak with Christa by Skype every two weeks or so, as so much has happened over the past few years, including some serious health issues. I am entering another phase of my life.

I wrote this section on Taiwan a week after the San Francisco Jung institute sponsored a conference on Jung and China, where several people from Taiwan, mainland China, and Hong Kong spoke about their experiences with aspects of Jung's psychology in relation to traditional Eastern philosophies. I was the conference coordinator and extended invitations to participants to come to San Francisco. With the generous financial support of Jenny Chang from Taiwan, we at the Jung institute were able to hold the conference here. San Francisco seemed the natural place for such an event, as it is really the gateway to the Orient and has been so for over one hundred years.

In many ways I feel that I have done what I started out to do in Taiwan and Asia, but there is still a yearning to go back one more time. Asia energizes me, though what the future holds is uncertain.

15

THE RED BOOK

The Red Book was somehow always in the background when I was growing up. I did not know anything about it except that it was spoken of in hushed and revered terms. When *The Red Book* was published in 2009, Sonu Shamdasani mentioned that my father had been shown the book in 1929, shortly after Jung had stopped working on it. There is no other documentation that suggested anyone else outside the family had actually seen *The Red Book*, but certainly Cary Baynes and others had access to it. Jung had been ambivalent about publishing *The Red Book* in his lifetime, and it remained in a bank vault in Zürich for many years.

In 1999 Sonu Shamdasani received approval from the Jung estate to translate and publish *The Red Book*, and he wrote an extensive introduction to orient the reader. This meant the publication of Jung's inner dialogues as well as printing the fifty-three paintings that Jung created in association with *The Red Book*. There were various production problems, which didn't concern me. However, I was concerned that Jung's private journal was being published at all. I expressed my opinion about that openly, which I am sure did not sit well with Sonu and the others who were busily working on translation and getting the book into production. Finally, in October, 2009, the book was ready to be launched. By that time, I was in conflict with Sonu and Beverley Zabriskie because of my dissident point of view.

Two weeks prior to the launch *The New York Times Magazine* ran a lead article on *The Red Book*. Suddenly the book had sixteen thousand pre-publication orders when only two thousand had been printed. A contract had been signed to print the book's images in Italy, which took longer than domestic printing would have, guaranteeing that at the outset there would be a shortage of books. This built the demand even further. Many members of the Jung family were invited to New York city for the launch, and Beverley encouraged me to attend.

Effectively I was invited to attend a single cocktail party at Beverley's, but was excluded from other special events associated with the launch. The hoopla associated with the weeklong events reinforced my belief that the book should not have been published at all, and I reacted negatively. However, I did go home with a copy, and I commenced studying *The Red Book*. The material is so dense that it is difficult to stay with more than a few pages at a time, and the images are often disturbing. Jung really plumbed the depths of the psyche in his confrontation with the unconscious.

Soon after *The Red Book* was published, I was asked to speak about it in various settings, including an interview with Michael Lerner at The Commonweal in Bolinas, California, a National Public Radio program with Michael Krasny, and a donor program at the C.G. Jung Institute of San Francisco. Around the same time I received a phone call from Andrew Samuels, who encouraged me to edit a series of papers on *The Red Book*, based upon the forthcoming conference on *The Red Book* in San Francisco. This made me extremely anxious, but I thought that if I had a coeditor who was a scholar in philosophy and religion as well as analytical psychology, it would be manageable. I thought of my friend George Hogenson in Chicago, who is a Jungian analyst and has a PhD in philosophy. He agreed to be the coeditor, and together we organized the conference in San Francisco in June, 2010, to bring together a number of scholars and Jungian analysts to give their perspectives on *The Red Book*. In doing so, we were going against an edict Sonu had delivered that no one should write anything on *The Red Book* until after reading and digesting it for at least a year. The conference speakers included Ulrich Hoerni, Jung's grandson and the member of the Jung family most responsible for the publication of *The Red Book*; Paul Bishop, professor of German languages in Glasgow and a Jung scholar; John Beebe, a well-known local Jungian analyst; Susan Thackrey, a local Jungian analyst and a former art dealer; Christine Maillard, a professor of medieval philosophy at the University of Strasbourg who had translated Jung into French; Korean professor and Jungian analyst Bou-Yong Rhi; Joe Cambray, Jungian analyst and president of the IAAP; and George Hogenson from Chicago. The crowd filled a large auditorium at the Hotel Kabuki in San Francisco, and space was standing room only.

The papers were uniformly wonderful, and everyone had a fairly polished paper ready for publication. We turned the papers over to Routledge a month after the conference. Many of the speakers had used images from *The Red Book*, and our major concern was that Norton, the publisher of *The Red Book*, would want a substantial fee for permission to use them. At the same time, there were internal changes at Routledge, and the manuscripts lingered for months with no action on their part. Finally, in 2012, I contacted the permissions authority at Norton and found, to my great surprise and relief, that the costs for using the images were not prohibitive after all. Norton asked for one hundred dollars per image, which was manageable. We requested funds from the group of authors, and from among them all we came up with the money. The project was now proceeding full steam ahead. The problem for me was that I had developed a serious health issue, renal clear cell carcinoma, so I no longer had the energy to work on it. At that point George stepped in and took over the project. He arranged the final editing of all the manuscripts, organized the images, and did all the detail work so that the book would be ready for display at the international congress in Copenhagen in August, 2013. I am extremely grateful for all the work he did to bring this important publication to fruition.

In 2010, *The Red Book* was brought to the United States and displayed in Los Angeles and at the Library of Congress. The Library of Congress began organizing a conference on Jung and *The Red Book* that was scheduled for the latter part of June. Planning this event was not easy. My assumption was that Beverley Zabriskie thought she should choose all the speakers, perhaps because her husband, Philip, who had passed away not long before, had been a classmate of James Billington, the director of the Library of Congress. Jim Hutson was the Library of Congress person planning the conference, and we had worked together previously on several projects, mainly adding the correspondence between my father and Jung to the Library of Congress. Jim also needed financial support for the Library of Congress event, and I was able to assist him with this. However, Beverley wanted certain people to speak, and she seemed puzzled that Jim was listening to me at all. The speakers chosen were of a high quality, and they each presented well. I felt like a bit of an outsider because Sonu, Beverley, and Jim Hillman were major speakers. At the end of the day I tried to speak with Sonu, but he just turned to me and said, "I never want to speak to you again." I took him at his word, and have never again tried to contact him.

The Library of Congress event was also my last meeting with Jim Hillman prior to his death in 2011. I had seen him in New York in 2009 at the time of the publication of *The Red Book*, and I remember that warmly as the most meaningful connection we had had since 1968. However, our brief exchange at the Library of Congress event was cool.

Overall the Library of Congress event was a great success. The largest auditorium at the library was completely full, and I felt satisfied with my presentation on Jung's "The Transcendent Function," which he wrote shortly after having gone through his "Confrontation with the Unconscious" as represented in *The Red Book*.

The Red Book has now been out for several years, and it has been translated into numerous languages. It has proven to be most popular in the United States. It does not matter now whether I thought it should be published or not. It is out in the public domain, and it will find its place over time.

16

RELATIONSHIP TO MY PARENTS
DURING MY ADULT YEARS

Going into the same field as my parents meant that I spent a lot of time working out my relationship with both of them. They were first-generation Jungian analysts who brought Jung into new geographical areas, and I was supposed to have similar interests to theirs, although we were dissimilar in many ways. The expectation growing up was that I would continue the work that they had started, and this made it difficult for me to leave the Los Angeles area.

The crucial change in my relationship to my parents came in the years 1966 and 1967, the period of the separation and divorce from my first wife. As I worked through the process of separating from her, I also separated emotionally from my parents, especially my mother. I realized that I had been too close to her and that this had inhibited my own masculine development. However, that meant that, at the time of a most difficult personal crisis, there was minimal contact between me and my parents, and that was difficult for all of us. However, it provided me the space and independence to live my own life. They knew that I was all right, but for the first time they knew few details about my personal situation. During this period San Francisco and the Bay Area became my home, and I found my place within the Jungian community there. The transition was particularly upsetting for my mother, who was used to having intimate conversations with me about a host of topics.

Although my parents had a great deal of respect for the San Francisco Jungian community, there had been a long-standing tension between the two groups because their makeup was so different. The Los Angeles Jungians were chiefly German Jewish refugees with a strong personal attachment to Jung and Zürich, while the San Francisco group was largely comprised of Protestant Californians who had gone to Zürich for analysis and training but were rooted in the Bay Area. The two groups had shadow projections on one another, and they did not meet for many years. Beginning in 1953, they began to have yearly meetings, and gradually the shadow projections lessened and the two professional societies accepted their differences. The early Los Angeles Jungians were like one big incestuous family, while the San Francisco society was less familial and much more professional and collegial. The analysts in San Francisco tended to have more of a relationship to psychoanalysis, and many taught at the two local medical schools, where interaction with new potential candidates helped draw others into Jungian training. The San Francisco organization appealed to me in part because of its more open relationship to the collective and more professional attitude toward analysis.

This context also influenced my relationship to my parents during my adult years. Over the years I continued to visit them for most major family occasions, and my two children both had positive relationships with my mother and father. In fact, my daughter Susannah named her own daughter after her grandmother, my mother. I did not know that she was going to do that until after the baby was born, but I was profoundly touched by it.

However, pulling back from my mother had a definite impact on our relationship. At some deep level she was hurt that our intimacy had changed, and after that she was generally a bit defensive with me. I tried to communicate the significance of our relationship in other ways. For instance, in 1977 a Festschrift entitled *A Well of Living Waters* was created in honor of her seventy-fifth birthday. I contributed a small piece to that endeavor, and I was pleased to do that. But her defensiveness continued until she was diagnosed with pancreatic cancer in the summer of 1978. At the time of diagnosis, the cancer had already metastasized, and it was clear that she was terminal. I made a point of visiting her several times in those last months before her death. She was extremely upset that she had cancer because she interpreted that as meaning that all her analytic work had not been successful. She could not be dissuaded from that point of view.

One week before my mother's death, my parents met with the rabbi to discuss the funeral arrangements. They ended up deciding that my mother and father should have a religious wedding. So exactly a week before my mother's death, they had a wedding in the house, and my mother wore a white wedding dress. It was very moving. The next week she died, and we had an orthodox funeral service that was clean and simple. I spoke at the funeral regarding some activities not related to the world of Jungian psychology that she had particularly enjoyed, ranging from small things like going to professional football games to her deep involvement with her extended family.

When my mother died, she left a letter for me to read after her death. In it she related a dream I had when I was a very young boy, age five or six, where there was a danger of me being swallowed up by the moon. In this last communication from her, she hoped that I would avoid this happening. With the help of Joe Henderson, I realized that being swallowed up by the mother would always be the danger for me. It is a warning that I have taken seriously all my life. The polarity between my sense of being both understood and swallowed up by my mother colored our entire relationship, but I have always been aware that it was through her that I found my interest in the unconscious and analytical psychology, and for this I have always been grateful.

My relationship to my father was on a different level from my relationship with my mother. As a lecturer, writer, and spokesman for Jung on numerous occasions, my father was much better known to the rest of the Jungian world. He attended any lecture that I gave in Los Angeles. Initially, this was very difficult for me. During the first lecture I gave at UCLA in 1971, he was seated very close to the front of the auditorium. I had been advised to pick out someone else in the audience and speak to that person so that I would not get distracted by my father. I did pick an elderly bearded man, and I directed my attention to him, but he promptly fell asleep! Needless to say, that was quite unnerving, but by that time I was into my lecture, and I was able to go on.

Over the years I continued to meet many of my mother's and father's patients, some of whom were quite famous in the movie industry and others who might have something that my father wanted. For instance, my father loved to go swimming, and if one of his patients had a lovely swimming pool, he would swim there on a regular basis. If I were in town, I would go swimming with him. I never would have gone swimming in a patient's pool in Palo Alto, but when in Los Angeles, I continued the pattern of my youth. One patient I came to know reasonably well was Sam Francis, a well-known modern artist, who was both a patient of my father's and friends with my family. Sam also exhibited at a gallery in Palo Alto, so I came to know him and the gallery owner fairly well. I feel free to write about Sam because in numerous biographies of him he openly stated that he was in analysis with my father, so I am not revealing confidential information.

Six months after my mother died, my father married his new secretary. She was forty years younger than he was, and it was a difficult adjustment. They continued to live in the house where my parents had lived for the past twenty-four years, and his new wife, Sandra, was quite withdrawn. It was very difficult to form a relationship with her. The marriage did not last, but they saw each other at times, and she tangentially remained in his life. In the last two years of his life, my father softened toward me and let me into some of his deeper emotions. He was really quite affectionate with me. The quality of his life had decreased markedly because he had lost his hearing, his vision was reduced, and he could not walk because of severe pain in his knees.

When he was eighty-seven years old, he developed bacterial pneumonia and decided not to treat it. I respected him for that. Shortly before he died, he had a vision that he was riding on the back of a bird and was only waiting for me to visit him to be released. When I heard this, I immediately rushed down to see him, and I arrived ten minutes before he died. I held his hand those last ten minutes. It was a most meaningful experience.

I was the executor of his intellectual property, which meant that I had to go through all his books and papers. He had a huge library and books in English, German, Hebrew, and French. I gave away most of the books to various individuals and libraries, and kept about 10 percent of them for myself. There were also literally several hundred tapes of seminars that he had given on a weekly basis on Jung's later alchemical works. There was an expectation that I would do something with these tapes, but I knew that was not for me, and I gave them to a former patient of his, who still has them.

I also found forty-four letters from Jung to my father, some of them originals and others copies. I thought that most of the important letters had already been published, so initially I thought I did not need to do anything more with them. Then in 2002 I received a letter from an American woman living in England, Sasha Rosen, who was doing research at the Jung archive in Zürich. She noted that all of my father's letters to Jung were in the archive and suggested that I might be interested in seeing them. I then wrote to the archive at the ETH and asked them to send me copies of all my father's letters. I had my secretary, who was Swiss, translate them, and I realized that the 1934 correspondence contained an extensive discussion between my father and Jung about Jung's statements about Jews and Jewish psychology. As I had seen only limited discussion of this material, I thought it would be important to publish both sides of the correspondence.

Most of Jung's significant letters to my father had been published in Jung's collected letters in 1973. I knew that Ann Lammers was preparing the correspondence between Jung and Victor White for publication and was nearly completed with that project, that she knew the Jung family, and that this correspondence would be a natural follow-up to her present work. She was very interested in the project, and so in 2005 we signed a contract with Routledge and the Jung family to publish the correspondence. Ann is an extremely careful researcher, and she found many other letters between my father and Jung, so the correspondence grew to about one hundred fifty letters, with Jung writing ten more than my father. Raising money for this project was not easy, because Ann needed a salary for herself as well as funds for the project. We each had one large donor who helped make a go of the project, and Ann went to the same foundations that had helped her with the Victor White correspondence. She had some success in obtaining further grants, although not as much as she had hoped. We both put small but significant sums into the project to bring it to its conclusion. The correspondence came out in English in 2011, but unfortunately it only came out in hardcover form, which made it a very expensive book. Ann has been working toward publication of a paperback version in English with a new foreword and other additions.

After working with the letters, I had to decide what to do with the forty-four letters from Jung to my father that I had inherited. I had developed a relationship with Jim Hutson, head of the manuscripts division of the Library of Congress, and, after talking with Jim and Len Bruno, I had decided that I would donate them to the Library of Congress rather than to the Jung archive in Zürich. My thinking on that was that my father had lived the majority of his life in the United States, and also that the Library of Congress made access to the letters far easier than if they had been in the Zürich archive. I had waited ten months after requesting my father's letters to Jung for them to arrive, and I hoped future researchers would not have such delays.

In May of 2014, a German publisher, Patmos, released a German translation of the letters. I sense that the German edition will be of more interest than the English version. In addition, a group of Jungians in Berlin, headed by Joerg Rasche, arranged with the city of Berlin to have a plaque placed at the site of my father's Berlin psychiatry office where he had practiced prior to his leaving Germany in 1933. I was asked to give a speech about my father at the dedication of this plaque in May, 2014, and I agreed and arranged to be there.

On the day we left for Europe, I began to have symptoms of nausea, diminished appetite, and urinary frequency and urgency. I ascribed all the symptoms to nervousness and the excitement of travel and never considered that they might have an organic cause. Our first stop was in Copenhagen, where Jean and I both gave seminars. My presentation was a joint lecture with Aksel Haaning, a scholar on medieval alchemy as well as a student of Jung. We spoke about Jung in the 1930s, a topic about which Aksel knows a great deal. Both the lecture and the seminar went well, but by the end of the second day I was speaking slowly, and my symptoms had gotten worse. I ended up in an emergency room, where within five minutes they had diagnosed a severe case of diabetes, the first diabetic episode I had ever had. My blood sugar was so elevated that the reading was off the charts, although I could not translate the Danish readings into a scale I was familiar with since they use a different system of blood sugar measurement than the US system. I spent four days in the hospital, where they gradually brought down my blood sugar and rehydrated me so I could go on to Berlin and deliver my major speech. However, by the time I got off the plane in Berlin, it was clear that my symptoms had returned. Beate and Joerg Rasche met us at the airport, and, after checking us in at the hotel, brought me to the teaching hospital of Humboldt University, where I was again admitted. There I stayed for six more nights, and they were much more aggressive in lowering my blood sugar.

I did not know whether I would be strong enough to give my speech at the unveiling. The doctors worked very hard to bring my blood sugar under control, and two days later they had me propped up to give my lecture for the conference. I was seated for delivery, and I softened the lecture a bit, so that the negativity I felt with respect to my father's relationship with women, which I had felt all my life, lessened. I discussed his lifelong search for meaning and how he had wandered the world looking for a place to settle down both internally and externally. He found that most in Switzerland, where he could come close to his German roots along with his connection to Jung and other first-generation colleagues. After my talk I received a standing ovation, which was really something. My wife, son, and friends like Andrew Samuels, Beate, Joerg, Linda Carter, Ladson Hinton, and Joe Cambray were in the audience, and I really felt good about the experience.

I returned immediately to the hospital, where I was to remain another three days as my blood sugar was gradually brought under control. I was let out one more time to attend a book reading of the Jung-James Kirsch correspondence, which had just come out in German. This was a two-hour discussion of the contents of the letters, as well as the general cultural conditions under the Third Reich and how difficult it was to practice psychoanalysis under these conditions. It produced a very spirited discussion which many people did not want to stop. Later we had dinner with Beate, Joerg, and Ann Lammers. After my discharge from the Berlin hospital, I returned to Palo Alto to the care of my local doctor at Stanford Hospital, and we managed to control my blood sugar with increased doses of insulin.

When I was admitted to the hospital in Berlin, I was told by the admitting doctor that I had almost died from brain swelling in Copenhagen because my blood sugar had been so high. It was a brush with death, and I was reminded of what my mentor and analyst Joe Henderson had said to me about working on my father's letters. He warned me not to get too involved with my father's material, saying that it would not be healthy for me and could send me into a regressive state. I thought of Joe Henderson's statement many times when I was lying alone in the hospital in Berlin. It was a very strange experience to be in a hospital there, hearing the birds sing, peering out to the green of the trees and being reminded of my parents all the time. I was reminded how often my mother complained of living in Los Angeles surrounded by concrete and cars with no access to the natural world that is everywhere in Berlin. I found myself fascinated with this place my parents and I had avoided all my life, fascinated with how I was now stuck in a hospital in the middle of this city. I felt all the layers of Berlin's overwhelming history, including the Weimar Republic period when my parents were young adults, and the many significant historical figures who have lived there. Now Berlin feels beautiful and exciting, full of new culture and growth, but beneath that one still feels the Nazi era, which is inescapable in the city. For example, the Holocaust memorial runs through the center of Berlin, and there are so many other subtle reminders of the Nazi period everywhere. Berliners were wise enough not to try to get away from that history. Instead they have really tried to come to terms with it, particularly with what it did to the Jewish population. Modern Berliners are aware of the wide range of intellectual development that was under way in Germany prior to the Nazi era, and they grieve for the loss of knowledge in so many fields of study that were being pursued by those who left Germany and went on to develop their disciplines in foreign lands. Present-day Berliners were so eager to treat me properly, and I appreciated that, but at the same time I could feel their almost obsessive need to repair all that had been lost.

And so I survived the experience of giving the speech for my father in Berlin. I cannot remember ever getting a standing ovation before, but more importantly, I felt that I had completed the circle with my parents. Spending close to a week in a Berlin hospital left me lots of time to think about what it must have been like for them there, and, although it was not easy, in some ways it was a most healing experience.

17

CONCLUSION

Going back over my life as a Jungian has been an emotional and exhausting ride. I watched my parents being marginalized for their complete devotion to Jung, yet growing up I never heard a single negative comment about him. Their idealization was at times difficult to take. I was the youngest and at that time was the only one of their five children who took to Jung's ideas, and then it was only through my relationship with my mother. She had a "witchy" understanding of my behavior, and she seemed to anticipate changes that were going to happen to me before they actually occurred. This represented a kind of closeness which was compelling but not entirely healthy, and I had to work many hours in analysis to separate myself from her. On the other hand, her uncanny intuition fascinated me and drew me to the world of the unconscious. Growing up I had great difficulty sympathizing with my father, and I was extremely critical of much of his behavior. It was only as a late adolescent that I began to respect and appreciate his deep scholarship. For the whole family, the move from Europe to the United States as the war raged around us placed a tremendous stress on everyone. My parents never adjusted to American life and always felt more comfortable in Europe. I was the one who was expected to make the adjustment to living in the United States, and for the most part I have done that. My parents encouraged my education and supported me financially until I was able to support myself and a family as a psychiatrist.

There was an enormous expectation placed upon me to follow in their footsteps as a Jungian analyst. It was clear to me that in order to do that I had to leave Los Angeles, yet leaving my family of origin was not easy. San Francisco was the ideal US location to receive that Jungian training. I began analysis with Joe Henderson when I was 26 and he was 59. Our relationship developed from an analytic one to a collegial one, and finally, as he aged, I began to take care of him. The analysis I had with him was the foundation for all my later work as a Jungian analyst.

When I qualified as an analyst in 1968 in San Francisco, the professional Jungian society there was mainly comprised of medical doctors, and they had a good relationship to the rest of the medical and psychiatric profession, which was strongly affiliated with the Freudian movement and psychoanalysis. Their professional persona relationship was very important for my own developing psychiatric and Jungian identity, having grown up in a community where there was little regard for the persona and men were often on the periphery of the Jungian scene. Realistically, there was not another location in the world where I could have formed the kind of relationships that I did both within the Jungian community and with the larger psychoanalytic and psychiatric communities.

I began my Jungian training in 1962 and completed it at the end of 1968, a most interesting time in the San Francisco Bay Area. First of all, the Jungian and psychoanalytic communities were friendly with one another. Only in London was there the kind of mutuality between Freudians and Jungians that existed in San Francisco. In most cities during this period, Jungians and Freudians generally did not speak to each other. On the other hand, it was a time when long-term depth psychotherapy and analysis was valued, and, as a result, Jungian analysts were in demand for that long-term depth work. Although at that time most people went into Freudian psychoanalysis, Jungians still had their share of patients. I was the first full-time Jungian analyst in Palo Alto, thirty miles from San Francisco and the home of Stanford University. Being the first analyst there seemed to satisfy my missionary spirit, and I found the challenge of having a Jungian practice in Palo Alto enough for me.

The sixties were also the time of the psychedelic and hippie revolution, and that brought a whole new wave of popularity for Jung. I was part of a workshop on dreams at the University of California, Berkeley, in 1968 where there were at least six hundred people in attendance, and the entire audience was full of enthusiasm. I was the youngest speaker on the program, and I cannot begin to describe how nervous I was doing my presentation. From the late 1960s through the 1970s, there were many programs at UC Berkeley and UC Santa Cruz that attracted large audiences. Jung was part of the psychedelic revolution that took root in the Bay Area and spread to the rest of the country and the world. The psychedelic approach was a fad that passed with time, but its popularity left Jung with a more solid status in the psychological world.

I found teaching and writing very fulfilling, and, before I knew it, I was receiving many local invitations to speak. In 1974, I was nominated to be president-elect of the C.G. Jung Institute of San Francisco, although I had only been a full-time member for six years and was still under forty years of age. Serving as president when all my elders were still active in the institute was a huge challenge. Sometimes it meant taking a stand against their positions, which was most difficult for me to do.

The presidency of the San Francisco Jung institute led me in turn into the larger political structure of the Jungian community, the International Association for Analytical Psychology, or IAAP. Jo Wheelwright promoted me to the international Jungian professional community, where I became vice president and then president of the IAAP, serving for the next eighteen years. Those were dramatic and exciting years for me and a period of enormous historical change. The highlight of my service in the IAAP was the fall of the Iron Curtain, the rise of Boris Yeltsin, the storming of the Russian White House, and then the fall of communism itself. Suddenly, interest in Jung emerged from Russia and all the former satellite countries of the Soviet Union.

As an officer of the IAAP, I traveled to many foreign places I never would have seen otherwise, and I found most of them fascinating. To go to these foreign places with a mission meant that I never went as a tourist but immediately got inside the culture. Along the way, I met many people, and some have become lifelong friends. I am thinking of Andrew Samuels, Murray Stein, Bob Hinshaw, and others. My visits to Europe gave me a chance to spend a lot of time in Zürich and the Alps; those times in the mountains are memories that I will cherish to my dying days. Although I enjoyed the time I spent in Zürich, I was rooted in the Bay Area, and though the thought of a professorship at the ETH in Zürich was appealing, I don't have any real regrets about not applying for it.

When the opportunity arose to go to Taiwan in 2006, I was most reluctant to accept the invitation. To me Taiwan, or Formosa as I remembered it from my youth, was a land that had lived under the dictatorship of Chiang Kai-shek, and I did not feel that system was something to be supported. How was I to know that I was going to fall in love with both the people and the place? For Jean and me, it was a shared delight. We had not expected what we found: a country that had become a thriving but imperfect democracy, and the experience of age-old Chinese wisdom, which has enriched us greatly.

In writing this memoir I realized that my life has intersected with the larger currents of history many times. The first was when we traveled across the North Atlantic at the height of the Battle of Britain, as Britain was holding on for dear life. This was a crucial event in the early part of World War II, when Britain stood alone against the Nazi onslaught. Had Britain fallen to the Nazis, it could have completely changed the outcome of the war and perhaps the face of Europe.

Second, when I first became a psychiatrist in Palo Alto, the San Francisco Bay Area was the center of the hippie and psychedelic revolution that eventually spread throughout the world. I was in the thick of the turmoil produced by these changes in the larger culture.

Third, I was scheduled to travel to the book fair in Moscow in 1991 to announce the translation of Jung's *Collected Works* into Russian when Boris Yeltsin overthrew the Communist regime of Mikhail Gorbachev. During the ensuing struggle, the Communists reclaimed power for a two-day period, during which they called off the Moscow Book Fair I was scheduled to attend. I was not sure if it still was important to go to Moscow, but eventually decided that I still needed to make the trip in order to sign the book contract. Unfortunately, with all the chaos of those early years, only one volume, volume fifteen, was ever translated. However, as events transpired, I ended up being in Moscow as Boris Yeltsin and the "Moscow White House" reclaimed power. It was a very intense and unforgettable experience.

Finally, in 1992, I was in South Africa during the election in which apartheid was voted out forever, and I was able to celebrate with the rest of the nation the death of that system. I feel very fortunate both to have witnessed these important nodal points in history and to have survived them.

Although I have enjoyed all my travels and the many interesting people I met during the course of them, I have been contented living in Palo Alto all these years. When Jean and I arrived here, Palo Alto was a rather sleepy university town, while now it is the center of Silicon Valley and a bustling metropolis. As a result, housing prices have become so high that we could no longer afford to buy a house here.

As I look back over my life as a Jungian, I feel blessed to have been one at this time. I had a definite connection to the first generation of Jungians, who were courageous in their support of Jung at a time when he was under attack from various sources. In those early years, however, the collective still valued long-term therapy, and many people sought Jungian analysis. Today more people want a quick fix that includes drug therapy. Over the course of my career, Jungian psychology has moved on to include post-Jungian thought, and the term *analytical psychology* now seems a more appropriate name for what still goes under the umbrella of Jungian thought. Today those who are drawn to Jung find many different Jungian viewpoints. Some follow the classical archetypal view, using amplification of dreams as the central foundation of their work; others are influenced by Jung's clinical formulations on transference and countertransference; others are interested in his views on the spiritual and transcendence; still others are interested in his work as it relates to modern neuroscience and basic science in general; yet others are drawn to Jung's work on national character and the psychology of nations. Jung's theories touch many areas of life, and no one sector can say that it represents the "true" followers of Jung.

Having been identified as a Jungian from an early age, I have witnessed dramatic changes in what that term has meant. From the perspective of my original family, it meant that they were marginalized and most often dismissed by the larger collective in Los Angeles. When I was in medical school, my interest in Jung was tolerated but not generally encouraged. At that time the only legitimate Jungian known to American psychiatry was Jo Wheelwright, whom I first met in 1959 at Yale when he was speaking there. My own interest in Jung was tolerated during my residency because I had shown the ability to do psychopharmacological research while I was in medical school. That could have led to an academic career in psychiatry, but the pull of my own psyche led me to a career as a Jungian analyst.

At first I was a kind of curiosity: a Jewish man who became a Jungian. In the worldview of the time, that was an oxymoron, because Jung was supposedly an anti-Semite and a Nazi. Throughout my Jungian career I have had to answer that charge, and my answers have evolved over the years as new information has become available. Jung's view of the Jewish psyche is subtle and nuanced, and that was the major reason why I wanted the correspondence between my father and Jung to be published. In it Jung speaks directly to similar questions raised by my father, and the reader can make his or her own decision about Jung's ideas on these questions.

As psychoanalysis evolved to include new theoretical models, such as object relations theory and relational theories that emphasized intersubjectivity, Jung became more palatable to students of psychoanalysis. That did not mean that Jung was read or accepted in most psychoanalytic circles, but it did mean that one could mention him and others might listen with respect without immediately dismissing him out of hand.

However, collective interest in psychoanalysis has waned. When I first entered my psychiatric residency, psychoanalysis was the predominant theory in psychiatry. All heads of institutional psychiatry departments were psychoanalysts. Today, not a single head of a psychiatry department is a psychoanalyst. As Freud has become a historical figure and psychoanalysis has evolved into something quite different from its historical roots, Jung has continued to be of interest to many people, and that interest has increased over time. The popularity of the ideas of Joseph Campbell and James Hillman are just one example of how Jung has exerted indirect influence. Over time terms like *complex*, *introvert/extravert*, and *individuation* have become part of our general language.

Despite this general interest in Jung's ideas, interest in depth psychology as a clinical profession has diminished, and the focus is chiefly on short-term fixes, including medications and behavioral therapy. Today Jung's message is viewed as a cultural critique rather than focusing on his clinical insights, but I think that will change again in time. I think that there is an ebb and flow to the psyche and that there will be a time when there is more interest in long-term analysis.

Relationships have been central to my life, and I have formed most of my deepest and most important relationships through my Jungian experience. Jean, my life partner of forty-six years, has been supportive of the path that I have taken and, while not always agreeing with my choices, she has been a steady trooper in my life. My two children are married, and both have terrific children of their own. Each has found meaningful work as well, and I could not ask more from them.

I have felt a real inner need to write up my Jungian life, and others who have heard some of the stories that are in this memoir have asked me to write them down so that they are not lost. My life has not been an easy one, but for the most part it has been extremely gratifying.

APPENDIX A

JOSEPH L. HENDERSON, M.D.

I came to San Francisco in 1962 with the specific intention of going into analysis with Joseph Henderson, M.D. Over the ensuing years he was by turns my analyst, my teacher, a professional colleague, and a close friend. Ultimately, he was the single most influential individual in my personal and Jungian development. Where I did my psychiatric residency was secondary in importance to my being able to begin analysis with him.

Prior to my work with Joe, my analysis had been piecemeal. As a student I had traveled back and forth from the West Coast to the East Coast and on the East Coast from New York to New Haven and to Boston. I came to the Bay Area with the idea that I would make it my home. Although I realized the probability that I would have to fulfill my military obligations in the US Public Health Service after my three-year residency, that eventuality seemed distant. Time passed quickly, though, and halfway through my residency I had to plan ahead. It was a challenge, but I arranged to change my military service assignment in order to stay in San Francisco.

I had been awarded a choice position with the National Institute of Mental Health in Bethesda, Maryland; no young male doctor turned down that plum! Many people thought I was crazy for trying to make the change. I actually had to fly to Washington, DC, to personally see the associate director of the National Institute of Mental Health, Stanley Yolles, to make the change. I spent less than two minutes with him, but he did engineer matters so that I could serve in the US Public Health Service and be stationed in San Francisco. Thus, I was able to continue my Jungian analysis and begin my Jungian training at the San Francisco institute, too.

This was a choice that set my life on a completely different course. Who knows what would have happened to my marriage had I returned to the East Coast at that time? Yet my analysis with Joe Henderson was extremely important to me. Joe's primary analysis had been with Jung, and given my family history, I definitely needed someone who had been directly influenced by Jung. The importance of that fact had been deeply ingrained in me by my parents, especially my mother. Henderson was probably the only person who would have been acceptable to my parents. Joe had known my parents in London and Zürich, but they had never been personal friends.

In spite of my eagerness to see Dr. Henderson, I felt a lot of resistance to begin this analysis. A month passed, and I had not called him, until I finally received a call from his secretary wondering if I still intended to see him. And so I began my twice-weekly analysis in the middle of July, 1962. Since my first wife and I had previously seen the same analyst, we persuaded Dr. Henderson to see both of us twice weekly. However, he made it very clear that he would like Marguerite to choose her own analyst. Nonetheless, we continued this arrangement for the next three years.

But I am getting ahead of myself; after one month of analysis, we received a call late on a Sunday evening notifying us that Dr. Henderson had some kind of heart problem and had been admitted to the hospital. The heart condition turned out to be minor, but I did not know that at the time. Finally, I had made a commitment to this analysis, and now my analyst was going to die on me! At the time Joe was nearly 60, and I was 26. Shortly after he was released from the hospital, he and his wife left for a long trip to Europe, and so we did not see him from the middle of August until the beginning of November, 1962—an eternity!

Looking back over fifty years, it is hard to recall the initial stages of analysis. Henderson was formal and reserved. He dressed in English suits, and he was neither personal nor outgoing. I brought him my dreams and gave my associations, and I recall that his interpretations were both personal and symbolic in nature. However, they seemed to hit the mark emotionally. I was extremely pleased with how I felt after each session and how I felt overall. In fact, I became inflated by the process of opening up to my unconscious under his aegis, and, as a consequence, I thought that all my fellow psychiatric residents also should have Jungian analysis. I became quite the proselytizer for Jung. Some residents did go into Jungian analysis, but I always steered them to other analysts because I wanted Dr. Henderson for myself. At the time the Jungian community was small, and I would meet Dr. Henderson at Analytical Psychology Club lectures and occasionally at other social events. I came to know his English wife Helena, a dancer, and I liked her very much. Sometime near the end of my residency Marguerite and I invited Dr. Henderson and his wife to our house for dinner. That was a huge occasion, and what I remember most affectionately was Dr. Henderson going to our piano and starting to play some of the pieces that I had studied as a child.

Another important connection with both Dr. Henderson and his wife Helena was Mary Crile, who lived in Big Sur. She had formerly lived in Pasadena, where she had befriended my parents. Later she had moved to a remote part of the Big Sur coast, where she had built an A-frame house on property abutting Pfeifer State Park. Marguerite and I visited Big Sur as often as possible. One of our visits coincided with a visit by the Hendersons, and we had a lovely lunch together with Mary Crile. I remember how exciting this was for me, because it really tweaked my transference. I was beginning to see how different the Hendersons' marriage was from that of my parents. They seemed to communicate with each other much more easily than my parents did. There seemed to be more affection between the two of them. Around that time I asked Dr. Henderson if I could call him by his first name "Joe." He said, "Of course, you can call me by any name that you feel like." So for a while he was still "Dr. Henderson" and other times he became "Joe." During those first three to five years of analysis, he remained formal in his manner. Even though he would sometimes include personal statements about himself, he did it in such a way that it did not seem very self-revealing.

By 1966, we had a two-year-old son. I had finished my psychiatric residency at Stanford and had gone on to work at the National Institute of Mental Health Regional Office in San Francisco as part of my military payback. Marguerite was doing a postdoctoral fellowship at Stanford. At this time Joe and Marguerite decided that it was time for her to see another analyst. She began with Elizabeth Osterman, who had originally trained as a microbiologist but had gone into medicine, eventually training as a psychiatrist. She was a senior Jungian analyst in San Francisco.

I did not realize it, but Marguerite had become very unhappy. She had been trying to "work through" her issues with Joe Henderson, who never revealed to me what was going on. This must have been very difficult for him.

For Christmas of 1966, Marguerite and I celebrated the holidays in Death Valley. She had been increasingly irritable, and I finally asked her what was going on. At first she was evasive, but finally she told me that her feelings toward me had changed and she felt that we should separate. I was completely decimated by this news. The symbolism of being in Death Valley was not lost on me, as I felt that I experienced this as my death. Very desperate, I called Joe from Death Valley on Christmas. He was responsive, supportive, and very encouraging. He did not mind my calling him, although I felt like a weak person for not being able to handle this catastrophic information on my own.

What happened over the next two years became the most significant part of my analysis. On the outer level Marguerite and I decided not to reveal publicly what was going on so that if we worked out things there would not be a lot of explaining to do. We both put on the persona of being together. Meanwhile, I moved to San Francisco for a while, and then back to Palo Alto in a separate apartment, where I opened a private practice in Menlo Park on

July 1, 1967. I was depressed and the structure of my life had completely broken apart. My marriage was a failure, and failure was not something that I was used to. During this period of being alone I was able to break off my dependency on my parents, mainly my mother. I spent many hours alone with my thoughts, dreams, and fantasies, which led me into profound early memories, as well as deeply spiritual moments. I questioned everything that had happened in my life up to that moment, including my being a psychiatrist, a Jungian, a father, a husband, and a son. All I can say is that it was a profound death and rebirth experience, initiatory in nature, and without Joe's presence, I wonder what would have happened to me. He made himself available as much as possible, and I cannot remember another time in my life that I have felt so vulnerable. After a year and a half of argument, Marguerite and I decided to go on with our separate lives, since we were not working out things in our marriage, and we made the separation public. As sad as that made me feel, I simultaneously felt an incredible relief from the awful pressure cooker of indecision. I wanted to socialize again, begin new relationships with women, and get on with my life. My private practice had started well, and I was eager to finish my Jungian training.

Very soon after the final separation from Marguerite, I met Jean, who was to become my second wife. We have been married for over forty-six years now. At the time I knew it was too soon to begin another serious relationship, but I followed my dreams with Joe. My unconscious was responding well to the new relationship, and Joe saw that it was good for me. There was also the issue of reconnecting to my parents, with whom I had not said much except to say that I was alive and kicking. With the breakup of my marriage, my unconscious tie to my mother was also broken. That tie had to break for my own maturation and growth.

One way that expressed itself was in my allegiance to sports teams. I left my allegiance to the Los Angeles Dodgers and Sandy Koufax, the greatest left-handed pitcher ever in the history of baseball, and became a devoted San Francisco Giants fan. Joe had been blind in one eye from age three months and had never been interested in sports, since depth perception is essential for any sport. However, he had a keen and highly developed inner eye, which I needed desperately for my own inner growth.

My analysis continued as my life evolved after the breakup of my first marriage. By now Joe was working only three weeks a month, taking off the fourth week for writing or free time. I was seeing him three times a month, which sometimes felt insufficient. I still suffered strong dependency issues, which had been transferred from my mother to Joe. Other issues included my coming to the completion of my Jungian training and working out the many differences in my relationship with Jean. Jean was extremely introverted and not Jewish, which was not a problem for me or for my father, but it was to my mother. Joe told me that I had tried the traditional Jewish marriage, and it had not worked, so having another Jewish woman in my life was not essential. Perhaps marrying Jean was another part of breaking my tie with my mother.

In May of 1968, Jean and I were married by a liberal rabbi in the backyard of the house where Jean had a studio apartment. He had not required Jean to convert to Judaism, and she never has. It was a small wedding of less than forty people, but it included Joe and Helena and both of our families. In October of that year, I took my final exam to become a Jungian analyst. I presented a case to three Los Angeles Jungians, who I knew very well, and three San Francisco analysts. At the time, Joe was serving on the certifying committee, and we discussed whether he should be there. I wanted him to be there, and he wanted to be there. His presence at the exam was just fine as he was silent during the exam, although the others certainly put me through my paces.

My analysis continued until the autumn of 1973. At that time I had a dream in which Joe came to "my" house—not a house I had ever lived in but some symbolic house—and observed what was going on. Joe interpreted this to mean that I had integrated the inner Joe and that the dependent phase of my analysis was finished. He suggested a rather quick termination, which lasted only another two or three sessions at the most. It all happened very quickly. It was an interesting time in my life in that Jean and I were having real problems in our marriage, and I was going to have to handle it on my own without my analyst and also, of course, without my parents. It had some similarities to the breakup of my first marriage, but on the other hand it had a very different feel. The door was left open for me to see Joe whenever I felt the deep need, and I did see him two or three times during the next year and a half while Jean and I worked out our difficulties. Then over the next several years I only saw Joe in professional or social situations.

The next important encounter with Joe occurred in 1977. Sue and George Wagner were interviewing people who had known Jung to examine the influence that Jung had had on their lives and to provide an impression of their experience with him. Joe Henderson was a prime candidate for their film project. I am not sure how I became Joe's interviewer, but the interview occurred in the backyard of his home in Ross, California, and it is a part of the *Matter of Heart* archive. Parts of the interview are in the DVD that the Wagners ultimately released, which contains bits of all the interviews. I felt I drew Joe out on a number of important topics like initiation, his views on Native Americans, Jungian analysis, and what I saw as a more objective view of Jung than many others, who were still caught in a complete idealization of him.

In 1977, I was elected second vice president of the IAAP, my first office in the organization. I was beginning to be pulled into the international Jungian arena, and I was feeling the urge to have someone to talk to. At first I thought it would be better to see a woman, and so I contacted Elizabeth Osterman since I had seen her a few times during the breakup of my first marriage. I called her, and she said that she could not see me. She came all the way to Palo Alto to have lunch with me and let me know her decision. At first I was disappointed, but then I thought I could call Joe and see him again. I did, and we began a different kind of analysis. We still discussed many dreams, but I described to Joe what was going on in the international scene among the Jungians. Joe had always had strong international connections, and my discussion of these issues was of great interest to him. For the next twenty-five years, Joe and I continued to see each other at least two times a month. Our relationship evolved over the years into one of a younger colleague speaking with an older colleague. Joe continued to charge me a nominal fee. The decision to resume seeing Joe was one of the best of my life. Simply being in Joe's presence grounded me. The work of the IAAP can lead one many places, both psychologically and globally, and one can feel scattered and groundless. During the first term of my presidency, the Eastern Bloc and the Soviet Union opened up to the West. Groups in Moscow and Leningrad wanted me to be there for several important functions. Being there when the Soviet empire was disintegrating was extremely intoxicating. I had a dream that I was hanging on to the tail of the plane, commuting between San Francisco and Moscow! We discussed this dream in terms of my thinking of the trip between San Francisco and Moscow as a flight between San Francisco and Los Angeles. The dream made me realize how I was taking my travels too lightly. I was not realizing what an effect it had on me to make such a long trip so often. In effect I cut down on my long-distance travel after that dream.

As our relationship developed into a friendship, we did more social events together. Occasionally we went to the San Francisco symphony or opera, and sometimes we would go out for dinner together. Especially after Joe's wife Helena died in the early 1990s, we did more social things together.

As Joe aged, he needed some help when traveling by air. We made three memorable trips together. The first one was to London at the time of the first Iraq war. Joe was asked to give a memorial lecture for the four London groups. I arranged the flights and hotel, etc. I remember our arriving at the Durrants Hotel just north of Oxford Street. Opposite the hotel was a small museum containing the Wallace Collection. Joe had been there on his first trip to Europe with his aunt when he was seventeen years old. On this trip he was eighty-nine years old, and he could remember the collection very well. We also saw Chekhov's *Three Sisters* with Vanessa, Lynn, and Jemma Redgrave. Joe was thrilled to see that performance. It was a truly memorable week for both of us.

Michael Fordham came to Joe's lecture, and we had dinner together along with Rosemary Gordon. Michael and Joe knew each other from the mid-1930s, and they were good colleagues. On this occasion he was extremely provocative toward Joe, the sort of behavior that had earned Michael the reputation of being an *enfant terrible*.

In the spring of 1995, Jean and I traveled with Joe to participate in a conference in New York put on by the New York Jung institute. One evening we had dinner in the café of the Ritz, which Joe thoroughly enjoyed, and then we heard the Guarneri Quartet at the Metropolitan Museum of Art. The first violinist, Arnold Steinhardt, was a friend of mine from high school, and he had arranged for the tickets. We came back to the hotel, and Joe thought that we needed a nightcap. So while Jean and I had drinks, Joe downed two cups of double cappuccino. He said that it would make him sleep better!

We were seated near him on both legs of the flights. What was amazing to see was that Joe just sat in his seat, not reading, not moving, and not disturbed by any of the movement going on around him. Meanwhile I either had to be reading, talking, or watching a movie. It was a real eye-opener to see how Joe grounded himself amid the excitement of the flight.

My third trip with Joe was to Eugene, Oregon, to visit with Robin Jaqua, who with her husband John had a large working farm or ranch along the McKenzie River, which flows through Eugene. John Jaqua had been the lawyer for Phil Knight when Nike shoes had been formed, and Robin told the story of how the first Nike shoe was built on the Jaquas' kitchen table.

One of the Jaquas' sons was a filmmaker, and Robin wanted to interview Joe and also wanted him to speak about the archetype of initiation for national ARAS, The Archive for Research in Archetypal Symbolism. She had asked me to do the interview. I liked the Jaquas very much, and staying with them was very pleasant.

Joe Henderson's One Hundredth Birthday

Joe continued to practice three weeks a month, and I continued to see him at his San Francisco office. However, he was becoming increasingly hard of hearing, and he finally had to stop driving. This meant that everyone who was seeing him had to travel to his home in Ross. For me that added half an hour to the trip, and it was exhausting. I cut down on the frequency, but it was still very worthwhile psychologically for me to continue to see him. Joe continued to see patients and supervisees and to write papers. In 2003, he was to have his one hundredth birthday, and a committee was formed to figure out what we would do to celebrate. I was the head of this committee. We finally decided to have a Sunday afternoon party at the Marin Art and Garden Center, a venue very close to his home in Ross. We decided to charge a small attendance fee to cover the expenses, and we also included a line on the invitation for contributions in Joe's honor. The party was very successful, and there were many speeches. Joe's grandchildren spoke as well as some members of the institute. We raised about ten thousand dollars in donations, and the committee made the decision to put out a new edition of Joe's book *Thresholds of Initiation*, which had been out of print for several years. This was Joe's seminal clinical work, and it had first been published in 1966. Murray Stein and Chiron Publishing in Chicago agreed to republish the work. This was a most satisfying way to use the money, and Joe was very pleased with the result.

The next year the extended education committee of the institute decided to have a conference on initiation in honor of Joe's work in that field. Speakers included Dyane Sherwood, Tom Singer, David Tresan, Virginia Rutter, and Murray Stein. I was the moderator for the daylong conference. Joe attended and sat in the front row taking in all of the papers.

In 2003, twenty-six years after the first interview for the *Matter of Heart* series, Suzanne and George Wagner decided to have a follow-up interview with Joe, and they asked me if I would again interview him. Joe was in amazingly good form, and we did a two-hour follow-up interview in which he talked about the current state of the world and of Jungian psychology. Suzanne also did a second follow-up interview.

Final Years

When Joe was 102½ years old, he developed a case of pneumonia and was hospitalized. It was touch-and-go whether he would make it. He had some important initiatory dreams while in the hospital, which he told Jean and me about when we went to visit him. I think 99 percent of people would have died at this point, but Joe recovered physically. However, he was not the same mentally. He began to have vivid waking fantasies. For instance, once he said that he had been to China the previous night, and another time spoke of having just attended a meeting in Carmel. It was clear to his friends and colleagues that he was no longer able to do analytical work. The well-being committee of the institute came to him to advise him not to practice. He took it with equanimity, yet people continued to have "visits" with him, but it was no longer called analysis or supervision. Joe had a steady stream of visitors who have many fond memories of these months. One still saw the essential Joe underneath all the fantasies.

During this final stage of life, Joe was cared for by a Filipino woman named Lita, who became completely devoted to him. She somehow understood Joe's very special nature and realized that he was truly a "wise man." Soon, Joe could no longer walk and required a wheelchair. Earlier, when Joe no longer could drive, he had hired a retiree named Kenny, who drove Joe around to different places. Joe and Kenny had a wonderful relationship, and when Joe died, I continued to have contact with Kenny, who really missed Joe after his death.

As Joe's health failed, the question of whether to take Joe to the hospital arose. Finally in November, 2007, when Joe was 104½, he was taken to the hospital, where he died on November 17, 2007. Joe's grandson-in-law was there, as were David Tresan and myself, as well as Lita and Kenny. Joe had signed up for the Neptune Society, and so his body was taken to Oakland, where all the final arrangements were made. Tom Singer and Lita took care of that lugubrious task. The following spring, a memorial service was held for Joe at his house, where we all paid our last respects.

A decision had to be made about the house the Hendersons had lived in since 1956. The house itself was not in good shape, but the grounds were absolutely beautiful. Joe's grandson-in-law decided to make it ready as a rental to neighbors who were building a new house next door. So on one weekend he invited me to go into Joe's pavilion, which he had made thirty years before, and go through all his books and letters. This was a very difficult task, and I am sure that I made some mistakes in the choices. However, it had to be done that weekend, and I had done something similar with my father's papers as well, although with my father I had had more time. Joe, on the other hand, had not kept as much material as my father had. Joe had tended to throw away letters after he answered them. That was why he had not known that his correspondence with Jung was available in Zürich. As I have mentioned earlier, he loved going through the correspondence again, and it perked him up for many months. I have what is left of Joe's papers in two boxes in my office at home. I have not wanted to go through all the personal papers. I do not want to find out anything that I don't already know. The papers and books should go to the C.G. Jung Institute of San Francisco for their archives.

What I have described is my own relationship to Joseph L. Henderson from 1962 until his death in 2007. He had a remarkable life, which I have not fully chronicled here, and he knew many famous people in various fields, many of them patients of his. I have tried to describe what this man meant to me, and how he helped to transform my life. I know that he did this for many people in our Jungian community and beyond. What I have attempted to portray is my own experience with Joe over a forty-seven-year period and how the relationship changed over time. No wonder I resisted beginning analysis in 1962! I had no idea what an impact this relationship would have on my life. What an amazing person, and what an amazing life!

APPENDIX B

JAMES HILLMAN, PH.D.

Jim Hillman was one of the first people that I met on my own without being introduced through my parents. Of course Jim knew my parents, and at the time that I first met him, he was still a student at the C.G. Jung Institute in Zürich. He had a tremendous reputation as a brilliant student, and he was obtaining a PhD in psychology at the University of Zürich at the same time as he was getting his Jungian training. His thesis topic, "Emotion," was considered brilliant, and it was to be published in both German and English, which in those days was considered remarkable. The year was 1958, and I had returned to Zürich for a second summer of analysis to try to deal with a love relationship which was tying me into knots. It so happened that both Jim and I were seeing the same analyst, Professor C.A. Meier. Jim, along with Bob Stein and Marvin Spiegelman, played tennis regularly during the summer months, and they were looking for a fourth. At that time I was a dedicated tennis player, and so I made a suitable fourth for doubles. Jim and I partnered against Bob and Marvin, and we played fairly regularly over the course of the summer. Jim and I always won, but a good time was had by all. The three of them were about a decade older than me, and I was called "kid Kirsch." Afterward we would go and have a drink and start talking about the Jung Institute and the various people involved with it. It was a rich opportunity to hear about their experiences as students at the C.G. Jung Institute. I had my first taste of Jungians who did not completely idealize Jung as all those people around my parents did at the time.

My next encounter with Jim was in the fall of 1963. By now I was a psychiatric resident at Stanford, and I had begun my analysis with Joe Henderson in San Francisco. I had heard that Jim and Adolf Guggenbühl-Craig were making a cross-country tour of the United States, speaking at various Jungian centers. At that time San Francisco was not on their map, but I wrote to Jim and suggested that I could arrange for him to speak at the Palo Alto Veterans

Affairs hospital at their grand rounds, and he could also speak at the Analytical Psychology Club in San Francisco. He accepted those invitations as well as another one from Jim Whitney in Berkeley.

His lecture on the subject of emotion was outstanding, and he very clearly outlined his thesis on the importance of emotion to these hospital psychiatrists, who for the most part had very little connection to either Freud's or Jung's concept of the unconscious. That lecture was a rousing success. His lecture for the Analytical Psychology Club in San Francisco was equally riveting. His subject was "Hope, Growth, and the Analytical Process." In this passionate lecture, Jim lowered the expectations of what one could expect from analysis. At that time in the minds of many Jungians, analysis could cure the problems of the world. Jim persuasively counteracted that notion of Jungian analysis while at the same time emphasizing what the value could be. This lecture to the Analytical Psychology Club became part of his book, *Suicide and the Soul*. It was the first time I'd seriously grappled with the limits of analysis.

When the book *Suicide and the Soul* came out in 1966, I was gripped by it, and a review of that book became my first public lecture in Los Angeles to the Analytical Psychology Club. In the book Jim carves out a unique position for psychology in terms of suicide. He states that the archetype of death and rebirth is at the core of suicidal ideation, and that we as Jungians have a unique perspective on the topic of suicide. Little did I know at the time that I was shortly to experience my own death and rebirth experience, which would result in a divorce as well as a psychological separation from my parents. During that tumultuous time, Jim's voice was with me constantly.

In the fall of 1967, I had just begun my private practice in Palo Alto, and I was an advanced candidate at the Jung institute in San Francisco. I received a call from a woman at San Francisco State University who was putting on a large conference on suicide. She wanted to have Jim Hillman as a keynote speaker, and she wanted to know how to get in contact with him. The connection was made, and he agreed to be a major speaker at the conference.

By this time Jim had become director of studies at the Jung Institute in Zürich. However, he had gotten into difficulties by having an affair with an American woman who was a student there, and he had written her a letter that had been intercepted by her husband. The husband was determined to bring Jim up before the American Psychological Association as well as the Swiss Psychological Association. It was a very tense situation in Zürich. What to do? At the time there were patrons from each of the major institutes who were driving the ultimate decision on how to handle this situation. My father was one of those patrons, as was C.A. Meier, who had been Jim's analyst. This situation had been brewing for two or three years, but by the time of the suicide conference, it had surfaced, and the small international Jungian group was in conflict about how to resolve it. Many different solutions were suggested to Jim, and he finally decided to resign his position as director of studies at the institute. I was extremely sympathetic toward Jim, because I knew that most of the patrons who were being so critical had been involved in sexual acting out themselves, and they had never been reprimanded or forced to resign any position because of their behavior. I attempted to make clear to Jim that I was fully supportive of him and that I found the behavior of the patrons remarkably duplicitous. However, I don't believe that I really convinced him of my position.

The 1967 conference on suicide at San Francisco State University was a huge success, and Jim gave an excellent paper. I cannot remember the exact content of the paper, but I am sure that it was connected with his book, *Suicide and the Soul.*

My next interaction with Jim came at my first official attendance at an IAAP congress in August, 1971, in London. Jo Wheelwright, who was then president of the IAAP, made me a delegate from San Francisco, much to the consternation of some older members of our group. I had no idea what it meant to be a delegate. I attended the delegates' meeting, and without my knowledge, Jim Hillman and Jo Wheelwright nominated me for second vice president. I ended up losing by one vote to Hannes Dieckmann. There was some question about the correctness of the voting, but the vote was never challenged. At the time I was relieved not to be elected. I was really too young to become a vice president of the IAAP. But having had my name put into nomination did make me a front-runner the next time that a vice presidential position would open up, which was in 1977.

My next interaction with Jim was at the 1977 international congress in Rome. We may have met in between somewhere, but if so, it was not a significant meeting. In 1977 both of us were invited as major speakers for this conference. My speech was to be on dreams and Jim's on alchemy. All of the speakers were invited to a round of parties at various Roman Jungian analysts' houses, which was quite exciting. At this congress there were to be significant elections, as the pattern up to that time had been that each president served two terms. The delegate meeting was governed by Swiss law, which meant that the nomination for each office did not require a second on the nomination. In those days the only contested election was who was to become the second vice president, because once one was elected, the ascendancy to the next rung of the ladder was the rule, although it was not guaranteed. However, no one had been knocked off the ladder once they were on the bottom rung. Jo Wheelwright nominated me for the second vice president position, mentioning that I had been president of the San Francisco Jung institute and that I had done a good job there. Much to my surprise and amazement, C.A. Meier got up and seconded my nomination. Others were nominated, but I won the election without a runoff. Later that evening at the banquet ending the congress, Jim came up to me, and he was furious. He asked, "How could you let Meier nominate you for the second vice president position?" He was angry that I was even on speaking terms with Meier. I knew the story between Jim and Meier, a very complicated account that is detailed in Dick Russell's biography of Jim. Both Jim and his wife Kate were in analysis with Meier at the same time, and they also traveled to Greece together. There were indiscretions in the analytical relationships, which Russell describes in his biography. Having heard the story, I was totally sympathetic with Jim for not remaining friends with him. However, in seconding my nomination in 1977, Meier had been extremely generous to me, and he had done nothing personally at that time to warrant my breaking off a relationship with him, although later he did tax our relationship.

During that election in 1977, Adolf Guggenbühl-Craig had been elected president, and he had chosen his longtime friend Jim to be his honorary secretary. This meant that Jim and I were going to be working closely together for the next three years at executive committee meetings and preparing the next congress, which for the first time was to be held in the United States and in San Francisco. Although I was the youngest and newest member of the presidential committee, I was going to be very busy helping to organize the congress for September, 1980. I cannot remember how Jim and I made peace around that incident with Meier, but I do remember Jim, along with Adolf and Hannes, coming to San Francisco in order to prepare for the congress. We all went to the kabuki baths, and Jim, Adolf, and Hannes came to our house for a meal. I have discussed the congress at another place, so I won't go into any detail about it here. There were no other flare-ups between Jim and me in the preparation for that congress. For Adolf's second term he chose Niel Micklem, and Jim and I did not see each other for a while.

By this time Jim had moved back to the United States, and he was living in Dallas, Texas. He had taken over the publication of the Jungian journal, *Spring*, and he had requested a San Francisco Jungian representative on the editorial committee. Since I had had a lot of contact with Jim over the years, our institute appointed me as the San Francisco representative to the editorial board of Spring Publications. I soon found out that this was a position in name only. I attempted to put forward a paper of a good friend of mine, and Jim wrote me a note stating that he alone decided what got published in *Spring*, and that he was not going to publish the paper that I had forwarded to him. Within a few years of this episode, Jim decided that he no longer needed a San Francisco representative, and my name was taken off the masthead.

Living in Texas, he became a popular speaker at our San Francisco institute public programs. He would always attract a large crowd, and so he came frequently. When Jim was in town for the seminars, we rarely found time to see each other on a personal basis. On one occasion we were both asked to speak at the annual American Academy of Psychoanalysis meeting in San Francisco. I gave a small talk on several clinical examples of women who had gotten divorces after more than twenty-five years of marriage. It basically was presenting four clinical examples, and Jim came to the presentation to support me. Afterwards we had lunch at O'Doul's, a San Francisco baseball hangout. Jim and I always had a connection around sports, beginning with our playing doubles together in tennis, but Jim was really a sports fan in a more general way. We had a nice low-key human connection.

The next significant meeting was in 1985 in Boston at the time of the national Jungian conference. The conference was around Halloween, and again, both Jim and I were speakers. At the banquet, which was a costume party, Jim dressed up as a preacher. I dressed up as a Viking. Jim came over to the table where I was sitting along with the Zabriskies and some other people whose names I cannot remember, and he said that this was the "power table." I found it very curious, because fourteen years before he had nominated me to a vice presidential position in the IAAP, and at that time he had been very interested in the power and political structure of the IAAP. However, those were the years when he was moving away from the collective Jungian group and forming his own school of psychology called *archetypal psychology*, and during this time he was critical of the official Jungian line.

Between 1983 and 1995, I made frequent trips to Zürich, always staying with the Guggenbühls at their house. I probably saw Jim at an average of once every year and a half during this time, and he was always very cordial to me, but we never got into any really meaningful discussions. We both attended Adolf's seventieth and eightieth birthday parties at Adolf's old guild in the heart of Zürich. At each of these, Jim gave a wonderful speech about his longtime friendship with Adolf. One saw the deep connection between these two men. Jim gave a lot of credit to Adolf's ideas, which was good to hear, because many people thought that Adolf just mimicked Jim's ideas. I knew this was not true, because I had many deep conversations with Adolf over the same years. When Adolf had his eightieth birthday, Jim came with Margot, and we were both there early before others arrived. Jim did what he had been known to do, and he just walked right past Jean and me, barely introducing Margot to the two of us. Many of Jim's friends and acquaintances have had a similar experience. The fact that we were almost the only ones in the room at the time made this more painful.

By this time Jim had moved to Thompson, Connecticut, and was living there with Margot, a very fine artist. Together they wrote a book on animal symbolism, and they did a book tour across the United States which included a stop in Palo Alto. My dear friend Neil Russack was also writing a book on animal symbolism and wanted to meet with Jim. I did not try to mediate a visit between the two of them, but Neil on his own came down to the reading in Palo Alto. Afterwards we went up to Jim, and Neil asked if he had any time to speak. Jim was fairly abrupt in saying that there just was no time and his schedule was too booked in San Francisco. Neil was disappointed, but Jim's response seemed appropriate to the circumstances.

Between 1996 and 1999, I was writing my book *The Jungians*, which was a personal history of the Jungian movement. I was interviewing many people for the book, and I tried on numerous occasions, both through faxes and phone calls, to contact Jim. He had been in Zürich from the early 1950s on, he had attended the first congress in Zürich in 1958, and he had a wonderful memory for these events. My last attempt was a phone call to Jim where Margot answered the telephone and said that he was sleeping. She said that he would call back in one or two hours. He did not call back in one or two hours, and I only heard from him when his friend Marvin Spiegelman was angry about my portrait of Marvin in the book. Jim wrote in support of Marvin, and I wrote back to Jim, saying that I had tried on many occasions to contact him without luck. Jim was slightly apologetic and realized that he had not taken my attempts to contact him seriously. I think he sensed that this was the first attempt at a history of the Jungian movement, and that people were reading my book.

In October, 2009, Beverley Zabriskie had a wonderful party at her apartment in New York to celebrate the publication of *The Red Book*. Jim and Margot were there, and Jim was as friendly to me as he had been back in 1958 when we were tennis partners. He introduced Margot to me very warmly and said how we had a long and complicated relationship. It felt good to experience the friendship from him which had not been there for many decades. I think he was trying to repair his relationship with me because, although there were some psychological and philosophical differences, we really had a long and continuous friendship.

In 2010, the Library of Congress was showing *The Red Book*, and in conjunction with that they had a one-day conference. Jim and I were both speakers in that conference, and so we had a chance to talk. He had fallen and broken his elbow as well as a bone in his foot, and he was essentially immobile. I arrived on the East Coast a few days before the conference at the Library of Congress, and I was hoping that I could go up to Thompson to see him. With his broken bones and failing health, it did not work out. I was disappointed, but I could understand his situation.

The Library of Congress conference was really the last time that I had any significant interaction with Jim. For a long time in our relationship I would have liked to have had a closer connection with him. However, after those first few years in Zürich, it was not to be. He was always very pleasant to my wife Jean, and they had many interesting conversations together. I did not have many dreams with Jim in them, but in the couple of dreams in which he did appear, the feeling toward him was always extremely positive. I remember in one dream I said that I loved him, which was a big surprise to me. But I did love Jim, and in retrospect I see how hard it was for him to show a similar response in himself.

APPENDIX C

ADOLF GUGGENBÜHL-CRAIG, M.D.

Adolf Guggenbühl-Craig came from an old and established Swiss family with roots going back to the Engadine in the eighteenth century. By the time of the twentieth century, Adolf's family had moved to the cities of Switzerland, including Zürich and Berne. His father was a well-known editor of a conservative weekly magazine. Adolf was born in 1923 and had tuberculosis as a child. He spent several years in a sanatorium as described in Thomas Mann's *The Magic Mountain*. Adolf's father was an ardent anti-Nazi prior to World War II, which he expressed forcefully in his weekly magazine. Adolf remembered his father receiving death threats for his views on Germany.

Adolf became a doctor and married Anne Craig, a young Scottish woman he met in a camp when they were both young. Adolf did his psychiatric residency in Omaha, Nebraska, and they were torn about whether to remain in the United States or return to Switzerland. Adolf had picked Omaha because it was exactly in the middle of the country, and that is where he wanted to be. They ended up returning to Switzerland, where Adolf, who had a strong interest in religion, went into Jungian analysis and a Jungian training. He also met Jim Hillman during their time as students at the Jung Institute in Zürich, and they remained lifelong friends. Adolf quickly rose to become president of the Jung Institute in Zürich and an officer in the IAAP. I first met Adolf when he and Jim Hillman made a lecture tour across the United States in 1963. He did not make much of an impression upon me at that time. The next time I met him was in 1974 at the second IAAP congress in London, during a banquet where the food ran out before everyone was fed, and we commiserated together. Our first real meeting was in 1977, after he had been elected as president of the IAAP and I had been elected second vice president. We had an IAAP executive committee meeting in December, 1977, and Adolf invited me to stay at their house in Pfaffhausen, a suburb of Zürich. I remember hiking to their house in snow and ice, and wondering why I was doing this. I could have stayed at a comfortable hotel in town and avoided all this walking in the snow! However, once I arrived at their house, I could not have been treated more graciously and openly. From that time on through the next twenty-five to thirty years, my wife, my daughter, and I stayed there in their separate downstairs at least one time per year. They also had a family-owned, traditionally styled house in the Engadine, where we vacationed with them many a summer. The Guggenbühls had five children, and every Wednesday all the grandchildren would descend on the Guggenbühl residence, so that eventually all thirteen grandchildren grew up knowing each other. I experienced many of these Wednesdays, and, in spite of the chaos, it was a magical kind of experience. I felt that I became a part of the larger family, a sense which has continued to this day. We recently had one of the Guggenbühl grandsons, now in his mid-twenties, and some of his friends visiting us here in Palo Alto.

One of the Guggenbühl sons, Alastair, stayed with us in Palo Alto for a wonderful week in 1980. We have kept in contact with Alastair all these years, and I went to Istanbul for Alastair's wedding to Yoncia in 1995. That was a memorable occasion when a planeload of Swiss all descended on Istanbul for a magnificent three-day celebration of Alastair and Yoncia's wedding. I felt very honored to be invited because I was the only other Jungian analyst in attendance.

Adolf was a remarkably practical and wise leader and analyst. Almost everyone in the local Swiss and international Jungian community went to Adolf for advice. He became my most trusted mentor and advisor during my six years as president of the IAAP. I would use the occasion of the frequent visits to Zürich to talk about the various issues involved in the IAAP. In retrospect I probably relied on him too much, because in hindsight some of the decisions which he helped me with did not turn out as well as they could have. As I have mentioned elsewhere, I found dealing with Hannes Dieckmann particularly difficult. Adolf tended to be much more lenient with him, and I wonder if some of that did not have to do with the fact that Adolf had had a series of heart attacks during his presidency, and Hannes had filled in admirably. I think Adolf was overly grateful for what Hannes had done in his stead. It must have been a big disappointment to Adolf for his presidency of the IAAP to have been interrupted by his heart attacks and finally end with an emergency, seven-artery bypass just prior to his last congress as president in 1983. I visited him on the way to that 1983 Jerusalem congress, and seeing him shortly after his bypass surgery, I did not think that he would ever recover. How delightfully wrong I was! Recover he did, and he lived with that bypass operation for twenty-three more years!

Adolf was a man of great integrity and loyalty. He was completely devoted to his family and his friends. I felt honored to be part of his circle of friends, and both on the professional and personal side I felt a deep connection. I am so glad that my wife and I have continued to be friends with the next generation of Guggenbühls.

I have often wondered what made for this deep connection between us. I do believe that it was mutual. Adolf and I were pragmatic people, and when there were problems to solve, we both thought of practical solutions. Adolf was much more the psychiatrist than I was. As soon as it was financially possible, I attempted to limit my practice to psychotherapy and analysis, whereas Adolf loved the psychiatric part of his practice, evaluating cases for the courts of Zürich and being a psychiatric consultant. I did as little of that as possible. Although Adolf was very well-known in the Jungian community, he did not immediately identify himself as a Jungian in the larger world. It was not that he hid this part of his identity, but he did not talk about Jungian things outside of Jungian circles. On the other hand, he was deeply concerned about Jungian ideas and the Jungian organization both in Zürich and elsewhere. We certainly connected in our discussions about the international level of the Jungian world, and we were very much in agreement most of the time. I was much more interested in the transference relationship than he was, but I was not close to the developmental school emphasis on transference or on frequency of sessions. Adolf did not write much, but what he did write was basic and essential. His book *Power in the Healing Professions* I consider one of the fundamental books for any psychotherapist.

I saw Adolf for the last time just three weeks before he died. Adolf tended to be a pessimistic person, but at that time he was really morose. It was sad to see him that way, but I have so many wonderful memories of him in different situations and places. We shared so much. I loved his wife Anne and being a part of the larger clan.

APPENDIX D

JOSEPH B. WHEELWRIGHT, M.D.

Jo Wheelwright was a name that I had already heard as a child growing up in Los Angeles. Jo was the only extravert of that first generation of Jungian analysts, and to many, that made him not a "true" Jungian. Also, he hobnobbed with Freudian psychoanalysts at a time when the relations between Freudians and Jungians were frigid. That fact also made Jo suspect among Jungians. In terms of my own family, Jo had not seen my half-brother, Jim Silber, in analysis when Jim was in psychiatric residency in the Bay Area. Jo could not see Jim in analysis because he was being treated for tuberculosis at the time, but my mother was very unhappy about that. She thought that Jo should have done more.

There was also a complicated family connection between my cousin Gerhard Danelius and the twin brother of Jo's wife, Jane. Neila, who married Gerhard in 1952, had been married to Clint, Jane's twin brother. It had been a messy divorce, and so the Wheelwrights' name in our household had mixed meanings. Jo and my father had known each other in London in the late 1930s when my father was already a practicing Jungian analyst and Jo was a struggling medical student. They had both been members of the Analytical Psychology Club in London. Their positions in the United States and California were completely reversed, with Jo being a professor at the Langley Porter psychiatric clinic in San Francisco, and my father struggling to get licensed in any way as a psychotherapist.

Jo was a member of the prestigious Group for the Advancement of Psychiatry, known as GAP. At the time the membership of GAP was made up of the most famous psychiatrists and psychoanalysts in the United States. Jo, because of his long association with Freudians, had been made a member of this auspicious group. Jo was involved at the University of California Student Health Service, and he became a part of the team that wrote up *Sex and the College*

Student, a monograph which became very popular in the 1960s. As a member of GAP, he lectured all over the country to departments of psychiatry. At the time he was the only Jungian who lectured in departments of psychiatry in the whole United States. That gives one the impression just how marginal Jung was in American psychiatry and psychology at the time. In the spring of 1959, he came to Yale University to speak to the student health service. Somehow I was notified about his visit, and I arranged to have a private meeting with him. During that meeting Jo strongly urged me to come to San Francisco for my Jungian analysis and analytic training. So from that time on until July, 1962, everything I did was to make sure that I ended up in San Francisco. He did not advise me to go into analysis with him, but rather with Joe Henderson. That was one of the two or three most crucial and best decisions I ever made in my life.

Joe Henderson and Jo Wheelwright practiced in the same building at 2206 Steiner Street, and the training seminars were also held there in a back room. This was the first center of everything Jungian in San Francisco. I would see Jo Wheelwright on many occasions when I would go up the stairs to see Joe Henderson. As an extravert, he would talk to me about all kinds of things that were going on in the international Jungian community, as he was involved in the IAAP. He had not yet been elected to the presidency. We liked each other.

I became a candidate at the institute in 1963. I was going through the training smoothly, but then I had an interview with Jo, who was on the certifying committee, and he suggested that I take off a year of training. The reasoning of the committee was that I was too young, and that I needed more clinical experience in seeing patients before I became an analyst. I protested that I had quite a bit of clinical experience, and that I was ready to become a Jungian analyst, but to no avail. I was held back a year, and in retrospect I am very happy it happened that way. Jo was right in that I really had not had enough clinical experience with long-term psychotherapy and analysis. Furthermore, my personal life went through a major upheaval, including a messy divorce. I became quite depressed during this period, but, I was able to come out of this depressed state and begin to think about opening a private practice in the Palo Alto, California, area. I finished my analytic training and opened up an office on the mid-peninsula. At that time it was easy to start a practice, as there were so few psychiatrists in the area and insurance helped pay for psychotherapy.

The Jung institute had monthly dinner meetings, and there I had many pleasant and intimate talks with Jo. Those early meetings of the institute were lively and chaotic, lasting until well after 11 p.m. Jo was president of the IAAP between 1966 and 1971, and he laid down the blueprint for the election process from then until 1995. In 1971 I attended my first IAAP meeting in London. Jo was managing the delegates from San Francisco, and he insisted that I be a delegate, much to the chagrin of some older senior analysts. What I did not know was that he and Jim Hillman were politicking behind the scenes to get me elected as second vice president. When the elections came, Jo nominated me as second vice president. I lost by one vote to Hannes Dieckmann, but it set me up to be the favorite at the next election in 1977. Jo nominated me again, and that time I won.

When I remarried in 1968, my introverted wife Jean decided to go into analysis with Jo Wheelwright. That was her introduction to Jungian analysis and how she became familiar with the San Francisco Jungian world. It is not my place to discuss her analysis here, but to honor her analytic experience I saw less of Jo during the years of her analysis with him. He was, of course, eager to hear what was going on in the IAAP, and I was happy to keep him informed.

As both Jo and Jane aged, they began to spend more and more time at the Hollister Ranch near Santa Barbara. It was a very remote area, and one had to travel eighteen miles on a dirt road to get to their property. It was a magnificent property overlooking the Pacific Ocean. Jane had grown up on the ranch and was in her element there, communicating with the animals and native plants. In the late 1980s, they moved permanently to the ranch, and I basically lost contact with Jo and Jane. They did this with almost all their Jungian contacts in San Francisco, so I did not feel that it was anything personal. However, for me not having contact with them was a big loss. Jo and Jane were one of the most remarkable and unique couples I have ever met. In spite of all their quirkiness, I still miss them dearly.

APPENDIX E

C.A. MEIER, M.D.

C.A. Meier was considered to be the "crown prince" to C.G. Jung. He had taken over Jung's position at the ETH, and he had been the first president of the Jung Institute in Zürich, as well as taking over some of Jung's patients when Jung retired from practice after his heart attack in 1944. My parents both saw him in analysis, but my mother was the main analysand of the family. I have already written about having seen him in analysis once in 1953 and regularly during the summers of 1957, 1958, and 1960. I had a long relationship with Meier from that time until his death.

Because of my parents' strong positive relationship with Meier, and given my propensity to accept many of their values, it was only natural that I would see Dr. Meier when I needed therapy. So, as I have already described, I began to see Dr. Meier in the summer of 1957. Meier was an extremely classical analyst. One brought in one's written dreams and gave one's associations, and then Meier, puffing away at his pipe, would think long and deeply about your dream. He did not say much, but in the temenos of the session often something productive psychologically would occur. Meier said much less during the sessions than any of my other analysts, but I felt that I got a lot out of the sessions. There were some funny moments. I generally came at 10:15 in the morning, which was the time that his wife Joan would bring in the mail and a glass of orange juice. He would often spend a couple of minutes opening the mail and drinking his orange juice. One morning I saw a letter from my mother, because I knew her handwriting very well. I did not comment on it, but all these years later I still remember it with a sense of humor and irony. Looking back on it, I see just how incestuous the relationship with Meier was, and how difficult it would have been to say negative things about my parents.

I returned in the summer of 1958 to resume my analysis with Dr. Meier because my life was still in disarray and disorder. Some life decisions were decided, such as the breakup with my girlfriend and the transfer to Yale medical school. I have written about this when I discussed my Zürich analysis. In the summer of 1958 I was excited to have been given an opportunity to have an appointment with Jung. Meier suggested some dreams which I had discussed with him. They were about intersecting circles, or were they moons? Meier thought that Jung would be interested in these dreams because he was working on UFOs and their meaning. What I did not know at the time, but I found out subsequently, was that Meier and Jung had gone through a falling out and were no longer friends. I only found this out from another source much later on. I never had a hint that there was any problem between the two of them.

One other significant event of that summer was that the first IAAP congress was to be held in Zürich. Meier, who rarely gave any kind of advice, suggested strongly that I not be in Zürich during the time of the congress. He was adamant that I did not belong anywhere near the premises. I left for four days in England.

In the spring of 1959, Meier made a trip to the United States. He visited Francis Braceland, the director of the Institute of Living in Hartford, Connecticut. I am pretty sure that I tried to get him a speaking engagement at the Yale department of psychiatry, but they showed little interest in having him. I drove Meier from Hartford, Connecticut, to New York, where he lectured for the Analytical Psychology Club. What I remember was going to a party after his lecture and meeting a number of the senior analysts in New York. The whole experience was pretty heady!

In the summer of 1960, when Marguerite and I were supposedly on our honeymoon, we required his services while in Zürich. He was helpful in getting us moving along on the trip and in our lives. This was to be my last analytical experience with him. I had minimal contact with him for the next nine years, because that was the next time that I went to Europe.

In the spring of 1969, I brought Jean, my new wife, to Zürich, as I wanted her to meet important people from my past. The Meiers were most gracious hosts, and we had a lovely meal with them. I saw that Meier liked his wine and Campari, and we joined him in that pleasure. The next time we saw him was in September, 1971. We traveled to Switzerland after attending the IAAP congress in London. Our daughter Susannah was nine months old, and it was wonderful to see Fredy playing on the floor with Susannah. It was amazing what a little Campari did for Fredy. I should mention that by then it was fine to call him "Fredy" instead of "Dr. Meier." By this time I felt as if Fredy and I were developing a separate friendship from the one my parents had with him. Both Jean and I were well treated when we were invited to the Meiers' house for lunch or dinner. There were usually a couple of interesting people there in addition to us. But this was many years ago, and I cannot remember anyone in particular.

The next very meaningful contact came in the fall of 1973. Meier had become the head of the Klinik am Zürichberg, and there he had set up a laboratory to do neurophysiological experiments. One of the areas of common interest was the new interest in sleep and dreams from a neurophysiological point of view. Earlier he had gone to a major conference on sleep and dreams at the University of Cincinnati, where he had presented Jung's view of dreams. I had also presented a paper on a similar topic in 1967 at the annual meeting of the American Psychiatric Association. The paper, "The Relationship of the REM State to Analytical Psychology," had been vetted by Bill Dement and had been published in the American Psychiatric Association journal, *The American Journal of Psychiatry*. It was most unusual to have a Jungian subject published in *The American Journal of Psychiatry*. Meier saw that I had the potential for an academic career. He wrote me and asked me if I would be interested in the professorship at the ETH, because he was about to retire. It was a very tempting offer because I dearly loved Zürich, but I had just firmly planted my roots in Palo Alto and the Bay Area, and I really could not see making that change. I loved visiting Zürich, but I thought life would be very different living there. Jean had only rudimentary German, and I am not sure that she would have even come to Zürich if I had been offered the position. In the end I turned down the invitation to apply for it. Interestingly enough, after Meier's retirement that position was not filled for many years, and when it was finally filled, a non-Jungian received it.

In 1977 the IAAP conference was held in Rome, and Fredy, loving Italy, attended parts of the congress. He invited Jean and me for a lunch which just happened to be before the delegates' meeting the same afternoon. I was excited about the delegates' meeting because I anticipated that I might be elected to the vacant second vice president's position, having lost by only one vote at the election six years earlier. When the nominations for second vice president were opened, Jo Wheelwright put my name up. What happened next was most surprising. Fredy Meier got up and seconded my nomination for the position. The IAAP is governed by Swiss law, and a second to a nomination is not required.

As I have mentioned earlier, Fredy's nomination of me brought up a wave of anger toward me from Jim Hillman, who said that I should have broken with Fredy by now. What was I doing still being on good terms with these older, first-generation Jungians? I could understand his distrust of Meier given Meier's indiscretions in their analytic relationship. However, it was not fair of him to think that I had to feel the same way he did. I don't think Jim could ever forgive me for still being on good terms with Meier.

My mother died the next year, and just before she died, Fredy flew from Zürich to visit her in Los Angeles. Six months after my mother's death, my father remarried a much younger woman, and they naturally went to Zürich to see Fredy for analysis. I was not involved in any of these arrangements, but it was difficult to take the change in my father, who went from being married to my mother to now being married to this thirty-nine-year-old woman who was extremely aloof and withdrawn.

As IAAP vice president, I continued to visit Zürich at least once a year and would always have some encounter with Fredy. He was most generous in inviting me, or Jean and me, for some meal. Probably in 1985 or 1986, at one of these dinners, Fredy told me in confidence that my father and Sandra, his young wife, were going to get divorced. Again, I was shocked, and I thought that Fredy had no business telling me this information. After all, Sandra was his patient, and this really broke doctor-patient confidentiality. I was extremely upset by this news and called my wife back in California to tell her what was happening. I found out directly from my father when I returned to California and spoke to him. I was very angry with Fredy for leaking that information to me, and I saw for the first time directly why so many people had had difficulties with him. It was completely unprofessional for him to tell me that information.

Nevertheless, we continued to meet socially, and I remember celebrating a lovely ninetieth birthday lunch at the fish restaurant just down the street from their apartment.

I had one more significant encounter with Fredy when I began to do research on my book *The Jungians*. Fredy was very elderly by then, and I was in the ETH Jung archive and wanted to look at the correspondence during the 1930s between Jung and the International General Medical Society for Psychotherapy, of which Jung had been the president. Fredy had been Jung's corresponding secretary for most of those years. I wanted to look at the correspondence, and so the archivist called Fredy and asked him if it would be okay if I looked at the correspondence. Initially, Fredy was extremely defensive and wanted to know why I wanted to see the correspondence. He calmed down after a while and gave me permission to look at the correspondence. I have always wondered why he was so defensive initially and only became reasonable later on.

Fredy Meier and I remained on good terms until his death. Six months after his ninetieth birthday, Fredy developed an esophageal cancer which quickly killed him. The 1995 IAAP congress was in Zürich, and so I had an opportunity to say goodbye to him. He was already in a very weakened state. In retrospect, he had been an ambivalent figure for me. He was a terrific analyst when I first went to see him as a young man. He had been a charming host and a very cultured person from whom I learned a lot. I appreciated his independence and the fact that he was not just one of the Jungian crowd around Jung. On the other hand, I saw him as defensive, narcissistic, and also unprofessional at times, and he often was not able to get along with people. I am left with very mixed feelings about this man who was such an important figure in the early Zürich days.

APPENDIX F

JOHN WEIR PERRY, M.D.

John Weir Perry was the best teacher that I had during my Jungian training in the 1960s. John was a decade younger than the founders of the San Francisco Jung institute, Henderson and Wheelwright, but he had also had significant contact with Jung. He had first met Jung when Jung came to the United States in 1936. During that trip, Jung spent time with John's father, who was the bishop of Rhode Island, and stayed overnight at the family's house. After World War II, John had studied in Zürich for a year, had analysis with C.A. Meier, and also had several meetings with Jung. John wrote a book, *The Self in Psychotic Process: Its Symbolization in Schizophrenia*, and Jung wrote the introduction. After a year in Zürich, John returned to San Francisco, and he practiced Jungian analysis in the same building with Henderson, Wheelwright, and Kay Bradway. I had heard that he had problems with women, and so I shied away from seeing him in analysis. Instead I listened to his lectures with great eagerness. I must have heard John lecture at least forty times in my life. I was particularly fascinated by his work with acute psychotic patients. I introduced him to Julian Silverman, a research psychologist, and together they began a project working with psychotics at the local state hospital, Agnews. It was called the Agnews Project and received funding from the National Institute of Mental Health. This was the late 1960s, and there was much interest in working with schizophrenics, especially first-time psychotics, psychotherapeutically.

I knew that I did not want to see John as an analyst because he reminded me too much of my own father. They both were brilliant scholars and had amazing breadths of knowledge, but at the same time they could not keep their hands off women. I felt that I could not trust John with my "anima" problem, because his seemed much bigger than mine. Besides listening to his lectures on schizophrenia, myths, and complexes, I wanted him as my supervisor for clinical cases. There I presented mostly male patients to him, and he was excellent with dreams and active imagination. I did my whole supervision with him, and it was a most satisfactory experience.

During the 1960s he was one of the most sought-after therapists in the San Francisco Bay Area. However, in the 1970s he lost his boundaries with patients, and he was brought up to the Board of Medical Examiners. At first he was allowed to continue to practice if he went into analysis, but he soon quit analysis, and he was back to his acting out with women patients. I was asked to be on the ethics committee of our institute, and before I knew it, he was brought up before our committee. By then I had become chair of the ethics committee, and so I had to preside over his situation. I absolutely hated being in this situation, because I had seen how he had behaved. Several of us had been on a charter to Europe for an international Jungian conference, and he had brought a woman patient along with him. She was absolutely lost while we were at the conference in Rome, because John could not bring her with him socially, although he was very busy since his work with schizophrenia had made him a big star of the conference.

So the decision by the other members of the ethics committee was to expel John from the institute. I felt that was too harsh, and so we ended up with "permanent suspension" instead of expulsion. John had a chance at a general meeting of the members to explain his point of view, and it was clear that sexual enactment was a part of his treatment with women. It was a sad day as the membership voted to accept the verdict of "permanent suspension," and John was no longer a member. After that I saw him occasionally on the street around the institute, because he still practiced psychotherapy even though his medical license had been revoked. He continued to be cordial and friendly toward me whenever we met.

In spite of his failings, he was an inspiring teacher and a major influence on my Jungian identity.

ABOUT THE AUTHOR

Thomas B. Kirsch is a Jungian analyst in private practice in Palo Alto, California, and the son of two first-generation Jungian analysts, James and Hilde Kirsch, who began their analytic work with C.G. Jung in 1929. He graduated from Yale Medical School in 1961, completed his psychiatric residency at Stanford Medical Center in 1965, and graduated from the C.G. Jung Institute of San Francisco in 1968. He was president of the C.G. Jung Institute of San Francisco from 1976 to 1978, served on the executive committee of the International Association for Analytical Psychology from 1977 to 1995, and was IAAP president from 1989 to 1995. He has also been a member of the American Academy of Psychoanalysis since 1976.

In addition to his private practice, Dr. Kirsch is on the faculty of the C.G. Jung Institute of San Francisco and has been a lecturer in the department of psychiatry at Stanford Medical Center. He is the author of *The Jungians: A Comparative and Historical Perspective* as well as many published papers on dreams, the history of analytical psychology, and the analytic relationship. He has written numerous book reviews, edited many chapters in books, and lectured worldwide. For more information on Dr. Kirsch, see his website at www.jungians. com.

Other Fisher King Press Titles

Marked By Fire: Stories of the Jungian Way edited by Patricia Damery & Naomi Ruth Lowinsky, 1ˢᵗ Ed., Trade Paperback, 180pp, Biblio., 2012
— ISBN 978-1-926715-68-1

The Dream and Its Amplification edited by Erel Shalit & Nancy Swift Furlotti, 1ˢᵗ Ed., Trade Paperback, 180pp, Biblio., 2013
— ISBN 978-1-926715-89-6

Shared Realities: Participation Mystique and Beyond edited by Mark Windborn, 1ˢᵗ Ed., Trade Paperback, 270pp, Index, Biblio., 2014
— ISBN 978-1-77169-009-6

Pierre Teilhard de Chardin and C.G. Jung: Side by Side edited by Fred Gustafson, 1ˢᵗ Ed., Trade Paperback, 270pp, Index, Biblio., 2015
— ISBN ISBN 978-1-77169-014-0

Re-Imagining Mary: A Journey Through Art to the Feminine Self by Mariann Burke, 1ˢᵗ Ed., Trade Paperback, 180pp, Index, Biblio., 2009
— ISBN 978-0-9810344-1-6

Sea Glass: A Jungian Analyst's Exploration of Suffering and Individuation by Gilda Frantz, 1ˢᵗ Ed., Trade Paperback, 248pp, Index, Biblio., 2014
— ISBN 978-1-77169-020-1

Transforming Body and Soul by Steven Galipeau, Rev. Ed., Trade Paperback, 180pp, Index, Biblio., 2011 — ISBN 978-1-926715-62-9

Lifting the Veil: Revealing the Other Side by Fred Gustafson & Jane Kamerling, 1ˢᵗ Ed, Paperback, 170pp, Biblio., 2012
— ISBN 978-1-926715-75-9

Resurrecting the Unicorn: Masculinity in the 21ˢᵗ Century by Bud Harris, Rev. Ed., Trade Paperback, 300pp, Index, Biblio., 2009
— ISBN 978-0-9810344-0-9

The Father Quest: Rediscovering an Elemental Force by Bud Harris, Reprint, Trade Paperback, 180pp, Index, Biblio., 2009
— ISBN 978-0-9810344-9-2

Like Gold Through Fire: The Transforming Power of Suffering by Massimilla & Bud Harris, Reprint, Trade Paperback, 150pp, Index, Biblio., 2009 — ISBN 978-0-9810344-5-4

The Art of Love: The Craft of Relationship by Massimilla and Bud Harris, 1st Ed. Trade Paperback, 150pp, 2010
— ISBN 978-1-926715-02-5

Divine Madness: Archetypes of Romantic Love by John R. Haule, Rev. Ed., Trade Paperback, 282pp, Index, Biblio., 2010
— ISBN 978-1-926715-04-9

Tantra and Erotic Trance in 2 volumes by John R. Haule
   Volume 1 - Outer Work, 1st Ed. Trade Paperback, 215pp, Index, Bibliograpy, 2012 — ISBN 978-0-9776076-8-6
   Volume 2 - Inner Work, 1st Ed. Trade Paperback, 215pp, Index, Bibliograpy, 2012 — ISBN 978-0-9776076-9-3

Eros and the Shattering Gaze: Transcending Narcissism
by Ken Kimmel, 1ˢᵗ Ed., Trade Paperback, 310pp, Index, Biblio., 2011
— ISBN 978-1-926715-49-0

The Sister From Below: When the Muse Gets Her Way
by Naomi Ruth Lowinsky, 1ˢᵗ Ed., Trade Paperback, 248pp, Index, Biblio., 2009 — ISBN 978-0-9810344-2-3

The Motherline: Every Woman's Journey to find her Female Roots
by Naomi Ruth Lowinsky, Reprint, Trade Paperback, 252pp, Index, Biblio., 2009 — ISBN 978-0-9810344-6-1

The Dairy Farmer's Guide to the Universe in 4 volumes
by Dennis L. Merritt:
   Volume 1 - Jung and Ecopsychology, 1ˢᵗ Ed., Trade Paperback, 242pp, Index, Biblio., 2011 — ISBN 978-1-926715-42-1
   Volume 2 - The Cry of Merlin: Jung the Prototypical Ecopsychologist, 1ˢᵗ Ed., Trade Paperback, 204pp, Index, Biblio., 2012
   — ISBN 978-1-926715-43-8
   Volume 3 - Hermes, Ecopsychology, and Complexity Theory,
   1ˢᵗ Ed., Trade Paperback, 228pp, Index, Biblio., 2012
   — ISBN 978-1-926715-44-5
   Volume 4 - Land, Weather, Seasons, Insects: An Archetypal View, 1ˢᵗ Ed., Trade Paperback, 134pp, Index, Biblio., 2012
   — ISBN 978-1-926715-45-2

Four Eternal Women: Toni Wolff Revisited—A Study In Opposites
by Mary Dian Molton & Lucy Anne Sikes, 1ˢᵗ Ed., 320pp, Index, Biblio., 2011 — ISBN 978-1-926715-31-5

Becoming: An Introduction to Jung's Concept of Individuation
by Deldon Anne McNeely, 1ˢᵗ Ed., Trade Paperback, 230pp, Index, Biblio., 2010 — ISBN 978-1-926715-12-4

Animus Aeternus: Exploring the Inner Masculine by Deldon Anne McNeely, Reprint, Trade Paperback, 196pp, Index, Biblio., 2011
— ISBN 978-1-926715-37-7

Mercury Rising: Women, Evil, and the Trickster Gods
by Deldon Anne McNeely, Revised, Trade Paperback, 200pp, Index, Biblio., 2011 — ISBN 978-1-926715-54-4

Gathering the Light: A Jungian View of Meditation
by V. Walter Odajnyk, Revised Ed., Trade Paperback, 264pp, Index, Biblio., 2011 — ISBN 978-1-926715-55-1

The Orphan: On the Journey to Wholeness
by Audrey Punnett, 1st Ed., Trade Paperback, 150pp, Index, Biblio., 2014
— ISBN 978-1-77169-016-4

The Promiscuity Papers
by Matjaz Regovec, 1st Ed., Trade Paperback, 86pp, Index, Biblio., 2011
— ISBN 978-1-926715-38-4

Enemy, Cripple, Beggar: Shadows in the Hero's Path
by Erel Shalit, 1st Ed., Trade Paperback, 248pp, Index, Biblio., 2008
— ISBN 978-0-9776076-7-9

The Cycle of Life: Themes and Tales of the Journey
by Erel Shalit, 1st Ed., Trade Paperback, 210pp, Index, Biblio., 2011
— ISBN 978-1-926715-50-6

The Hero and His Shadow
by Erel Shalit, Revised Ed., Trade Paperback, 208pp, Index, Biblio., 2012
— ISBN 978-1-926715-69-8

Riting Myth, Mythic Writing: Plotting Your Personal Story
by Dennis Patrick Slattery, Trade Paperback, 220 pp. Biblio., 2012
— ISBN 978-1-926715-77-3

The Guilt Cure
by Nancy Carter Pennington & Lawrence H. Staples, 1st Ed., Trade Paperback, 200pp,
Index, Biblio., 2011 — ISBN 978-1-926715-53-7

Guilt with a Twist: The Promethean Way
by Lawrence Staples, 1st Ed., Trade Paperback, 256pp, Index, Biblio., 2008
— ISBN 978-0-9776076-4-8

The Creative Soul: Art and the Quest for Wholeness
by Lawrence Staples, 1st Ed., Trade Paperback, 100pp, Index, Biblio., 2009 — ISBN 978-0-9810344-4-7

Deep Blues: Human Soundscapes for the Archetypal Journey
by Mark Winborn, 1st Ed., Trade Paperback, 130pp, Index, Biblio., 2011
— ISBN 978-1-926715-52-0

Phone Orders Welcomed
Credit Cards Accepted
In Canada & the U.S. call 1-800-228-9316
International call +1-831-238-7799
www.fisherkingpress.com

Lightning Source UK Ltd.
Milton Keynes UK
UKOW03f2018231114

242040UK00003B/28/P